To Wear
the Dust of War

To Wear
the Dust of War

From Bialystok to Shanghai
to the Promised Land

An Oral History

by Samuel Iwry

Edited by L. J. H. Kelley

First published 2004 by
PALGRAVE MACMILLAN™
175 Fifth Avenue, New York, N.Y. 10010 and
Houndmills, Basingstoke, Hampshire, England RG21 6XS.
Companies and representatives throughout the world.

PALGRAVE MACMILLAN is the global academic imprint of the Palgrave Macmillan
division of St. Martin's Press, LLC and of Palgrave Macmillan Ltd.
Macmillan® is a registered trademark in the United States, United Kingdom and other countries. Palgrave is a registered trademark in the European Union and other countries.

ISBN   978-1-4039-6576-9

Library of Congress Cataloging-in-Publication Data

Iwry, Samuel.
 To wear the dust of war : from Bialystok to Shanghai to the Promised Land : an oral history / by Samuel Iwry ; edited by L.J.H. Kelley.
  p. cm. -- (Palgrave studies in oral history)
Includes bibliographical references and index.
ISBN 1-4039-6575-7 -- ISBN 1-4039-6576-5 (pbk.)
 1. Iwry, Samuel. 2. Jews--Poland--Biography. 3. Holocaust, Jewish (1939-1945)--Poland--Personal narratives. 4. Refugees, Jewish--China--Shanghai--Biography. 5. Refugees, Jewish--Maryland--Biography. I. Kelley, L.J.H. II. Title. III. Series.

DS135.P631895 2004
940.53'18'092--dc22
[B]
2004040005

A catalogue record for this book is available from the British Library.

Design by planettheo.com

First edition: August 2004
9 8 7 6 5 4 3 2 1

Printed in the United States of America

Transferred to Digital Printing in 2011

Contents

Series Editors' Foreword

Oral history usually is defined as an interactive process. An interviewer asks questions and the person being interviewed, the interviewee, responds. Ideally, the questions are open-ended and the answers are lengthy and complete. The interview, however, is shaped by the interaction between the two participants. On the other hand, some practitioners who conduct life histories may begin by asking their subject to tell about their life and then refrain from intervening in the remainder of the interview or do so very infrequently. This oral history of Samuel Iwry combines both approaches with a greater emphasis on the latter. As described by Leslie Kelley, Dr. Iwry would hold forth and set the agenda for discussion. Her intervention emerges as an editor more than an interviewer. She shaped Iwry's story once it was transcribed, placed it in chronological order, checked facts, and filled in historical gaps. In many respects, this is the life story of Sam Iwry *as told to* Leslie Kelley. While this raises certain methodological questions for oral historians related to the purity of the interview and the desire to capture a verbatim and true account, it does not detract from the very dramatic and compelling tale that Sam Iwry tells. The substance of the story, its particular emphases and shadings, the unique voice—all are Iwry's, the result of hours and hours of interviews.

Many of the critical issues of twentieth-century history erupt on the pages that follow, which tell the story of one man's resilience in the face of world peril. Pre–World War II Eastern European Jewish life, the tragedy of the Holocaust, the world of uprooted refugees, the humanitarian act of courage by a Japanese diplomat, the community as well as the danger and brutality of Shanghai under Japanese rule, the birth of the state of Israel, and immigration to the United States all are a part of Sam Iwry's sojourn through the twentieth century. Less dramatic, but of great historical significance, is his life as a scholar of Hebrew and Near Eastern Studies and his contribution to our understanding of the Dead Sea Scrolls. Iwry's coming to America completed a life that met its full potential at the

Baltimore Hebrew College and the Johns Hopkins University, where his teaching and research excelled.

One of the great values of oral history is its ability to humanize the story being told. Leslie Kelley's presentation of Sam Iwry's account does just that and accomplishes another important purpose. It offers a contextual framework for the narrative that is offered. In this sense also, it fits well with the Palgrave Studies in Oral History series, which is designed to make history accessible to the general reader as well as to students and accomplished scholars.

Linda Shopes
Pennsylvania Historical Museum Commission

Bruce M. Stave
University of Connecticut

Samuel Iwry, My Father

by J. Mark Iwry

The truth is, my father never was eager to write this book. Probably the prospect of reliving the Holocaust was too wrenching. He has never lost sight of the bitter reality: For every grateful survivor with a story of miraculous escape, there were 100 innocents, including his parents and sisters, and his wife's parents and sisters, whose lives were cut off (as he describes in his narrative) in a manner that was—for him, quite literally—unspeakable.

My father has always felt acutely the absence of the six million and their would-be offspring: how much more robust and creative our people, Israel and the world would be today had they not been cut down. At the same time, no one was more alive to the miracle of Israel's birth from the ashes of the Holocaust. In fact, he never made peace with the fate that took him to "the other Promised Land," America instead of Israel, where he felt he really belonged. And yet, as a new American, Sam became profoundly loyal to his new homeland.

Bemused by what he viewed as many Americans' naiveté, and put off by the hype and commercialism he sometimes saw here, my father nonetheless became an admirer and champion of the American spirit and character. He treasured America's freedoms and values as only one who lived so much of his life without them could. In contrast, his graphic narrative bears witness to the hollowness and mendacity of Soviet Communism, including its dispiriting effects on ordinary people, its impoverishment, and, more broadly, the evils of overbearing bureaucracy. My parents' experience (my mother's story is briefly recounted in the epilogue) explains their hard-won skepticism of politicians and governing authority and its potentially heavy hand under any system.

My father never could (or would) have put the Holocaust behind him; in his words, he would always "wear the dust of war." As the book describes, during his work in the underground he narrowly escaped death several times in Europe and Russia and endured physical torture in the Shanghai prison camp. (My mother saved his life on that occasion.) But his sharpest pain was self-inflicted. He never stopped torturing himself over his inability to save his parents—or his sisters and their families—from their horrifying fate, even as he was able to save many others.

After all four parents and most of their siblings were murdered for being Jewish, my parents hesitated to bring another child into this world, especially a Jewish child. And after deciding to have just one, they always sought to protect me from the horrors their families had suffered in the Old World. But they themselves never left those horrors behind: at age 93, my father's sleep was still disturbed by nightmares of his parents' fate and of the Shanghai prison camp.

Already a product of the European and Jewish enlightenment, experiencing the Holocaust made it harder for him to maintain a simple unquestioning faith in a providential Supreme Being. As a hard-headed but by no means hard-hearted rationalist, my father's identity was bound up in the unique character, history, and contributions of the Jewish nation, "walking in history under G-d," as he put it. His teaching stressed the centrality of learning, study, and questioning in the Jewish tradition.

At the same time, his bitter wartime experience convinced him of the ultimate importance of what he called "simple decency." His teaching brought out how decency and respect for human life and dignity have been integral Jewish values since the Hebrew people originally rejected polytheism and paganism in favor of monotheism and the single, absolute moral order. And he was vigilant against modern forms of idol worship and paganism--totalitarianism, political fanaticism, materialism, or a losing of self in the frivolous or ephemeral.

Deeply learned in Bible, Hebrew, classical and modern Hebrew literature, and Jewish history and culture, my father was devoted to his people, their unique civilization, and their new, hard-won national home in Israel. Accordingly, when he prayed, it was not so much to, as with—not to an anthropomorphic deity, but with his people, as an act of humility and a collective expression of gratitude, awe, fear, pain, hope, and rededication to the highest values of our tradition. His emphasis was less on pure faith than on learning, values, and action.

Action for him included dedicated support of Israel and the Jewish nation. Through public lectures, classes, organizational activity, and one-on-one discussion, he taught countless Americans—friends, contemporaries and students—about the Jewish heritage and the importance of Israel (where he spent time most summers). Defining Zionism as "the modern expression of the 1,900-year-old dream of rebuilding the historic Jewish homeland in Israel," he saw the Jewish state as "the only positive answer to the Jewish powerlessness of the past, to spiritual homelessness and to rampant, unavoidable assimilation."*

He succeeded in inspiring many Americans—including influential, dynamic and dear friends such as Chuck Hoffberger, Irving Blum, and Alvin Blum, each of blessed memory—to identify more and more actively with Israel, not only through major financial contributions but most importantly by contributing their exceptional talents, political support, and personal involvement. And he always viewed the Arab peoples as "our cousins" with whom Israel's Jewish community must share the land in peace and mutually respectful cooperation. Sam recounts his effort, after having been invited to lead a Biblical studies seminar at the residence of Israel's then Prime Minister Menachem Begin, to use his credibility as a world-class Biblical scholar to persuade Begin—Sam's old political adversary from pre-War university days in Warsaw—that Begin's particular policies toward the territories of Judea and Samaria were in fact not dictated by scripture.

In fact, for all his regret about never settling in the Promised Land, Sam might have accomplished more for Israel and the Jewish people through his wartime work in the underground and his later activities based in the United States than he would have done living in Israel.

When my parents reached America, he was 36, she 30. They had never before set foot in an English-speaking country. Their first task was not to master "English as a second language," but English as a seventh language. This was no small handicap for someone resuming his scholarly career, after a nearly decade-long interruption, in a high-powered, rigorously demanding, competitive PhD program in which all classes and papers were in English and most faculty and graduate students were American-born (and could type!). But Sam loved scholarship and had a passion for Biblical archaeology; before long, he learned to write, teach, and function fluently in English.

If Biblical archaeology is a kind of detective work, my father was an armchair detective. (Think Sherlock Holmes, not *Raiders of the Lost Ark*.) Not for him the long summers in the Middle East directing excavations under the broiling desert sun. The fruits of those labors were delivered to him and his colleagues in their air conditioned offices at Johns Hopkins, where they pieced those clues together with other textual and physical evidence to assemble the full mosaic: the social, political, economic, intellectual, and spiritual history of the Hebrew people, of ancient Palestine, of Judaism and the origins of Christianity, and of the Bible.

It seemed like a grand, multidimensional jigsaw puzzle. Building on a command of ancient languages, texts, and history, the work involved developing and testing creative hypotheses and powerful explanatory theories. When the pieces fit together, it was more than satisfying—it was exhilarating.

As described in my father's narrative, deciphering the Dead Sea Scrolls—considered by many to be the greatest archaeological discovery of the twentieth century (and on which my father wrote the first PhD dissertation)—or discovering the previously unknown exile to Damascus had the feel of a dramatic breakthrough. The drama included the 1948 telephone call from Jerusalem in which excerpts from the Scrolls were read to Dr. Albright and my father; the scholarly controversy over their authenticity as the oldest version of the Bible; my father's examination of the Scrolls and euphoric 2 A.M. phone call to announce to Dr. Albright that their authenticity and antiquity were clear; and the scientific confirmation of that conclusion, through carbon-14 dating, announced the day my father retired from Johns Hopkins, more than four decades later.

My father was a brilliant scholar and a spellbinding teacher and speaker: impassioned, inspired, and inspiring. Much in demand as a public lecturer and a scholar-in-residence at congregations, he knew instinctively how to share his learning, insight, and passion. A 1985 volume of course evaluations, prepared by Johns Hopkins undergraduates to give other undergraduates candid appraisals of professors and their courses, referred to

the plethora of positive comments bestowed upon [Professor Iwry] and his course [in this case, "Modern Hebrew Literature"]. Everyone recommends this course for others. The . . . best [aspect of the course] by far is the professor and the subject matter. One International Studies major remarked, "Don't be afraid to take it—I got more out of it in terms of learning about philosophy and human relations than from any other class . . ."

As his son, I too was his student—but outside the classroom. It was a remarkable education. He taught me far more than I learned.

The proverbial absent-minded professor, my father came to America too late to adapt to many of our ways. He had trouble remembering names, for example, including those of his many students. But he always enjoyed American informality and humor. When teaching, he refused to be distant or impersonal, often addressing the "boys" by their last names ("Robinson!") or by a nickname of his own devising. Unwilling to expose the "girls" to the same unceremonious treatment, he struggled to recall their first names. Once, before the modern women's movement and much to the amusement of the young men in his classes, he made a special offer to the female students: "A majority of girls in my classes seem to be named either Debbie or Susan. So I will let the rest of you choose, each one, to be called in my class either Debbie or Susan. And this is what I will call you." This was intended at least partly in jest. But while many of the women students were amused (and a few even accepted the offer), others, understandably, were not. My father got the point, and quickly recanted. In truth, he respected and took his women students every bit as seriously as the men, both in point of intellect and character.

In his academic career, as in his personal life, my father straddled different worlds. His love of modern Hebrew literature involved him in a field far removed—by two or three millennia—from Biblical and ancient Near Eastern studies. But he saw literature as "the key to the inner soul." And "[o]nly through Hebrew literature can one understand the Jew in modern times." He loved the works of I. L. Peretz, S. Y. Agnon, the Nobel-Prize-winning Hebrew writer, and other great Hebrew and Yiddish authors. A friendship developed between Agnon and my father when he was a Visiting Professor at the Hebrew University in Jerusalem, and Agnon told my father that no one better understood or appreciated his work.

My father delighted in small children and young people, and seemed to have a special understanding with them. He conferred his own nicknames on my grade school classmates: "The Genius," "The Red Hair," "The Scientist's Daughter." When my contemporaries reached college age, many came to view my parents as friends and counselors, visiting them even in my absence, for advice on problems, relationships with parents, and careers, for adult companionship free of conventional American attitudes and parental postures, for greater depth, a broader perspective, a more objective take on their and their parents' culture and society. In particular, they came to my mother for a loving soul and sympathetic ear, to my father for an honest, unvarnished, tough-minded reaction to personal issues and dilemmas.

For my father, with old age came a sense of affirmation, continuity and *nachas* (joyful pride). The 85-year-old Hebraic scholar watched his 3-year-old grandchild reach for the colored plastic Hebrew letters and try to form them into words. And certain things have come full circle: Sam saw several of his former students become his grandson's teachers at the Charles E. Smith Jewish Day School in Maryland. By the time my father was 91 and his grandson 9, Jonathan had acquired his grandfather's love of languages and began regularly conversing with him only in Hebrew. When Jonathan turned 11 and was invited to deliver his own sermon (*Dvar Torah*) to the congregation at Sabbath services, his grandparents were able to hear the child say,

> We all cherish being with grandparents, if we still have them. They bring us wisdom, knowledge, love and joy. They have survived the Holocaust and have discovered many things about our religion. They have experienced many things we can only dream about, and carry a wisdom that, if obeyed, could make this world paradise for everyone. . . . In Judaism, each type of person represents something. A child represents learning and the beginning of something, an adult represents duty and striving toward success, and the grandparent represents wisdom and achievement.

I have said my father never wanted to write this book. In fact, he never did write it. It is genuinely an oral history, much like a first draft "dictated and not read." When he spoke these words, my father did not think he was dictating an autobiography or composing a work for publication, but simply recounting something of his life experience at his colleague's request. By the time L. J. H. Kelley had diligently transcribed the tapes and judiciously assembled the most appropriate passages into a chronological narrative, my father's vision was too impaired to read or edit.

For a scholar who took infinite pains with his published works, meticulously revising and editing numerous drafts, this, ironically, is the one work he never revised. It came straight from the heart. When I read him the manuscript, about 15 minutes at a time (his energy permitting), he suggested a few corrections, filled in a few names and dates, but lacked the strength to do more.

Of necessity, much original material was omitted from the text, including several wonderful disquisitions and mini-lectures on European and Jewish history and culture, discussion of my father's leadership activities in the national and worldwide Jewish communities, and descriptions of several additional honors, such as his Honorary Degree in Hebrew Letters and his invitation to be the only American corresponding member of the Israel Academy for Languages and Literature. Those omissions were of no concern to my father. Instead, his great frustration with this book was that the final text could not include his efforts to recognize personally and individually, and to thank, by name, his and our family's beloved friends and relatives, and his treasured colleagues. It was determined, understandably, that such material—without historical significance or interest to general readers—would not be appropriate for an oral history.

We have my father's distinguished colleague and friend, Dr. Kyle McCarter, to thank for persuading his reluctant colleague to dictate his memoirs. After repeatedly declining, my father quickly consented once Dr. McCarter arranged for a series of graduate students to earn financial aid by "interviewing" him. My family is grateful to Dr. McCarter for conceiving and launching this project.

May this oral history help to preserve my father's story. May his soul be bound up in the bond of eternal life. And may his memory be for a blessing.

May 25, 2004 (5 Sivan, 5764)

Samuel Iwry, Scholar

by P. Kyle McCarter, Johns Hopkins University

Samuel Iwry began his formal training in Vilna, Lithuania. Vilna had been the home of the great Elijah ben Solomon Zalmen (1720-1797), the dominant figure of Lithuanian Jewry and one of the most important Jewish scholars of the modern period. Renowned for his unsurpassed knowledge of the Torah, the *Vilna Gaon*, as he is known, was an Enlightenment figure who recognized the importance of text-critical study of the ancient literature of Judaism. His scholarship survives in an abundance of authoritative notes on the Mishnah, Talmud, Tosefta, halachic Midrashim, and other Jewish texts.

Sam Iwry became a scholar very much in the spirit of the Vilna Gaon. His erudition is a unique combination of traditional Jewish learning, deeply and broadly mastered, and modern secular scholarship judiciously applied. This combination came about in an extraordinary way, and it is the exceptional history of his intellectual formation—and the extraordinary life events in which this formation took place—that make Sam Iwry's story so compelling.

As a seminarian, scholar, and teacher in Vilna, Sam was exposed to the entire range of Jewish learning that was available in the "Jerusalem of Lithuania," and there he refined his exemplary command of the Hebrew language, for which he became so highly regarded later in life. From Vilna he moved on to teaching positions in Bialystok and Warsaw, where, under the influence of Moses Schorr, Professor of Semitics at Warsaw University and Chief Rabbi of Warsaw, he first encountered the rapidly accumulating knowledge of the civilizations of Israel's neighbors in the ancient Near East. It was in Warsaw that Sam began to appreciate the value of drawing on this "new" knowledge to augment his prodigious understanding of Jewish tradition.

At that time, however, the horrifying events of the impending world war overtook Sam and precipitated the long journey that brought him eventually to Baltimore. Here, while teaching at the Baltimore Hebrew College (now Baltimore Hebrew University), he embarked on the second phase of his dual education. Across town at Johns Hopkins, the great Orientalist William Foxwell Albright was then at the height of his prestige as a pioneer in the study of the Bible and the ancient Near East. Sam applied to study at Hopkins, and he was readily admitted by Albright, who recognized his impressive and already mature command of Hebraic scholarship. At Hopkins Sam mastered the new methods that had been developed for shedding light on ancient Jewish—and, more broadly, ancient Near Eastern—literature, history, and material culture. He became one of Albright's most respected students and, in due course, his colleague, friend, and confidant.

As the years went by, Sam continued to teach both at Baltimore Hebrew and Hopkins, refining the dual education he had acquired in the two worlds of scholarship that nurtured him, and passing it on to a new generation of appreciative students.

Acknowledgements

L. J. H. Kelley, editor

I am profoundly grateful to Dr. P. Kyle McCarter, professor of biblical studies at Johns Hopkins University, for entrusting this assignment to me and for his great patience in allowing me to work at my own pace. Dr. McCarter also granted me the most valuable compensation I could have requested: permission to attend classes in the Department of Near Eastern Studies where Dr. Iwry was a professor for so many years. In addition, he generously shared his perspective on Dr. Iwry's achievements as a scholar, providing the material for the introduction and notes to chapter 9.

My thanks also to Nina Iwry, who tolerated my phone calls and made her own contributions in the background. And I am especially grateful to their son, Mark, whose enthusiasm for the project made getting to the finish line a breeze. Mark also made countless trips to Baltimore to read and review the entire manuscript with his father, and enabled me to add some valuable final corrections and comments to the manuscript. Most important, he wrote his own introduction, the epilogue relating his mother's story, and also collected and prepared the photos on his father's behalf.

My thanks also to the several graduate students at Johns Hopkins who began this oral history. They had collected many hours of this story on cassette tape before I arrived, and gave me a valuable jump start on this project.

Voice to Print

When I joined this project, Dr. Kyle McCarter, then the chair of the department of Near Eastern Studies at Johns Hopkins University, had already arranged for the recording of many hours of Samuel Iwry's story. He had related enough of his life to nearly fill eight cassette tapes, and I began by transcribing the contents of these tapes.

These eight tapes carried his story up to his arrival in China and the pleasanter times in Shanghai. I do not know who handled the recording of these initial tapes, as the only voice I heard belonged to Dr. Iwry. No questions were asked by his listener, and the only interruptions to the steady flow of Sam's narration were the telephone in his office.

After transcribing these tapes, I knew his voice, knew his style, and had many questions that I hoped would clarify what he had already told. At this point, I met with him weekly to resume recording and transcribing.

Dr. Iwry had not lost his European elegance even after more than 40 years in the United States. He sat erect and with perfect posture, leaning back and gently rocking a little in his swivel desk chair. He still loved inhabiting his book-lined and paper-filled office in Gilman Hall. He always wore impeccably tailored, vested suits, and spoke with the manner of someone who loves teaching and who is accustomed to being listened to by attentive, eager students.

I did not need to actively interview him, and Dr. Iwry would not tolerate my setting the agenda. He always had his own mind prepared as to what he wanted to talk about and to relate. After a few minutes of pleasantries, he would pause, signal to me to turn the tape recorder on, and then he would begin to speak with no other prompting. I was at times only a human fixture, making his story-telling into the tape recorder feel a little less odd. I often interrupted him with questions, and he would graciously answer, while also waving his hand to indicate that my question was an unnecessary interruption. He would then continue exactly where he had left off.

Dr. Iwry was in his 80s when he recorded his story, and although his mind was perfectly clear, his command of four-decade-old details was sometimes, understandably, incomplete. It was also still painful to recall some of the times he experienced, and he often simply stopped, unable to speak, and would either abruptly end the session or after a long and emotional pause, begin speaking of something else. I approached the more painful subjects by researching what I could and then asking him at the next session for correction or clarification in small doses rather than trying to get him to spill the details in their painful entirety.

The greatest challenge was that Sam's incredible flow of narration was connected by logical links in the ideas and details, but not by the years in which the events occurred. He would mention an acquaintance in Israel from his year there as a Fulbright scholar, then tell an anecdote of how things were in Israel then, then talk about a similar thing in Poland, and so on.

So after transcribing the many hours of cassette tape, my first task as editor was to put his account into chronological order. This, fortunately, was not difficult, as so much of what Dr. Iwry experienced and spoke of is well documented by historians. The dates of *Kristallnacht*, the bombing of Shanghai by the Americans, the day the Soviets rolled their tanks through Lithuania, and many other events were easily put in their proper time frame. The biggest part of the task was moving the little puzzle pieces of text from file to file until, after disassembling and reassembling 24 files of raw text, Sam's account had become an oral history.

Once the raw material was arranged and divided into chapters, I began to fact-check and fill in any missing gaps where Dr. Iwry's references to historical events were obscure or confusing. This was necessary to ensure that the story went into print with utmost accuracy. The gaps and obscure details were mostly items such as names of people he knew less well, like Nathan Gutwirth and Jan Zwartendijk, the two Dutchmen who had "invented" the idea of Curacao as a destination for a transit visa. He remembered Laura Margolies, the relief worker in Shanghai, only as "Margaret." These details were easily researched and I filled in the information where clarity was needed.

I added little material, in terms of numbers of paragraphs, to this oral history. But it was material I deemed important to the reader. For instance, Dr. Iwry mentioned a passport from World War I called the *sauf conduit*. When I asked him more about this, he said that was all he remembered. After finding more information, I added three sentences to Dr. Iwry's story, giving more detail on this unique document. So to his account of "The league of nations had once designed, at the end of World War I, a refugee passport. They called this passport the *sauf conduit,* which means safe conduct, for refugees. Its purpose was that it matters less whether you are a Jew or a Pole, only that you are a refugee who is now in danger. . . ." I added: "It was also called the Nansen Passport because it was invented by a Norwegian called Fridtjof Nansen, who was the commissioner for refugees at the League of Nations in the 1920s. He made this passport for people who had been thrown away by their own countries. It was a great success at the time because there was a labor shortage in many countries after the first world war and refugees at that time were welcomed by many countries."

When the story was in chronological order and the facts complete, I then moved most carefully to editing Dr. Iwry's own words. He is a colorful and entertaining storyteller, and his account for the most part was too wonderful to be improved upon. Most of my changes consisted in shortening. He spoke extensively, slipping into professor mode, on the Dreyfus trial and the growth of Zionism in Europe. He also delighted in giving me three full hours of tape on his favorite stories by Shalom Aleichem, and a survey of Modern Hebrew Literature. On two occasions, he provided lectures on the Hebrew alphabet and its origins. I made his account more concise, preserving the expressiveness of his account as much as possible.

Dr. Iwry never failed to find the exact words to express himself, and his voice could not be improved upon in that respect. However, his thick Polish syntax, which sounded musical to the ear, looked quite odd in print. The essential problem was his use of verbs, and beyond reducing the length, that is the primary place where I edited. For instance, "This train of ours was going slowly, but surely. We were told it will disembark us in Moscow. It is there we will be to wait, after a new inspection, of course, for a train, which will bring us, perhaps . . ." I edited to: "Our train went slowly but surely. We were told it would eventually arrive in Moscow. And there we will have to wait, after a new inspection of our papers, of course, for another train which would take us . . ."

However, I did not fully correct his verb usage. Dr. Iwry tended to narrate in present tense, switching to past tense at times in a way that, though perhaps grammatically incorrect, was logically consistent with the manner in which he told his story, and in order to preserve his voice, I left his usage alone unless it was jarring. The primary concern throughout all the editing was that Sam's story should reach the reader in as close to Dr. Iwry's own spoken words, if he could have perfectly chosen them, as possible. I hope you enjoy *listening* to him as much as I did.

Chronology

IWRY	EUROPE	ASIA
Born December 25, 1910 Lives in Ukraine from age four to 12		
	World War I begins in 1914	
August 15, 1916: Nina born		
	Poland regains indepen- dence in 1919	
		Hirohito comes to the throne in 1921
1922: Returns to Poland		
1926-1930: Student in Vilna		
		Japanese at war in China from 1931
Spring 1937: Iwry gradu- ates from the University of Warsaw, becomes director of a Jewish School		
	Evian Conference, 1938, reveals poor opposition to Hitler	1938: Japan installs a pup- pet government in Nanking
	November 10-12, 1938: Night of Broken Glass (Kristallnacht) in Germany	
	January 1939: Sugihara opens a Japanese consulate in Lithuania	
	September 1, 1939: World War II begins, Hitler takes western half of Poland	
	September 17,1939: Soviet Russia takes eastern Poland	
December 1939: Iwry escapes to Lithuania, becomes a refugee in Vilna	October 29,1939: Vilna given back to Lithuania. Several days of riots against Jews follow	

IWRY	EUROPE	ASIA
	Spring 1940: Sugihara begins issuing transit visas	1940: Hideki Tojo promoted to war minister and in September, Japan signs military and economic pact with Germany and Italy, creating the Rome-Berlin-Tokyo Axis
	April 1940: Germany invades in turn Norway, Denmark, Holland, Belgium, Luxembourg and enters Paris on June 14	
May 1940: Sweden closes its door to refugees; Iwry and friends get copies of sauf conduit (Nansen Pssports)		
	June 15 1940: Soviets take control of Lithuania	
August 2, 1940: Leon Ilutowicz gets transit visa from Sugihara, Iwry and friends copy it and apply to Intourist for exit visas	August 1940: Soviets order all foreign consulates in Lithuania to close	
March 1941: Iwry and friends cross Russia by train, and arrive by ship in Kobe, Japan Sam appointed JA (Jewish Agency) representative by Ben-Gurion	1941: Germany fighting in North Africa; invades Russia June 22	
June 1941: Iwry arrives in Shanghai, continues refugee work		
		December 7,1941: Japanese bomb Pearl Harbor, Shanghai and other points around Pacific; United States declares war on Japan; Japanese take full control of Shanghai
December 15, 1941: Nina escapes Japan, arrives in Shanghai		December 9–25, 1941: Japan takes Philippines, Guam, Hong Kong, Malay Peninsula, and Borneo
1942: Shanghai economy crippled, inflation begins, support for refugees from overseas ends because of war in Pacific		April 1942: Tokyo bombed by General Dolittle (operation Shangri-La)
		June 1942: Japanese defeated at Midway

IWRY	EUROPE	ASIA
	Summer 1942: Germans hold Kiev and Minsk	August 1942–February 1943: Fighting between Japan and United States on Guadalcanal
	September 1942: Germans attack Stalingrad	
February 1943: Japanese announce refugees are to be moved to ghetto	Winter 1943: Germans (and Russians) freeze to death at Stalingrad	
	Spring 1943: Hitler begins retreat across Russia	
	August 16–21, 1943: Bialystok Uprising	
May 18, 1943: Refugee ghetto goes into effect in Shanghai		
		November 1943: Japanese lose the island of Betio to United States
	January 1944: Germans forced out of Russia; Hitler's armies retreat across Poland from the east and across France from the west	
	June 6, 1944: British and Americans land at Normandy	July 1944: United States captures Saipan, Premier Tojo and his cabinet forced to resign
	August 1–October 2, 1944: Warsaw Uprising	
	December 1944–January 1945: Allies fight Germany in the Ardennes	
		February 1945: Battle of Iwo Jima, followed by bombing of Tokyo
		August 6 and 9, 1945: United States drops atomic bombs on Hiroshima and Nagasaki

IWRY	EUROPE	ASIA
	April 28, 1945: Mussolini executed	
	April 30, 1945: Hitler commits suicide	
	May 7, 1945: German army surrenders to Allies	
July 1945: United States bombs Shanghai, ghetto is hit		August 14, 1945: Emperor Hirohito announces that he is ending the war
August 14, 1945: Japan quits fighting and ghetto residents freed		September 2, 1945: Japan formally surrenders
1945: Iwry marries Nina Rochman, receives visas to the United States as a wedding present		
Iwrys leave Shanghai and arrive in San Francisco on January 30, 1947	April 1–November 25, 1947: UN debate on the establishment of Israel	1947: Dead Sea Scrolls discovered in Palestine
September 1947: Iwry resumes his career as a teacher and begins studying with W.F. Albright	November 29, 1947: The UN vote to create the state of Israel passed by 25 to 13	
1951: Iwry completes doctorate, writes first dissertation on Dead Sea Scrolls		
October 1958: Iwry named New American of the Year		
1985: Iwry honored with Festschrift by fellow scholars		
April 1991: Dating of Dead Sea Scrolls confirmed, Iwry retires from Johns Hopkins		
1999: Blum-Iwry chair established at Johns Hopkins in Iwry's honor		

ONE

Three Worlds, Three Lives

Samuel Iwry (pronounced "EE-vree") was born into the eastern region of Poland, which since 1797 had been occupied by the Russian Empire. Western Poland had been divided between Austria and Prussia. When Poland became an independent republic after World War I, its many decades under foreign rule were readily apparent. Not only was Poland a mosaic of ethnic minorities, but the Poles living under the Tsars barely recognized those living under the Austrians. The new country inherited six different currencies. The war had left the land devastated and looted, and a third of the population was near starvation. Yet the country's economic and political achievements between the two world wars were stunning.

Poland's Jewish citizens were vibrant contributors to every element of Poland's life, politically and economically. Half of Poland's doctors and lawyers were Jewish, and Zionist representation in the Polish Seym (the Parliament) grew steadily until the breakdown of democracy in the country prior to World War II.

In the years after World War I, Zionism grew into the dominant force in Jewish public life. This was especially true in the Tarbut Schools, which had 40,000 students and used Hebrew as the language of instruction. Aliyah (literally, "the ascent"), as migrating to Palestine was called, was the focal point of Polish Zionism, and Polish Jewry was strongly represented among new arrivals in Palestine between 1919 and 1939.

I have enjoyed—and not enjoyed—many great adventures, but I will start with a smaller one in 1958. One day in October, I was teaching a class at Johns Hopkins, in Gilman Hall, in Hebrew literature I think. It was in the morning, and I had quite a large class of undergraduates. So I am in the classroom teaching, and the door opens up, and I was with my back to the door, and I hear all the students say, "Look here!" And I look, and then I completely lose my tongue!

Somebody came in and with them was a television station—a whole television station. It is not like today, one person pops in with a photographic bag. It was going on four wheels, it was like a big desk, cameras and everything, rolling into the classroom, and we saw the two men behind it, pushing it. Before I could speak, I saw the face of Milton Eisenhower, the president of Johns Hopkins and also the brother of the president of the United States. He was the man who really made Johns Hopkins great in many respects, and he comes over to me and I was still losing my tongue. And he greets me, and he says, "Congratulations! You have been elected nationally as the New American of the Year."

The idea was—whose idea, I don't know—but it was an idea that here after World War II there came a lot of people to America, as a result of the war. Refugees, from Europe, like me. So, it was worthwhile to ask, is the American idea that the new people, these immigrants, all these strange-sounding people like me who came here to escape the Nazis and the Communists, are they a burden or do they contribute to this country? Who are these people, and what are they doing?

Somehow they found out about me, because of my business with the Dead Sea Scrolls, which of course I will tell more about later. Apparently I caught the eye of some people and they recommended me, and a committee named me the "New American of the Year." I didn't know anything about it. As a matter of fact, nobody came to interview me. They must have talked to Professor Albright[1] or some other people, they must have found out what they wanted.

Well, at the time, there wasn't any great prize in it, it was just a recognition. Congressman Emmanuel Celler of New York gave me the award, and the mayor of Baltimore, Thomas D'Alessandro, awarded me the gold key to the city. Then, some of the people involved had arranged an interview over the radio in New York. So I sat before a microphone, and I answered some questions—how did I come here, what were my difficulties, and so on. The whole thing was a week or two of celebrations, and I was invited here and there, met different groups of people, told them some of my story. But only a little. Now, I will say more because now I have time.

I have lived in three distinct worlds, three distinct lives. Not as an individual on the edge, but in the mainstream of movement of my generation. I would say that I was one Sam Iwry in the first 30 years of my life, growing up in Poland and being educated in the old European way, and in middle-class Jewish ways. And I was another person in the most unpleasant and terrifying part of my life, the ten years of Hitler and Stalin and Tojo—I was snared by all three of them! I was a refugee then, in those years of homicide and persecution and survival. And I became another Sam Iwry in my third world, when I came to America, when my wife Nina and I entered the country through the Golden Gate and walked together for the first time on the streets of San Francisco.

I was born in the city of Bialystok, in Poland, which was then occupied by Russia, on December 25, 1910. My mother was born Deena (or Dinah) Epstein-Hepner. My father's name was Jacob. My earliest memory is of my father taking me to a school. I was four, and my father took me to a private school called Boyalskys, if I remember the name correctly, and left me there. I don't remember whether or not I cried.

It was also when I was four that World War I began. Germany declared war on Russia. Now, at the time, Germany occupied the western half of Poland, and Russia occupied the eastern half. So Poland was their battle-field! A year later the Germans were nearing Bialystok. My father left his business, and my mother packed us up—Benjamin and I, my sisters had not yet been born—and we went to the Ukraine, nearly 500 miles south and east of Bialystok. My mother had a sister, Azrika, who was now widowed and had two grown children, and they lived in the city of Uman. There was a sizable Jewish community there. Because of this large, well-established community, my family could lead a normal existence. My brother Benjamin and I were sent to a good school, where we received our first grounding in Jewish and general studies. And I grew up speaking both Polish and Russian very well. The childhood experiences and years I spent in this lush part of the Ukraine left me with many fine memories. We used to go to the Sofiefka National Park, which extended from Uman to another city. The war was far away. It was in Uman that my four sisters were born. (The youngest died shortly after birth.)

Suddenly, in February of 1917, the Russian revolution broke out. The Romanoff ruling family was no more, and Kerensky became the premier of Russia.[2] When the revolution came, it was truly traumatic. The whole social, political, and economic structure of the country broke down. Even the army fell apart. We felt that we entered an unpredictable sort of existence, which became unbearable because of Kerensky and Lenin. The war created complete disorder in the land. They were the *Doctor Zhivago* days.

Hordes of former soldiers started to invade every little community, becoming a daily threat and creating a complete breakdown of order and supervision. Then came an avalanche of pogroms—organized attacks on Jews and Jewish communities as well as the general population. Even though I was barely ten years old, I knew the names of those generals whose forces were a danger to physical life and existence.

The White Russian Generals were Anton Denikin and Ataman Petlura, who was later shot and killed by a Jew in Paris. The Whites were mostly counter-revolutionaries and anti-Bolsheviks. They fought the Red army, which was led by Trotsky, Lenin's commander-in-chief, and many had been soldiers in the old army under the Tsar. All of them were plunderers. They went even into the little towns, and they devastated them indiscriminately. Children, women, men—all killed.

These Russians had no ideological guide for persecuting Jews. It was sheer hooliganism and the hatred that was cultivated among the Cossacks and the southern Ukrainians, which had been the place of a Jewish bloodbath in the 1600s.[3] Because we were with our aunt and her children, who were local people, we found a way to be transported to a smaller village, where our relatives had friends. And miraculously, we withstood all the dangers and pogroms. The soldiers never came to that small village. But it was still very difficult. The soldiers lived off the land and destroyed everything. There was no livestock, not seed even to plant crops.

1921 was a bad year, a bad year in all our memories, a date of desperation in the history books. There was complete social breakdown. Weeks went by without bread, there was nothing to buy. There were times when all normal life stopped, and my father and Aunt Azrika smuggled some food and potatoes to live on. It was later estimated that five million people starved to death in Russia in that year.

When finally the Soviet government was established, my parents began a concerted action to get a permit to leave Russia and be returned to Bialystok. It was nearly a miracle that we were allowed to leave. But we had our Polish documentation, and some additional documentation also came from Poland for us. So we were able to show the Bolsheviks that we really belonged in Poland and they let us out. But we couldn't take our relatives.[4]

And so we returned to Poland in 1922, when I was 12 years old. During World War I, the Germans did not get as far as Bialystok. But they did get as far as Lodz, where my wife Nina was born in 1916. Before World War I, the German border was near the city of Poznan. But in late 1918, the Paris Peace Conference carved out Poland again, away from its German and Russian landlords. So when it was resurrected as a nation after World War I, Poland got back its western cities, which Germany considered theirs, and all of its Russian-administered territory as well. So when we returned to Bialystok, we found Poland a country reborn again.

Now, after those *Doctor Zhivago* days of the Russian Revolution, Poland seemed like paradise. But I was only 12, and didn't understand how desperate Poland's existence was. The political situation was chaotic. Poland got a lot of territory by the Versailles Treaty, which resulted in a lot of other nationalities suddenly becoming part of Poland, so there were these territorial minorities—Ukrainians in the southeast, white Russians in the northeast, Lithuanians in the north, Germans in the west. Then, they had a large minority, the Jews, who constituted more than 11 percent of the population.

Now, when the Polish people were given their independence again, they celebrated with pogroms against the Jews, and they were generous with their violence toward the other minorities as well. This shook up the international community a bit, so the Paris Peace Conference[5] told Poland that they had to guarantee the safety of their minorities. The Poles didn't like being told this, but the new government finally signed the Polish Minorities Treaty, reluctantly, in 1920. This treaty also gave these minorities the right to vote. And they all organized into a political coalition against the Poles, all the minorities—Germans, White Russians, Ukrainians, some Lithuanians, and the Jews also.

The situation was very unstable. By 1925, the banks were failing and the country was paralyzed by unemployment and inflation. The zloty lost half its worth. In the first eight years, Poland had 14 governments come and go. When they finally elected a president in December 1922, they reached outside the borders to a Pole in Switzerland, a professor, Gabriel Narutowicz. And the party of the minorities and the small peasants tipped the election against the latifundias, the wealthy Poles who owned large parcels of land. So Narutowicz was really elected by the poor Polish peasants and the minorities.

Now, Narutowicz, being a liberal and a scientist, didn't go, as you would expect in a Catholic country, to the cathedral, and give thanks to God for his success. Instead of going to the cathedral, two days after his inauguration he went to the Warsaw Gallery of Fine Art, and stood before the canvases of the great Polish painter, Jan Matejko, and he paid tribute to the Polish art and spirit. But Narutowicz didn't understand that to most Poles this was unacceptable. So they did not like the fact that he was elected by the minorities, who were not native Poles. And as he was standing in the museum, a young radical, who was also an artist, was waiting with a revolver and shot and killed him.

This was my own great political surprise. I was barely a teenager and found this to be astonishing. This is the way it was. But after that, they elected another president, Ignacy Moscicki, who was a little more to the right.

Back in Bialystok, my father was a supplier of raw materials for the textile industry. Bialystok is an industrial city that is centered on the production of textiles, and all kinds of wool and garments. There were thousands of workers in huge factories as well as people who worked for themselves in small cottage industries.

My father had a small business, perhaps two dozen people worked for him who unpacked, sorted out and sent these raw materials away—this is as much as I remember. My connection with this business was (and this is very difficult to understand) when he had to pay out every week his workers. There was a need to go to the bank and write out a check, and bring it back to him. Since Friday afternoon my Jewish school was closed and my general school let us out earlier, I could do this because I was now older than 12.

The reason that I had to do it was that according to Jewish law, a certain Hebrew inscription from the Talmud was necessary to provide on every I.O.U. or transaction like this to the bank, since it is biblically forbidden to take interest [usury] or deal with usurers. The rabbis had learned how to go around it, because in their time commerce was already developed and you wouldn't do it any other way. So I had to write out the amendment to this law. The amendment says "I thereby make the lender or the borrower a partner in my business, for this sum," let's say for 550 zloty. This way, the usury was removed.

In the Christian world, which condemned very sharply this business of usury and called the Jews bloodsuckers, usury dogs, and all kinds of things, not only did they not understand it, the ways Jews permit themselves to take or pay interest, but when they appeared finally on the scene of great commercial dealings of the sixteenth and seventeenth century, it was the Protestant businessmen who found a way to enter into commerce and to make it legal, who found a way of opening banks, paying interest, charging interest, and went ahead with this. In the Middle Ages when there was one shepherd and one flock—the Catholic church—only the Jews were the usury dogs and bloodsuckers.

We lived in a roomy apartment. This is how in Europe they lived mostly, in apartments, in these buildings full of tenants and full of children. The yard in the middle is a great playground for all the children, of all ages and description. When somebody lives in a little cottage within the confines of the city they call it a "villa," although it is far from being a villa.

However, I was lucky not to be confined always to the city life, to our "yard." My mother came from a little town, a shtetl, called Zabludow, or Zabludova in English. It was surrounded by woods. These woods, and the little town itself had some 300 families. Everyone lived in small houses, it was all little houses with little vegetable plots. Each family had a cow to provide them with milk and butter and cheese. And in the morning a non-Jewish boy or boys or men called shepherds, would come and take all these animals far away into the fields and bring them in the afternoon, late in the afternoon, back. This was a procession! The town was covered with stone pavements—you can imagine the sound.

People lived by some small livelihood and managed to feed themselves though Poland was a poor country. My mother was the daughter of one of the "richest" people in this little town. They had there a tannery, they had stalls in the market, which was in the middle of the little town, and also a special place in their front room where they transacted their daily businesses. Their house was very big. At the back were two more little houses amidst gardens and trees. My mother grew up amongst eight children: Most of them who married remained in this little town. My mother, who went to school in the big city, was the one who married out into a large city. But all my aunts and all my relatives were very happy to see us come for two months in the summer. And my mother was very happy to come out of the city and to be with the children in the place where she grew up.

Nobody knew me there by the name of Iwry. My name there was Shmuel (Samuel) Deenas, after my mother's name. And everybody in the town of the 300 families knew me. In this little town the last name was only a necessity for paying tax to the government, otherwise they called you by your first name and patronymic, or in this case by my matronymic because they didn't know my father. My father came there on the weekends during those summer weeks and was hardly known in the town. But everybody knew my mother.

What is nice to tell about this little town in which I grew up for many years is that they had one of the oldest synagogues in Poland, one of the well-known, much-photographed buildings of the area. It was a wooden synagogue, made entirely with penknives. It had three or four roofs that

Samuel ("Shmuel") Iwry as a youth in Poland. This photo gives little hint of Iwry's subsequent distinguished academic career as a scholar of the ancient Near East, Biblical archaeology, the origins and history of the Hebrew language, Jewish civilization, and modern Hebrew literature. Among other things, Iwry was the first scholar to decipher and translate the Dead Sea Scrolls; his doctoral dissertation was the first ever written on the Scrolls.

looked like a Chinese pagoda. The interior was done with a pen knife, and the exterior also—how they did it, I really don't know. But this was a wooden synagogue, and in my time they said, and it is most probably so, that it was built somewhere in 1660, or maybe 100 years earlier. But it is gone now. The Germans did not leave a single wooden synagogue standing.

My happiest memories of childhood are from the months which I spent there. Because we were a family of five children, my mother rented a very nice place in a mansion of two old people who operated the largest fruit orchard in the area. This fruit orchard was situated in the back of a Greek orthodox church. I remember every Sunday when the services were held and processions were conducted, my mother kept all the children inside. We were advised by the old people, the Jewish people, and by our family, not to come out alone at the time of this procession. Better to sit and wait until late afternoon or they would beat us up. Any sermon in the church could never be complete—and I have heard many of them—without saying that the Jews killed Jesus, killed our God. And this was a thing which was very much in the air.

These processions—the same thing happened at Christmas in Bialystok. The mothers would run out onto the street to remove their children, if they were near the activity. This being a strictly Catholic country, and we, the Jews, knew that we were not a part of it, there was a kind of seriousness in the air on these holidays. And we knew from old traditions that on these holidays, it is better not to stick around. Not that in my time they went out of their way to attack or to shout the slogans, no. Nothing happened in my memory, but really, the idea was that it is better to be home.

The anti-Semitism that existed in Poland at that time was not like the German anti-Semitism. In Germany, hatred of Jews was official policy and enforced by the government. In Poland, it was random hooliganism, practiced mostly by young men, the university students, and well encouraged by vodka. They would go drinking and then attack any Jewish male they happened upon. They left the women and children alone. So we were always careful at certain times. My father would take us home from a movie along certain streets, and sometimes we ducked down an alley if we saw trouble ahead of us. And on holidays like Christmas, we simply stayed home.

My mother used to joke that everyone had a birthday except Sam, because I was born on Christmas. But really, I just celebrated my birthday the next day. I didn't take it as a personal tragedy.

We lived in a girl-dominated house, and we knew it. My brother and I were in the minority. My sisters had the economy of the house in their hands, and we just got the leftovers. And there were times when we were sent away to school, but they were not. We went to a good private Jewish school in which you recited the Torah as well as the general disciplines. Later on when we grew up we all went to gymnasia, which is what we called high school.

My sisters Fanya, Naomi, and Leah all went to a classical gymnasia, which is a secular, more or less scientific high school. Fanya was very intellectual. When she grew up, my parents were able to send her to Warsaw

According to family tradition, the Iwrys are direct descendants of the Ba'al Shem Tov (b. 1700), the legendary, charismatic founder of the Hasidic movement in Judaism. Sam is pictured here in his early twenties with his eldest sister, Fanya. Their other two sisters and their husbands and children were murdered by the Nazis, and Fanya's husband was burned alive when the Nazis trapped 3,000 Jewish men in the Bialystok synagogue and set it afire. Fanya saved Sam's and her parents from the concentration camp for many months by concealing them in a cave in Bialystok. Eventually, a neighbor betrayed them to the Nazis, who opened the cave and machine gunned them. When Fanya was ordered into the concentration camp, she killed herself with poison provided by a physician friend, Dr. Tobias.

and to the Warsaw University with a concentration in Latin. She was supposed to become later a Latin teacher, but World War II prevented it.

Latin was taught without fail in every gymnasia in Poland. This was the second language after Polish. If you lived more to the east in Poland you knew Russian and French (besides Latin). If you lived in the center of the country and to the west you knew very well German and French, and Latin, again. So I studied Russian, French, and also English, as well as Hebrew.

A typical day was always spent in learning. My brother and my sisters and I were all students. No one floated about doing nothing. We played like other youngsters, but my father—he insisted that we always do our studies.

Perhaps because of my early studies in the Torah, I barely remember my bar mitzvah. On some Saturday I was called to Torah, and I am sure a kiddush was offered, but I have no great memory of it. At the time of middle school, and after my bar mitzvah, my father was very worried about me and my brother, that we had not been grounded so well in Talmudic studies as he had been.

Therefore we moved out into some kind of villa or cottage on the outskirts of the city. My father chose this place because of the attic, which had two or three little rooms where there could live a tutor. And my father hired an old retired scholar, a very fine and civilized old man, who stayed with us in the family for two years, when I was 14 until I was 16. So after school, the girls played some and helped my mother, but my brother and I had this Talmudic scholar waiting for us at home. For those two years, my afternoons were spent with the tutor, and evenings with regular homework. And we always at least looked at a newspaper of our city.

But it was not all school. We had little clubs. My brother was a champion checkers player, and like all European boys we kicked a soccer ball. As in checkers, my brother was the great master at soccer, who dared far more than I. Although I loved the sport as much as any other boy, I was not a talented player. When I played, I was a left side runner—a far left runner. At school, they sometimes made me a referee, because they knew I would be fair.

One summer, I remember we were staying in my mother's village and I learned that the HaKoach team from Vienna, the most celebrated Jewish soccer team in all Europe at that time, would be playing an all-Polish team in Bialystok. I thought if I was not there I would never forgive myself. So I got up at 3:00 A.M., left a note, and went out my bedroom window, which was on the ground floor. Bialystok was 18 or 20 kilometers away. I knew the peasants would be heading for the city with their daily produce, so I hitchhiked. One would let me sit on the end of his wagon, which was loaded with vegetables. When he made a turn into a town, I would get off and hitchhike on another wagon going closer to Bialystok. It took three or four hours to get there, and I had enough coins in my pocket to buy a little food and a ticket to kneel on the grass at the edge of the soccer field.

The Viennese were very elegant players. And I saw my hero, a great player who was also a Polish Jew, named Plavsky, play against the Viennese team. Afterward, I hitchhiked back to Zabludova.

In those two years when we lived in the villa on the outskirts of Bialystok, we were only five or six blocks from our grandparents who had a very nice general store. It was run by some of my aunts and we would go there to get something sweet. If we could, we would find 15 or 20 minutes several times a week to be there.

The days were always interesting. Bialystok was a wonderful city. It was not a beautiful place, but it was wonderful to me. Some evenings we would take a tram—you never needed a car to get about—and go to the movies. But we were always asked, "Do you have your homework done?" We could not go if we did not answer "yes." We had neighbors who were not so well off, and they did not give out movie money as easily. Their parents would tell them, "Those Iwry children, they're intelligent enough. Why should we pay for movies when they can tell you all about it?"

In our neighborhood was an older girl, and she was very beautiful. I was in love with her, like all the other boys. I learned many decades later from her brother that during the war, when she had grown into a beautiful and accomplished woman and was about to be married, that a German soldier saw her as she was crossing the street. The soldier declared that such a beautiful Jewess should not exist and he took out his gun and shot her down. This was many years later, of course. But even then, we were always aware that we were under some threat.

The fact that I was born in Poland has a lot to do with who I am. Poland is not so small. Poland in my youth had 33 million people. It lies in a very comfortable piece of land, touching the Baltic in the north and almost reaching the Black Sea in the south. But this comfortable piece of land is unfortunately placed between giant Russia and aggressive Germany.

Germany became more and more nationalistic after the Renaissance, when people in Europe were no more one flock and one shepherd under the Catholic Church, but instead the Europeans sculpted out their own territories and languages. Added to were the ideas of German Romanticism at the beginning of the nineteenth century, and the idea Germany had of being the central power in Europe and a *Drang nach Osten* [pressure to the east]. This was the fright and the nightmare of Poland. And at the end of the eighteenth century, the three powers around Poland—the Russians, the Germans, and the Austrians—carved Poland into three parts. In Poland, we would say that Russia, always on our eastern border, and also Germany, which was on our west and growing bolder and bolder, that these two were always looking to Poland as their *liebensraum*—their living room. This was never lost from our consciousness, from the consciousness of anyone born in Poland. First of all we were always aware of the threat from both the Russians and Germans, who hated each other almost as much as they both hated Jews. And secondly, we always had in our consciousness that as Jews we are living in a country where the majority of the population was either indifferent, or simply unfriendly and sometimes directly hostile. So there was always a threat.

As Jews we learned then that this has to be accepted as fate. Because this was the rule of God that the Jews as a group should be wandering in exile until this God sends the Messiah. For me, I would say that God especially watches this small group who have taken upon themselves to proclaim the name of the one God, and to wait until the whole world will see, will recognize the oneness of God and the Torah and the role of Israel. I think it will not be completely out of place if I say that I know for sure that a great part of the Jewish population, despite the persecutions and the problems, are still a very optimistic bunch, because many of them, I underline many, really believe with all their heart and all their soul that the Messiah will come. No matter how feeble the person is and how miserable his mode of life might be, he is better for believing that he may not die. In this circle I was born in, you shouldn't say "he will die, I will die," that's not nice to say. If you say so you are breaking the hope that the Messiah will come any day or any hour.

Since the Jews lived in Poland for a thousand years they were also very much affected by the German *Drang*. However, with the partition of Poland, even though they were considered one group, one minority, they were divided many ways. There were traditional Jews, religious, who spoke Yiddish. They sent their children to their own elementary schools, called *Heder*, and after this elementary education, they went to yeshiva to study Talmud. This was the largest group of Jews. There were also traditional Jews who considered Hebrew the proper Jewish language.[6] They had their own schools, called the *Yavneh*. There were secular Yiddish-speaking Jews who were Zionists and thought the solution to the Jews' dilemma was a national homeland in Palestine, and they had a school system called the YIVO, for the Central Yiddish School Organization, which was run from Warsaw. There were also Hebrew-speaking Zionists. This was where I belonged. These Zionists had a school system called Tarbut and we competed with the YIVO schools for the middle-class Jewish students. There were Jews who had completely assimilated and there were upper-class Jews and ghettos of Jews stuck in horrible, dismal, poverty.

And later, 100 or 150 years after the division of Poland these the different groups of Jews also showed the influence of these different cultures, the Russians, the Germans, and the Austrians. When Poland was united again in modern times, the groups of Jews that were for 150 years separated from each other became again one group. Middle-class Jews who had been part of Austria could barely recognize Jews who had been under Russia. So Polish Jewry was a mosaic, in some ways united for their common benefit, and in other ways hardly speaking to each other. This was my time.

Here comes a certain break in my secular education. My father was sure, and so was his father, who was still alive, that I as well as my brother were very talented young men, and after graduating from gymnasium, we should go to a great Lithuanian yeshiva, one of the academies of Talmud and Torah. These yeshivas taught the Jewish tradition of Talmudic scholarship that had existed from the Babylonian times some 1,500 years ago until now. My brother, who was a little bit younger, did not object very much, but I had to be cajoled to go to another city, to Lomzha, to a very famous academy there, which produced great rabbis.

It was in 1926. I was brought there by my father one day and a "great light" of Talmudic studies subjected me, alone, to a so-called *Leyenen*—the word means "to read." This is a reading much like is still given today to a new student who says that he wants to concentrate on Northwest Semitic and Biblical Studies, we ask him to read some passages in Hebrew from the Bible to see how well he is prepared. So he gave me something to read in a Talmudic book which he opened at random, and apparently my reading was not bad because he did accept me! And I spent there what we call here, three semesters, learning day and night at a fast pace, in a method not well known here.

I was young, and mostly I went because I was under constant encouragement from my father, who had also studied there. But in later years, I came to appreciate this additional education, which very few people of my age and time had. A few weeks of that time was spent in a little town called Radun, where one of the greatest lights of Polish Jewry used to teach. In fact, Radun was only a small place in what is now Belarus, but it was famous because this man, Israel Meir Kohen, lived there, although in my time he was almost fully retired. He was called not by his name, but by his commentary, which was "Hafez Hayyim."

To say a little bit about this yeshiva in Lomzha: It had its own dormitories and kitchen (it was a very fine and clean dormitory, as my mother came one time with my father to see how I lived there, and she found it to her full satisfaction). After the war, this institution was transferred entirely to Israel, to a little town called Petah Tiqwa, outside Tel Aviv.

A freshman like me who just came from a gymnasium would share living space with an older fellow who was already a rabbinic candidate, just to have a little supervision. I was almost 17 years old and already going out with girls at that time. My roommate was a very fine fellow named Gershon, and—this was very unusual then—he was about 30 years old. He treated me very nicely even though he often asked me, jokingly, "So, did you do well today? Tell me something you learned today." My father used to ask every day after he came home whether I had taken a book in my hands today. My mother had to always say "yes," whether or not this was the case.

Really, the idea was that frivolity and freedom—running around purposelessly as boys and girls would do—is not what befits a Jewish, educated person. We were supposed not only to do our homework, this nobody ever doubted, for this was a part of the evening with my father and mother and all the boys and girls when everybody helped each other. But what my father meant was, did I read on my own, whether I read some Hebrew novel or a historical book or some other things that would be edifying. And so did Gershon. He not only introduced me to the regime of learning at the school, but he also asked me questions inside and outside. I was interesting to him because I came from another academic environment, not strictly a yeshiva environment.

I never knew of this kind of confinement that I had in this yeshiva. I had lived in a large city with a lot of young Jewish people all going to school together, and reading the Yiddish as well as the Polish newspapers from Warsaw and Bialystok. So I grew up in a worldly environment, whereas there in the yeshiva, it was like a monastery.

This was a Lithuania-influenced yeshiva, which means it was mostly academic: you got up in the morning, and the attention to prayers was very short, in contradistinction to the Hasidic places. The Hasidim were a mystic, messianic group, built always around a holy man, called a rebbe rather than a rabbi, whom they believed at times could get the "red line" to God. The rebbe was a spiritual leader, while a rabbi was a teacher, a teacher of Torah.

The Lithuanians were the Protestants of the Jewish world, very practical and study-oriented. Their attitude to Judaism was not of piety and devotion, but one thing only—the study of the Torah. Learning the great mass of Talmudic writings took years of study. However, the purpose of the yeshivas was not to create rabbis. The students became rabbis as a compromise of practical needs, to get afterwards a job, but they weren't prepared just for this job. They were prepared to be learned people, scholars. The teachers at the yeshivas looked at their students as the future great scholars, who will by necessity become also rabbis, teachers.

Before coming to this yeshiva, my whole mode of life had been that of a young man who was independent, living in my own environment, knowing my friends, boys and girls with whom I grew up. Here, I was immediately regimented. I knew that I was in a school that can be vaguely compared to a divinity school in the Western world.

There was a code of behavior in which the unwritten things were more strict than the written. I had to become immediately attuned to a place where the whole life of these students, who were between 16 or 17 years of age, was devoted to one overwhelming thing—the learning of Torah. By Torah I mean not just the five books of Moses but all that was derived from it as well. It means the whole Torah, which we call the Mishnah, and the Midrashim, the Babylonian Talmud, the Jerusalem Talmud, and all the Talmudic works and expositions that were written over the course of history.

The Mishnah has six divisions, which elaborates the Biblical law into every corner of life. It existed first in oral tradition, from about 100 B.C.E. until 200 C.E. It was finally written down and sealed. The Gemara is the extension by the rabbis, who sat in the academies of learning and elaborated on each and every smallest portion of the Mishnah.

In the yeshiva one had to follow a certain regimen. First of all, one studied the Talmudic volumes that are related to the Mishnah, and every period another volume was taken up. Every morning you would see some 300 young fellows in one large hall, each sitting at a little desk, like in the parliament. The hall looked like a synagogue except there is no holy area or scrolls in it. And everyone sits in his own chair and has a little stand which was made to sway back and forth. And the 300 students, divided into sections according to the years of their stay there and their advancement, would all study the same volume of the Talmud.

The younger students would study the two commentaries printed to the right and the left of the text. One was Rashi, named for the French Talmudic scholar who wrote it, and the other was Tosafot, which was compiled by many scholars over about 200 years. Rashi was an explanation of the text, and its connection with other similar texts, while the Tosafot was purely analytical. The older students, would be taking up other commentaries, which were in addition to the Rashi and Tosafot.

They would learn it by humming, like a little tune, and anyone who would come in the hall would find that some students are swaying a little bit and others are sitting straight, but they are all repeating out loud. They learned by softly saying the text over and over and this would make a kind of a music, a hum. In the middle of this great room was an elevation, and on it stood a kind of administrative person who would make announcements from time to time, and make things easier by answering questions, not about the text, but about their needs at the moment. That way the students didn't waste time worrying about a book or looking up something.

Younger students could step forward and ask those who were sitting in the front, who know already. Everybody saw themselves as a great family engaged in learning, and it was the obligation of everybody to help those who are younger or who find something difficult. There was a great moral feeling that we all were engaged in an eternal thing. The atmosphere was not apocalyptic or messianic. It was strictly a study group, to study seriously— not to become a rabbi or be ordained, this word was never mentioned—but to learn for the sake of learning, to become scholars.

Twice a week there would be a summary, an explanation by the scholars of the yeshiva. Once a week one of the heads of the yeshiva would lecture strictly on textual things. The other day of the week, the leader of the yeshiva would talk. He would lecture in a way that not everyone could follow, by reaching outside of the texts in a circular way and connecting certain ideas that are mentioned in other volumes and in the literature in general.

In addition to this, I remember, when I reached a certain stage when I could be considered a young little scholar, I was permitted to participate in what we called a seminar. This consisted of a group of advanced students who would meet for two hours in a certain corner of the big room. One of them would start talking about things that had to do with this volume. This was the place where you could ask questions, you could answer, and you participated. This was called in Yiddish *redn in lernen,* which means "speaking in scholarship."

The yeshiva had another tradition that will seem strange to many but it is true. Those who were in their second year, who could be expected to participate in such a seminar, also came to participate in an all-night study. After seven o'clock in the evening, after your meal—which was always a one-pot meal, consisting of potatoes, barley, and sometimes pieces of meat or chicken—after that you got ready to come back, and this was Thursday night, all night from 7:00 P.M. to 7:00 A.M.

Some would disappear for an hour or two around three o'clock, but they would still come back at five. Some would sit all night without stopping, they would not fall asleep, they would not be dizzy or hazy, just taking in more learning, looking in other volumes, and deepening their scholarship. These were the people who wanted to achieve as much scholarship as possible, because the next day, Friday, the yeshiva took respite after one o'clock, for preparations for the Shabbat. So this is why you took Thursday for the whole night.

There was always a festive Friday night dinner in the yeshiva, with *zemirot*—religious songs composed especially for the Shabbat meal, with fine melodious tunes—and everyone sang. This is also a nice institution, that nobody was left having the Shabbat meal alone.

We had a relative near this yeshiva by the name of Iwry, who owned a nice delicatessen and wine store, and where I was invited from time to time for a Friday night meal. Many students were invited by local families to have the Shabbat meal with them. This was a tradition, that the head of a local family when he had enough room, when he had enough service or servants, would invite a student of the yeshiva on Friday night. Everyone, including my family, who was middle-class had a servant, usually a girl from a village whose parents wanted her to work in the city and become more or less urbanized and also to send home money. Some families invited always the same student, to give him a "second home" and since some families had daughters it made life a little more interesting.

Once, my supervisor found out that I came back late from dinner. And why did this happen? I took a girlfriend, and I went with her to see a movie. Nobody of course was supposed to find me in the movie. Very few Jews in the whole community went to a movie on Friday night, and those who did wouldn't know me. But somehow my supervisor found out.

So he started with me, to tell me that clearly it's not nice. I apparently had this fault, because I came from a secular environment and I had gone to a secular school. I should know that this is not permitted because this profanes the Shabbat. He asks, "You went with a girl?" I said, "Yes, I went with a girl." And he said that we don't look very nicely on these things, and besides, to be wicked he said, you bought two tickets on Friday, right? So I paid money on the Shabbat, which is absolutely forbidden. And when I started defending myself, saying "I didn't pay money, I bought the tickets ahead of time," he said to me a thing that requires some explanation.

He said, "Do you know that according to Kabala, a person gets an additional soul on Shabbat. It is the Shabbat soul, part of the presence of

God who comes down on a person. One is a weekday soul, but on Shabbat, one gets a new spirit for the Shabbat. And when you went into the cinema, you took in two spirits on the one ticket! So you are a cheater, too, in addition to all this!" Well, I had to promise him, it couldn't be otherwise, that I would not do it again. So even though this was a strictly academic yeshiva, focused on knowing the Talmud, it was still a little like a monastery.

For half an hour, every day around 5 o'clock, we set aside the Talmudic books and read some edifying literature, dealing with moral philosophy. They were written of course in Hebrew and were designed to address questions of morality, and to imbue the reader with a deeper piety. These were mostly the work of Rabbi Yisra'el Salanter, who wrote extensively on ethics in the 1800s.

Many students stayed for a number of semesters, and then they would decide to leave the school, perhaps to get married—to find a nice rich Jewish girl whose father will give them some five or seven years of support. When they decided this, they would themselves come to the head of the yeshiva and say that they wanted to change the order of their day and give their full time to studying the practical application of the Four Codes, which means to have and lead a congregation.

Then the student would come before a group of three, and at least one would be the academic dean of the yeshiva, and the others would be local rabbis. These three would have a long discussion, probing him both in his theoretical knowledge and the day-to-day applications that he should know. If he was up to the challenge, they would put their hands on him—this is called *semikhah* which means "the laying on of hands"—and declare him a rabbi in Israel.

But I witnessed in this yeshiva a completely different way. One day after breakfast when I had come up to my room, somebody knocked at the door. I opened the door, and to my great surprise—I almost fell on the floor—I saw the dean of the yeshiva! Plus two more! Three figures coming out of the blue, all with beards, very fine people. Well, they winked to me that I should get lost, and of course I went out. But being what I am, I thought that this must be a very important thing. They never came to the dormitories. So, of course I was behind the door, and I listened. And they said to my roommate, Gershon, in a loud voice, "Gershon, you will agree to us that the time has come that you should be a rabbi in Israel, and we want you to agree and to do it for the sake of Torah." I heard him call out, I could hear well, he said "No, Rabbi! No, I will not agree! I'm not ready yet, I'm not ready in Torah, I'm not ready in scholarship. I'm not ready!"

But he was already over 30 and he schooled students. All the people who studied there called him "rabbi" although he wasn't yet. So when I came in the evening back to my room, I wasn't bashful at all to tell him, "You have very nice guests, Gershon, today. What did they want from you?" He said—he didn't make it a secret—he said, "They want me to take *semikhah,* to accept ordination. But it is not right, I am not ready."

I said, "What do you mean you are not ready? Everybody here knows that you could be a head of an academy anywhere. How can you say you're not ready?" He said "You will never understand, because you cannot comprehend what it takes to know." And after that he walked in the room for hours, talking to himself, clarifying what his ideas were. I learned later that Gershon had moved to Palestine before the war. He spent the rest of his life in northern Israel. But when I left this academy he still wasn't ready to take *semikhah.*

Like Gershon, I didn't want to become a rabbi. I felt that the three semesters I spent studying at a yeshiva were enough. So I returned to secular studies. But this background in the yeshiva has never been lost for me, and when I look at myself, I think as a person and as a Jewish fellow, I would be incomplete and very superficial if I hadn't had this analytical Talmudic education.

However, I did have a great desire to continue studying in a different way, in a historical, critical way, and to study secular history as well as Jewish history. My next step then led me to continue my former studies in a teacher's seminary. So I went to a city that in my day was famous for its educational institutions, and which was the center of Jewish academics as well. In my world, the world of Eastern Europe and the Jewish world, the great centers of learning were not in Paris or London. No. They were in Vilna.

Into the Dark Tunnel

Vilna, as did all Lithuania, had a rich Jewish as well as Lithuanian culture in the early twentieth century. Like eastern Poland, Lithuania was home to a very large population of Jews, largely because imperial Russia in the late 1700s created a Pale of Settlement, regions where Jews were legally allowed to live. This Pale included Lithuania, most of the Ukraine, and parts of western Russia. During the early 1800s, however, Czar Nicholas and his antecedents began to reduce the Pale, forcing the Jews in newly illegal regions to relocate. Thus more and more Jews came to live in Lithuania. In 1981 (the most recent census available), 94 percent of Russia's Jews still lived in the region stretching between the Baltic Sea and the Black Sea.

During its years in the Russian empire, Vilnia was a major commercial center, connected by rail to Russia and the Ukraine, and to the Baltic by the Viliya (Neris) River. However, being annexed to Poland after World War I was an economic disaster, as Vilna was cut off from its markets in Russia and the rest of Lithuania. Although it remained a cultural and educational center, the poverty rate was high. When Sam Iwry began his studies there in 1928, people and goods still moved about on horse-drawn wagons, or droshkies.

In my time, Vilna was part of Poland, a city completely surrounded by Lithuania, but belonging to Poland. In 1920, after Poland was again a republic because of the Versailles Treaty, General Josef Pilsudski came with his army and decided that Vilna was really a Polish town and belongs to Poland.[1] He decided this because the greatest Polish poet of all time, Adam

Mickiewicz, started his wonderful epic poem "Pan Tadeusz," which the Poles compare with Homer's great creation, with the words "Oh Lithuania, my homeland . . ." And the tale speaks a lot of Vilna, like nothing else! Very few people have their own mythology, their beginnings, their holy and beloved places so well described and preserved as by this Polish poet.

However, before 1920, Vilna was, and is now again, the capital of Lithuania. In the 1300s the tiny Dukedom of Lithuania swallowed up the Kingdom of Rus, which is now called Belarus and the Ukraine. This territory had been—like Poland—overrun by the Mongols, but had not recovered as Poland had. So Lithuania suddenly was the size of France, and reached to the Black Sea, though outside Vilna it remained a backward, poor country. Not long afterward, however, Lithuania became part of a commonwealth with Poland. It happened this way: In 1382, King Louis of Hungary and Poland died, leaving two daughters and no son. The Polish gentry refused to accept the husband of Louis' eldest daughter as king, so they arranged a marriage between the younger daughter, who was only 13 years old, to Jagiello, the Grand Duke of Lithuania. So in 1386, Jagiello became King of Poland, and for 400 years[2] the land that is now Poland was the cultural and intellectual heart of the largest empire in Europe. And Vilna was the capital.

So even though Lithuania and Poland became different countries after World War I, the Poles took Vilna. So bad was it for the poor Lithuanians, losing their beloved city of Vilna, that they never created any diplomatic relations with Poland. Not even postal communications! It was a national wrath. So if I wanted to send a letter to my aunt who lives in Vilna, and I lived in Lithuania, I couldn't do it. I have to send the letter to Germany, and the Germans will take it and send it back to Vilna, through Poland. But these two would not directly communicate, for the 20 years between 1919 and 1939.

Under the Jagiellonians the Jews thrived. Yeshivas grew in Lithuania and Poland to become as great and creative as they were once in the third, fourth, and fifth centuries in Babylonia. The Jews also helped the Lithuanians solidify their rule in the south by becoming traders and business people of all kinds, opening stores, exporting and importing, as well as being wine sellers and innkeepers. In the late 1800s, the Russians moved the Pale of Settlement, the regions where they permitted Jews to live, to the west of Lithuania, and forced these Lithuanian Jews to move to Poland. They were deeply resented, and called by the world around, "Lithwacks" from the word Lithuanian. They were different from the Polish Jews.

So Vilna became a center of Jewish Enlightenment, and was considered the Jerusalem of Lithuania. In 1725 Vilna produced the greatest *gaon* of all *gaonim* since the time of Babylonia (*gaon* is a title that means great and excellent scholar). This Vilna Gaon, as he was called, not only did scholarship in Talmudic law, but to show that he is also in the modern times, he wrote a little booklet called "The Grammar of Hebrew Language," a thing that would not have been even thought of a hundred years earlier. And during this Enlightenment, people began translating their heritage in terms of modern European ways and to start writing encyclopedias, histories, dictionaries, and more than this, to examine their past.

There were two other great men who lived and worked in the 1700s. Besides the Vilna Gaon, there was Moses Mendelssohn, the great philosopher of the Enlightenment in Germany. Certain writers, poets, historians, and others grouped around Mendelssohn, who stated in his book *Jerusalem*, that Jews should see the world in the eyes of their contemporaries and should pay more attention to learning European languages, entering research, and seeing history and themselves with a scientific understanding. There was also Israel ben Eliezer (later called Ba'al Shem Tov), the father of Hasidism.

In Vilna I entered a then very popular and reputable academy for teachers and scholars, the Hebrew Teachers Seminary, which existed side by side with the Yiddish Teachers Seminary and the Yiddish Scientific Institute, which was affiliated with the CYSHO in Warsaw. This institution was known by its initials, YIVO, and still exists today in New York City. The years that I spent in Vilna, between 1928 and 1932, were great romantic years. Vilna has a central mountain around which the city is built, and a river, the Viliya, which flows with sparkling water. It is here, on this mountain and river, that most of the mythological stories of Lithuania took place. The Lithuanians have tried not to erase anything that is on the top of this green wooded mountain.

In my time, Vilna was very much a Jewish city, and more Russian than Polish. Like me, the middle-class Jews of Vilna were Zionists and spoke Russian and Hebrew as well as Yiddish. A third of the population spoke Yiddish, and there were many, many Jews living barely above poverty. Becoming part of Poland was, I must admit, a great disaster for Vilna. It was not an industrial city. Vilna had been a great trade center under the Czarist Russians, but when Pilsudski took Vilna away from Lithuania, the borders to Russia and Lithuania closed and the trade ended. Vilna became a very poor city, even by Poland's standards.

The Jews of Vilna opened a trade school and many Jews made a living in light industry, in very small factories of less than a dozen workers. So there was some light industry, and of course its famous educational institutions.

Vilna had in its past attracted another small group, a splinter of Judaism that has existed since the eighth century. These were the Karaites. Their name is called from the Hebrew word *kara,* which means "reading" and also "Hebrew text." In the seventh century, a man called Anan rejected the Talmudic laws and literature and called for a reform, a return to the Hebrew Bible, the Tanach, without the heavy crust of Talmudic interpretation. The Karaites claimed, like the Protestants today, that you derive everything from the Bible and the Bible alone.

The Karaites had remained a small group living in the Middle East. But a group of them, for unknown reasons, moved to Russia and established a synagogue near Vilna. It was in a nice wooded part of the territory, some ten kilometers or less from Vilna, in a place called Trakai.

When I was in my second year—I was 18 or 19—I volunteered one day to go to Trakai and learn more about these "non-Jewish Jews," who traditionally spoke Russian. I got my friend—we studied together, he was the son of the rabbi of Bialystok—and we ventured to leave the school. It was the night of Yom Kippur, Kol Nidrei night, and the school was a trembling atmosphere of prayers and supplications and a forest of burning candles, and the ringing of metal containers for giving charity of alms. Yom Kippur is a very heavy and tumultuous time in the Vilna Synagogue Yard, which is a conglomeration of 39 different synagogues (the place was called the 40 minus one).

I thought to say goodbye to this tumult since I wasn't with my family, and we started out first by foot and when we were outside Vilna, we hitched rides—one wagon to another—in the direction of this little place where we found the woods and the settlement.

We came in to find a group celebrating Yom Kippur both the same way and completely different—like a Reform synagogue in Detroit or Atlanta. There were a lot of lights and people who looked absolutely nothing like the Lithuanian Jews: no beards, no prayer shawls. They looked rather like middle-class Russians. They were dressed very nicely in suits. The women and the children were not separated to another section. I had never been in a reform synagogue, so this was new to me, but I took it as part of the culture.

Since we were strangers and therefore conspicuous, I and my friend, to these couple of hundred people, we decided at the first opportunity to go over to the *hakham,* their word for rabbi or minister, and introduce ourselves as students from the Vilna Seminary. And we asked if we could attend their services. He was very glad and happy to make us feel at home, and he even asked us if afterward we wanted to stay overnight, which would make it possible for us to be with them the next day. We accepted the offer.

They of course didn't speak Yiddish. They knew very little Hebrew. They had a prayer book, they had their literature. The *hakham* knew a lot of things about which I asked him, but he wasn't up to date in the scholarly work, and he asked me to come again and tell him more about this.

The Jewish world knew about their existence and in my day there was no enmity between them and other Jews. They were just a little limb that was dried up out of the main body of Jewry in the world. They believe that their form of the Israelite religion is the right form, the continued form since the Bible, without any additional embellishment. They also believe that their writings, which began with Anan, do not contradict anything in the Bible.

I wrote an article about the visit and sent a copy of it to a daily Yiddish newspaper. The editor kept it for the following year, when it appeared in a very conspicuous place of the paper on the eve of Yom Kippur. The title of the article was "Yom Kippur with the Karaites in the Vicinity of Vilna."

My education in Vilna put me straight into the intellectual center of the Enlightenment. I studied everything that happened in the 3,000 years of Jewish history. After I graduated from the Vilna academy, they asked me to stay on and be what is called today a teaching assistant. They influenced me to try and to help the older professors and also to see how their new methods of teaching could be tested in their experimental school. Professor Czarnow was the head of it. He was the theoretician of a new psychology attached to education. They had an elementary school of six grades and the seventh was forming. The name of it was the Gurevitch School. It was named for a woman who was famous for her work in progressive education. The leaders and teachers of this school were drawn from the Vilna University and from the city's other educational institutions.

One of them was Stanislav Borovsky, a Polish professor, very respected and moving on to the idea that education is a continuing experimentation, a continuing effort to find ways of coming to a dialogue with the young student and how to continue this dialogue in trust and in good will. He believed, like the Swiss educator Johann Pestalozzi and others, that a child is really a *tabula rasa* that can be written on. Borovsky also knew of Freud's theories.

Well, the atmosphere in Vilna was very interesting. Even though Vilna was the center of the Yiddish language, the intelligentsia, especially the

Jewish intelligentsia, continued to speak Russian. This is where I polished the Russian I learned as a child, to speak, to read, and to feel at home in this language that is quite different from Polish. Very few people in the United States can say that they read *Anna Karenina* in the original Russian!

The people of Vilna knew that they lived in a city that didn't abound in material goods, that hadn't a great industry. Even then, Vilna was made mostly of stone and the few streets that were paved, were paved with cobblestone. There were not many automobiles. Mostly people walked or rode in horse-drawn wagons. The people are not very rich but they lived very nicely. There were many fine cafes and maybe ten or twelve theatrical troupes, performing in many languages. There were always concerts.

And in the center of the city was the Strashun Jewish library. This library was a meeting place of intellectual life, both for the Jews and the rest of the population. There were a tremendous number of books and journals that were accumulated there by the philanthropy of one family called Strashun, like the Enoch Pratt Library here in Baltimore. It was rivaled only by the library in Warsaw. The Soviets and Nazis together tore it down during World War II.

I remember that it was one great room, and entering was like going into a small sanctuary, and a sanctuary it was par excellence. It was served with great love and understanding. We could go over to the librarian, who talked with the lowest voice possible, mostly with signs. The library had no card catalogue. I would write the name down of the book I wanted, and they would bring it. Many of the books, many places were not open to the public. But they would bring books to you. This was their policy.

The service was very simple. We all knew the several people there who answered us right away without a computer where this book is, or if it was taken out. They would also remind you that a book is in demand and please bring it back. Most of the reading, most of the work was done at the library. They were very reluctant to give up any book except novels and things that were not for reference. Books that were stamped for research or for study, remained there. You need it? You come there and read it.

There were two very long tables around which were sitting older, bearded talmudic scholars as well as young modern students, secular students. These older rabbis would sometimes mutter about this young frivolous generation, but they were ignored. And we really spent days and days, and nights and nights there. Every night some several hundred people would be sitting there. Most would come and go, but for the people who were studying, the tables were as if assigned. They weren't assigned, but I always went to the same place where I was always near similar people of similar interests. I never approached another chair, where I would find people whom I didn't want to meet.

In Vilna, I also played some soccer. I was a member of the Maccabis, a Zionist sport club, and they had a branch there. In school I was a left side runner, and when I was at that time already beginning to go bald I said this is because I deliver so many goals with my head! This wasn't true of course. I was not much of an athlete. I remember even in my younger days they wanted me to be a referee. I was more useful as a referee. I was not a good player, but they believed that I would be fair, as it should be.

However, my world of the early 1930s, this time of great youthful hopes, was also completely darkened with recessions, strikes, and the ascendance of Nazism in Germany. There were many dark clouds on our horizon. Soviet Russia was only a few kilometers away, and we could hear and fully understand the news in both the German and Russian languages on the radio. But we had no way of knowing what was ahead.

When I graduated in 1932, I left Vilna and returned to Poland proper. I decided to look for a position near Warsaw in order to continue my studies at Warsaw University. I found a position at the Tarbut cultural pre-gymnasium in a town called Suwalki, and in 1934, I entered the Institute of Higher Judaic Studies at Warsaw University.

This institute was headed by the great scholar Moses Schorr. Schorr was an Akkadian scholar. Akkadian is the language of Ancient Babylonia, written in the cuneiform script. He was an interesting teacher, who conducted all the preparatory classes in Near Eastern Studies. It was while I was studying with Schorr that I heard for the first time a name that was to determine the nature of many of my later years, the name that eventually pulled me away from Israel, the name of William F. Albright.[3]

The classes took place twice a week, and since the distance between Warsaw and Bialystok was not too far—it is like between here, Baltimore, and New York, or even less—I could be there twice a week, stay the two days, and go back home and teach. So I arranged it in such a way that I could work and be a student. Only the first year, I remember, I couldn't do it. I had to be completely busy with preparing and attending the classes. But the second and third year, I found a position as director of a gymnasium in Bialystok. I could commute from my home for the two days.

The class with Professor Schorr was a little bit different than those of the other professors. He was the Chief Rabbi of Warsaw, and also a senator in the Polish government as well as a professor. So many times his classes were canceled because he had so many other responsibilities, and I could save myself a trip.

Schorr required a paper at the end of every semester. On one of these papers, I had worked for a long time and I mailed it in, to save the trip to Warsaw. However—this is how strict was the protocol in Europe—Schorr's secretary didn't like the way I had addressed the envelope, and she sent it back. She enclosed a note: "A fellow who is with us for two or three years should know how to address an envelope to the professor!" I had written, "Professor Schorr, Rabbi of Warsaw." She wrote, "This is horrible! You have to write"— she gave me the order—"Rabbi, Senator, Professor, Doctor Schorr . . . There is an order!" She gave me a lecture. So I had to get a new envelope, and send it back with everything addressed according to her instructions.

Many years later, when I enrolled at Johns Hopkins, Albright's attitude was human, smiling, laughing. I thought then, what a difference! This pompous European way doesn't make you a better scholar. Doesn't give you better preparation. The European way is stultifying. Everything must be according to a certain protocol, especially for these professors. They were schooled in German schools and Austrian schools, and they followed a certain routine.

When I had to be in Warsaw, I stayed in the house of a family that my family had known for a long time, my father's second cousin or whatever. When they came to Bialystok, they stayed with us. They gave me a room and I could come and stay overnight if I needed to be there two days. I didn't need a hotel.

And being in Warsaw was an extraordinary experience. Warsaw had a population of a million people, and a third were Jewish. In my experience, the contrast between the little village where my mother grew up and a place like Warsaw was very educational and enriching.

Before it was leveled to rubble during World War II, Warsaw was a great and learned European city. There were three Jewish dailies for the Jewish population, two in Yiddish and one in Polish. Well, I would not read all of them, but I would see at least one Jewish and a Polish paper. In my trips on the train, I would try to get all the news. There was a large intelligentsia in Warsaw. There were many fine Jewish theaters, very fine forward-looking Polish theaters. And I liked to take advantage of as much as I could. The 1930s were a time of very bad news, yet the theater and all the rest of life went on in some way. So I enjoyed my time, I went out with my girlfriends, I was a young man in a great city that I came to know well.

In western Poland, including Warsaw, the Jewish population was mostly Hasidic. It was Israel ben Eliezer, the Ba'al Shem Tov (literally, "the Owner of the Good Name"), who called for a new spiritual awakening among the Jewish masses. His influence spread in the east and south of Poland where the Jewish peasants, although they were not learned, they could read some Hebrew. And there grew a mindset that the wealth of the Torah should not only belong to a Talmudic scholar, but there should be something for the people as well. In Hasidism, learnedness was combined with prayer, with devotion. This movement spread like a fire all through the little towns neglected by the scholars.

Although the Ba'al Shem Tov is considered the founder of Hasidism, it did not start with him. Hasidism put down roots years before, when the Jewish families were scattered around the vast expanses of the Ukraine, southern Poland, and the Black Sea, living as peasants on large estates. Jewish families saw each other only on the holidays of Yom Kippur and Rosh Hashanah. They came to experience an unexplained phenomenon, called the *Gute Yid,* the "good Jew."

A visitor would knock, the door would open and a man would kiss the *mezuzah,* the holy sign that marked the house of a Jew, and the woman, the *baleboste* of the house, would with surprise say "wash your hands and I will make you something to eat." The visitor never introduced himself or explained his visit. By his gentleness and the light of his face, they recognized that a different kind of a guest has come.

Then the whole family would take their place around him, before the fireplace, and he would begin by praying with them, and then he would ask about their situation. And they would pour out their worries to him. They stay there as long as the master tolerates them, but their children are wandering away. There is no one to prepare a bar mitzvah for the sons, the daughters stay out late and they don't know who may have taken hold of them. They live little better than animals—when it is cold, they have to share their house at night with the lambs and kids and calves, keeping them warm. And they are never sure what the next day will bring.

Well, the visitor tells them that with prayer, God will help them and things will change. And he disappears. But in a year's time, he returns, and he finds that things have indeed changed. The little animals have a shed and are not in the house. The sons and daughters are smiling and participate in the prayers with them. When he disappears as before, they all wonder if it was he that brought the blessings they have experienced.

They called this mysterious guest in Yiddish *Gute Yid.* And when more and more of them had experienced the blessings of this mysterious visitor, they went to the nearby cities to look for him. The *Gute Yid* later grew into the Hasidic movement, of which Israel ben Eliezer was the crowning phenomenon.

Besides ben Eliezer, the Ba'al Shem Tov, there was also his daughter Odel. There are a lot of stories of this great and spiritual woman and other great Hasidic figures. And there is a tradition in my family that my forefathers are descendants of this Odel. According to our family's tradition, as told to me by my father, and by his father to him, the Ba'al Shemtoph gave the name "Iwry" to his daughter Odel and his son-in-law when they married, to use as a family name. There were once records that went back five or six generations, from Odel to my grandfather, but these records perished in the Holocaust.

Hasidism was a movement that rolled like a warm fire into all the small Polish villages, a movement that rolled with great force and couldn't be stopped. The simple Jews believed the rebbes were holy men. But the Vilna Gaon didn't like them. He forbade them to come into his domain, and if one ventured into Lithuania, the gaon "put them in Herem"—excommunication. So there were much fewer Hasidic Jews in Lithuania and eastern Poland. But when this Vilna Gaon died, the Hasidic Jews that were there in Vilna celebrated in the streets, and then there was a riot.

Away from the Vilna Gaon, the Hasidim filled up western Poland, and they adopted later the traditional clothes, copied from the Polish estate owners. But in my time, there were still very few Hasidic Jews in Bialystok, because we were close to the Lithuanian border, and under the influence of the Vilna Gaon. Besides the influence of the Vilna Gaon, there was another movement, called the Mithnagdim, or "opposition," which was a counter to Hasidism. Now, my more recent ancestors were major exponents of the Mithnagdim, which emphasized the intellectual and literary nature of Judaism, rather than the mystical and inspirational focus of Hasidism.

In my day, there were in Poland more than a million Hasidic Jews. So besides the Zionists and others, there were also these contrasting movements among the Jews, between the Hasidim and the others. And I was one who was thrown into all these movements.

In Warsaw, you could see all these Jews. I saw it too in some of the fathers and sons of the Hasidic families. The father dressed as a Hasid, in a long black coat, nicely tailored, very fine, made to measure, with a black hat. Often the sons dressed this way, too. But some sons were assimilated. They broke with Hasidic tradition and had thrown off the long black coat. They would say that "they went short!" Short means the jacket is short.

In some families, those sons who "went short" were treated as if dead—they had a funeral for them. In other families, this was no big deal. This was the case in the family of my wife Nina, who lived in Lodz. Nina tells me her father was Hasidic, but dressed for work as a Pole. On the holy days, he put on his Hasidic clothes and spent time with the rebbe, and took her brother with him. However, Nina's mother and sisters did not observe the Jewish holidays and spoke only Polish. Nina alone learned Hebrew because she happened to attend a Tarbut gymnasia.

In Warsaw, I studied biblical, post-biblical, rabbinic and modern Jewish history, all taught like they do today—textual criticism and historical interpretation with a modern scientific approach. The Hasidim didn't come there. But for people like me, it was okay. It so happened that Schorr was very well known as an Akkadianist, and Akkadian supplies us with a lot of the background for the Bible. Hebrew alone is not enough. Akkadian is a Semitic language, older than Hebrew, which has a straight base in the Mesopotamian world, so he taught Akkadian and Semitic grammar, so I became a Semiticist because I knew Semitic grammar and not Hebrew grammar only.

After three years of being in Warsaw taking my courses, both at the Institute and at the University, I finished with a dissertation, "The Rise and Fall of Sephardic Jewry." Being an Ashkenazi Jew, I was very interested in Maimonides and others who made famous the Sephardic Jewry, and in 1937 I got my diploma, more or less an M.A.

But, unfortunately, there was much more to this time of my life than fun and schooling. All of Europe was stirring with hatreds and warlike ambitions. Germany and Russia, as they had hundreds of years ago, were threatening to gobble up Poland again. And within Poland, anti-Semitism was rising. I finished my schooling just in time because 1937 was perhaps the last year when it was even a little bit possible to be a Jew and still live a decent life of any kind in Poland.

Now, there had been some Jews in Poland for a thousand years. However, many more came during the late 1300s. It started after the Great Plague of 1348, which was followed by a widespread famine, which killed half of the population of Western Europe. The survivors went looking for a scapegoat, and there followed a terrible wave of anti-Jewish atrocities across Europe.

The plague did not have much effect on agrarian Poland. While Western Europe was in decline from failing agriculture, plague, pogroms, and economic instability, Poland was enjoying a time of great prosperity. King Kazimierz the Great built universities and cathedrals, art and agriculture flourished, the population grew and Polish literature was being written down. King Kazimierz welcomed the Jews and others from devastated Western Europe, to settle in Poland and help develop the economy. The clergy was against it, of course. The pope even sent complaints to the king, protesting the place of the Jews in Polish society, but the king persisted, thinking that over time the Jews that came would intermarry with the Poles, and assimilation would resolve any problems. However, that didn't happen.

And the Jews did come. Each latifundia, or large estate, invited a Jewish family to come and develop its business. They created small industries with the timber, meat, milk, whatever the natural resource was. This had previously been done to a small extent by German agents, who lived on the Polish borders. But now the Jews became the marketing people of Poland's natural resources.

Soon, every latifundia had a *moshka,* as these Jews were called. And the music of the Shabbat and other celebrations became well-known to all the Poles on the estates and to the peasantry. The song ma *yapht umah na'amt at Shabbat ha mulka* was very popular. Many times, the "great boss" or *poretz* of the latifundia would have a party with drinking and dancing at the estate. At the last minute, he would invite the estate's Jewish family to the party and order them to sing and dance this song.

Later, when the Jews were more established in Poland and no longer considered themselves bound to the latifundias, they would often refuse to perform when asked. They called those who did, whether willingly or unwillingly, *mevayesh* because they gave up their dignity.

But even though they became very established in the culture of Poland, the Jews did not assimilate. They built synagogues, they sent their children to be educated in a Jewish manner. In time the Jews became prosperous and no longer thought of themselves as invited. But even so, the Jews of Poland at that time had this idea of always living by the grace of others, in whatever conditions existed, because it was temporary. Any day, the Messiah may come.

There is a story that illustrates how immediate the Messiah was. One day the *moshka* of an estate comes to his wife as she is doing laundry, and he has a big dog on a leash. She sees him with this dog, and asks "Are you out of your mind?" The man explains that the dog belongs to the *poretz* and this boss had asked him to teach the dog Yiddish. "At first he wanted the dog to learn Yiddish in one year, but I said ten years," the man told his wife. "I agreed on three to five years in the hope that in five years the *poretz* will drop dead or the Messiah will come."

The point is this: The Jews considered Poland as the place where they stayed, but it was not their home. And they even Hebraized the word "Poland." "Poland" is English, but the German is "Polen"—so they made two Hebrew words of it. *Po* means "here" and *leen* means "dwelling overnight." So, to the Jews Poland means "Here you stay overnight" until the Messiah will come. So even though there were many Jews who did assimilate, most did not, and the Poles in turn never really considered the Jews a true part of Poland, even after many centuries.

By the 1900s, the Jews were the educated and worldly business people with contacts in almost every city in Europe. They were the importers and the exporters, and some in the cities were quite wealthy, though the ghettos were also full of very poor Jews. While the Jews in the small Polish towns were not wealthy or in poverty, they all made a living in the industrial and commercial life of Poland.

The big industries, as well as the latifundias, the large agricultural estates, belonged to the Polish aristocracy, or *szlachta,* which was strictly Catholic. These included the railways, the *hutas* [steelworks], banking, and the government. These were strictly Polish aristocracy, whereas the rest of the population, 75 percent of all Poles, were small farmers and peasants, or *piasts.*

The *piasts* had a difficult time entering the cities and finding a place in urban economic life. That place was occupied by the Jews. This alone was enough to create friction and jealousy, the idea that the Jews have economic power—unjustly so. Now, the cities of all Europe had ghettos of very, very poor Jews, but that did not stop the rest of the population from thinking of the Jewish people as rich at the expense of everyone else. The well-educated Jews were especially resented.

The Polish peasants did not often get a good education. The further to the east, the more uneducated and helpless was the peasant. Eastern Poland was for almost 200 years under the domination of the Russians, who themselves have a very deprived peasantry. More to the west and the center of the land the peasant went to an elementary school and got a reasonable education. However, the best education was to be had in the southern part of the country, called Gallicia. Unlike eastern Poland, which had been part of Russia, Gallicia had been "administered" for 150 years by Austria under a quite enlightened dynasty. In Gallicia it was said that if you threw a stone you could hit either a dog or a doctor. The peasants in this part of Poland were better off than those elsewhere.

But the Jews had built their own schools, and as they were forbidden to own land, had only an education to rely on. In my time, nearly half of all the doctors and lawyers in Poland were Jewish.

Poland was a poor country. The economy was very bad. The industries were backward and could not compete with the European countries around it. There was no money for a military. A third of the Polish peasants were illiterate and there was a lot of alcoholism, because there was also no hope. The Catholic Church taught that suffering was what you were supposed to do anyway. So you can imagine the condition of the people.

Well, there was also the big idea in Poland that the reason Poles were poor was because the minorities had more than their share, and in 1934 the government decided that the Minorities Treaty was not valid. To improve the lot of the Poles, they began to exclude the Jews from the economy, to force them out of business and the government. Jewish businesses had all my life been boycotted and picketed at times. Picketing Jewish businesses was a great pastime among the university students, as well as a profit-making enterprise. The students would stand outside a Jewish store with leaflets in their hands, threatening anyone who tried to buy from the owner. These leaflets had the names of Polish-owned stores where you were supposed to spend your money. The Polish store owners would pay the picketers to have their businesses listed on the leaflets.

Besides the economic reasons for anti-Semitism, Poland was a uniquely Catholic nation. In no other country as far as I know was the mixture of true Catholicism and strong nationalism so well combined together. A lot of their clergy, being fine theologians, gave a special coloration to their view of history. They brought the idea into their national consciousness of being the sacrificial lamb and waiting for the coming, the second coming of their redeemer. The Poles were always looking back to the time when they were a great country, stretching from the Baltic to the Black Sea.

And they had a reason to feel like a sacrificial lamb. The Germans, Russians, and others have been invading, carving and seizing parts of Poland for over a thousand years. Poland is different from Western Europe because the Romans never conquered there. Poland had no "dark age" when the Roman empire collapsed, and Christianity and the feudal system were never tied together there. At the beginning of the tenth century, as the rest of Europe emerged from the dark ages, the territory that is now Poland was occupied by a thriving, peaceful, agricultural, and pagan people who called themselves the *polenz*, the people of the fields.

Their isolation ended in the 900s, when Otto I, King of the Germans, invaded Poland and well into this century, Poland was repeatedly invaded, fought over, and chopped up between the imperialistic powers around it. The Polish people came to have a great messianic longing for the days of the Commonwealth, when it was at peace.

Even the literature reflected this attitude. Wladyslaw Reymont was one of Poland's great writers who received the Nobel Prize for a novel, *The Peasants* (1909), which only a Polish writer could produce. This book as well as the works of the three greatest poets of Poland, which are taught in every Polish school, all had the feeling that Poland was the lamb that was sacrificed on the altar of imperialism and there would come a time when they, who suffered and suffered very much, would become free again.

This gave a special twist to their anti-Semitism, which wasn't as brutal as that of the Germans. Their anti-Semitism was protesting, denigrating, boycotting, disorganized hooliganism. But their literature also shows that the Jews were part and parcel of their whole culture, of a colorful grouping together. It is seen in their poetry and also in their novels.

In 1933, Hitler became Chancellor of Germany and the boycotts of German Jews began. Right away there started a large migration of these Jews to Palestine. I was told in 1934 and 1935, 60,000 German Jews went to Palestine, besides those who left for other countries. But then, the British White Paper was in effect to limit this immigration. Britain was in charge of Palestine, and they supported the Arabs. And it was Britain that issued several so-called White Papers[4] that said how many Jews would be allowed into Palestine.

The Zionists had been at work for decades already, trying to make a national homeland for the Jews in Palestine. And the Balfour Declaration in 1917, which recognized a Jewish homeland in the Middle East, was a great victory. But then, in 1922, the first White Paper came out, the Churchill White Paper, to make sure not too many Jews entered this homeland. When the Passfield White Paper came out in 1930 to stop immigration completely, the Jews in Poland did not panic because the war was not contemplated. Germans could get to Israel easier—they could get around the matter that only so many certificates were issued by the Jewish Agency for Palestine as some were rich and went as capitalists. If you deposited a thousand pounds sterling in a British bank, you could go to Palestine as a capitalist, and didn't need a certificate. However, negotiations with the Germans were difficult as the Germans would only let them leave if all their possessions—to the last coin—stayed in Germany. They didn't want the British getting those pounds sterling. So it was tricky even for those who could be capitalists.

That last year before the war, all of us wanted to get out as soon as possible. I had wanted to leave Poland and go to Palestine all my life. There was one other way to go, besides being a capitalist or getting a certificate. That was as a student at a university. After graduating from the University of Warsaw, I sent my papers, everything I had from the Higher Institute for Jewish Studies, and applied to the Hebrew University in Palestine.

My brother was already gone. He went to Israel as a *halutz*—*halutz* means pioneer. This was a time when many young Jewish people, after graduating the gymnasium, would go to Israel, to live and work in a collective, a kibbutz, and build the country. My brother Benjamin did this and went to Israel in 1936.

The year 1938, after I graduated from the University of Warsaw, was the year all hope trickled away. In 1938, Poland became as bad a place for Jews as Germany. There had been pogroms against Jews in Germany already, and there were many Jews who were Polish citizens living in Germany during the 1930s. And in 1938, Germany began to kick them out in earnest. But the Polish government didn't want them to come back. So in March, the Polish government denaturalized these Jews, took away their Polish citizenship and stopped them from entering the country. There grew a refugee camp of displaced Jews at the border between Germany and Poland, and the appeals for financial help spread through the Jewish communities to help these people survive the winter.

In the summer of 1938, there was a great meeting between heads of state—the U.S. president and the leaders of most of the European countries were there—and it became known as the Evian Conference. They were supposed to find a place for the Jewish refugees forced out of Germany, but it became depressingly clear at this meeting that no one wanted the Jews. The Germans were not alone in wanting to get rid of them. So after this conference was held, Hitler knew no one would oppose him.

It was also in 1938 that the universities decided to get rid of Jewish students and as a first step, they made them sit on "ghetto benches" at the back of the classrooms. They began pressuring the Jewish gymnasia and pre-gymnasia to close. They wanted the middle-class Jewish families to send their children—but mostly their money—to the Polish-run schools. I was the director of a Tarbut school and we knew our time was running out.

In all of Europe at this time, Hitler made the mood terrible. He was insisting that any territory that had Germans living there should belong to Germany. This was the thinking of the time, that a country was defined by the ethnic background of the people. So sometime that spring of 1938, Hitler took the Sudetenland, which was a part of Czechoslovakia where there were a lot of Germans. It was called the *Anschluss,* the union, because Hitler claimed that it had been part of Germany all along.

Hitler a year before had insisted that the western Polish city of Danzig belonged to Germany, as well as the land on Germany's border because there were many Germans living there. The Polish government of course refused to return it. After he grabbed part of Austria we knew he would eventually take Danzig and some part of Poland by force. As Hitler became more threatening, the commander of the Polish army, Edward Smigly-Rydz, said "Not a button will we give them!" But this was the last notable reaction. There was no solution.

There was this same thinking about ethnic uniformity in Poland, and the idea of a country as a place where the people have the same ethnic identity grew stronger after World War I. This, I believe, was one reason why Hitler met such half-hearted opposition, because even people who hated him still liked this idea of ethnic unity.

In June there was the news about a ship, called the *St. Louis.* This ship was carrying over 1,100 Jewish refugees to America, but the U.S. officials would not allow it to dock. It was not allowed to go to Cuba, either. These refugees all had papers and some even had relatives who were willing to take financial responsibility for them, but this ship was still turned away. It proved that the Jews were not wanted anywhere, and Hitler and his Nazis became even bolder.

And this happened in Poland. In September 1938, President Ignacy Moscicki dissolved the government and called for new elections.[5] This caused great confusion, but when the elections were over, we knew what it meant. The Camp of National Unity, or OZN, had won a large majority, and they immediately began to push the Jews out of the economy. Jews were dismissed from their jobs in the government, and those running their own businesses could not get their licenses and permits renewed. They were made to sell out to Polish owners at a very low price. If they were very lucky, they could stay and work in their own business for a small wage.

Even in my small city in eastern Poland, people talked low to each other. Everyone knew changes were coming. Terrible changes. The newspapers reported constantly that all the countries of Europe were calling for men to report to the military. Italy and even England were inventing anti-Jewish laws. My oldest sister, who worked in a bank at the time, she saw it, felt the disaster coming. She would come home from the bank and fall on her bed. She wouldn't eat dinner.

But it was not until November that all hope disappeared. What happened was this: A young Jewish man got into the German embassy in Paris and shot a German official. He had intended to kill the German ambassador, but shot someone else instead. The Nazis lost no time. They called for retaliation, and that night thousands of Jewish businesses and hundreds of synagogues in Berlin were vandalized and looted. It was November 9, and it became famous as the *Kristallnacht,* the night of broken glass. But it did not stop there. The government said that the Jews could not use their insurance to fix their properties and the Nazis even placed a terrible fine on the Jewish community. They had to pay the German government a billion Reichmark. This was absurd! And we did not know it, of course, but Hitler was already arresting and placing the wealthier Jews in concentration camps and confiscating their property.

Kristallnacht told everyone clearly that a great danger had arisen, unlike anything before. Hitler was saying that he will "solve the problem of the Jews." But he didn't yet speak of his "final solution." That came later. We only knew that there was no more existence for us in Europe.

As the year ended, there was a sense that we were just waiting for our doom. When we heard in April 1939 that Germany and Russia had signed a nonaggression pact with each other we knew it could only mean one thing. Poland was to be divided between these two powers again.[6] War would break out any day. To make things worse, that spring, another White Paper came out, to reduce emigration to Palestine even more. Reduce emigration! This was a great disaster. Then I received word that I was accepted at the Hebrew University. But I did not get out in time.

The evil we knew was coming arrived on a Friday morning, September 1, 1939. The Germans invaded and took Danzig. They claimed that Poland had invaded Germany and they had responded in defense of the Fatherland. It was unbelievable. It turned out that the night before, the Nazis had grabbed some men out of a German prison and dressed them in Polish military uniforms. Then they staged an attack on a radio station in a little town near the Polish border. They claimed Poland had invaded Germany. No one believed it, but the Germans got what they wanted anyway.

Hitler sent his *Luftwaffe* to subdue Poland, but after the planes had dropped their bombs and destroyed the railroads, came the parade of soldiers who randomly grabbed and shot people—mostly Jews, but really anyone who got in their way. They entered the towns playing the Nazi music on their trucks. They thought the population would applaud their coming. But the stores closed right away. Everything shut down and everyone who was not clearly German hid inside their houses.

Poland's tiny military held out for only two days against the German army, which was more than ten times bigger. By September 9, the Nazis had arrived at Warsaw. They stopped there because of the nonaggression pact that they had signed with Russia.

When the Germans invaded, I was in eastern Poland, in Bialystok. The mood in Poland at the outbreak of the war, well, we didn't think it could get worse, but it did. Everything changed. The order and tranquility in the home, the order of the day, everything changed the moment it was known that Hitler was in power to our west.

Much later in my life, I heard this story from Nina's sister. I did not know my wife Nina then. But this is what happened to her family. Their father, like many others in Lodz, made a living in the textile industry. He had a small factory that employed 20 or 30 people, who finished out fine blankets, very fine blankets. The workers were Poles, Jews, and Germans. And the head of the workers, the foremen, was a German who had worked for them since Nina was born. He was a good man. He ran the factory. Nina's father ran the commercial side, selling, meeting with customers. And the factory had a good name.

When the war broke out, Nina was in Warsaw. But her sister said that this man, the first thing, this man who came to all their birthday parties, who was like one of the family, the very day that the war broke out, he came to their house like he did every morning. Only this time he did not remove his hat and ask politely for the boss. This morning, he stepped in and only held out his hand and demanded the key to the factory. And that was it.

Nina's family lived in an apartment building like everyone else. And the building had three sides, and there was a courtyard, and a man kept the gate to the courtyard. And this man—the residents of the building every year would give him presents at the holidays. And he knew every child, and watched them grow up, and scolded the older ones when they came in too late. But when the war started, and the Jewish residents were told to leave, they were kicked out of their apartments. They were told that they could bring with them only a blanket and other necessities. They had to leave their other possessions. Even so, this man, as they walked out the gate, he took from them their blankets, and even the hats from their head. And it was winter! How were they to keep warm? He did this.

Those in western Poland immediately fled to the east, to escape the Nazis. Many of my family's friends and relatives came to Bialystok. Some of them came on foot, hiding from the soldiers that were on every road. They talked of the hundreds of bodies already left lying in ditches across western Poland. And we knew that being in eastern Poland was not enough. The Germans had stopped at Warsaw only because of the nonaggression pact with Russia, and we knew it was only a matter of time before Russia took what was left of Poland. And Russia waited only long enough to be sure that no one—England, France or anyone else—would fight on behalf of Poland. England and France had both declared war on Germany, but they were not interested in freeing Poland. So Russia didn't have to wait long. On September 17, 1939, the Russians marched in from the east. Poland was gone, again divided up between two evils, the Nazis and the Soviets. We were trapped.

When the Russians arrived and all Poland was under these two powers, all the parents worried about their sons, that the Bolsheviks will take them to Siberia, or the Nazis would just shoot them. My brother Benjamin was already in Israel. So it was me that my family had to worry about. And they were all correct to worry. I learned later that in 1941, all the Jewish men who were still in Bialystok were snapped up by the soldiers, and put in the synagogue. The synagogue was set on fire and everyone inside was burned alive. My sister Fanya's husband was among them.

But at the beginning, the Soviets wanted everything to appear normal. Three days after the invasion, they ordered all the schools and businesses to reopen. So I went and opened the school again. But this was only a temporary kind of normal, while they put together their lists. The Soviets' first move was to confiscate lists of names from organizations that they consider to be anticommunist. They looted and confiscated everything— they would raid the shops and take away your watch or bicycle or anything they wanted—but also they entered offices and took lists of names. This included of course the names of members of the Zionist Organization and the other Jewish organizations, as well as members of political parties. Everyone knew there would be some arrests, and if your name was on one of their lists, you would be arrested and sent to Siberia. I was a known Zionist as well as the director of a Jewish gymnasium, and therefore in line to be gotten rid of. I began planning my escape.

To leave Soviet-occupied Poland, I needed to cross a border that was kept by either Germans or Russians, and that would not be easy. The border was a hot place, in which military armies, with full strength and equipment, were holding watch over every piece of land. I was also told that the Germans walk around with big dogs, whereas the Bolsheviks don't need big dogs because they shoot straight.

To go west, into Germany, was a faster death than staying put. And there was no going to Russia itself, even though we were now occupied by Russia. The saying when someone went to Russia was, "Well, we will never hear from you again." The Russians were so paranoid that anyone who entered their country, even to escape the most horrid conditions and enter what they themselves called "the workers' paradise" touted in Russia was shot as a spy. They even shot their own communists who tried to go back home to Russia.

The only place to go was north, to the Baltic countries, back to Lithuania. Anyhow, how could I do it? The help came from an unexpected source, my youngest sister. She was maybe 17 or 19 years old at that time and had a boyfriend whom I didn't like, because, I thought, he doesn't belong to our family, he is the son of a baker. I was a snob. I am telling it honestly, right? And to be serious, I thought that he was a communist. He was unlike her other friends and those of my other sisters. They were all fine people, nice families and more or less of the same outlook as me. But he in my eyes was an outcast.

I told my sister, very clearly, not to go out with him. Since I was much older than any of the sisters, my words somewhat carried, but they carried too far because she stopped seeing him. And one time, as I was walking on my way home, he stopped me and he said he wanted to talk with me.

And in this moment he told me that he knew I had a very bad opinion of him and that I'd told my sister I wouldn't like her to keep company with him. He didn't threaten me with anything. But he said that I am very much mistaken, that he loves her, that they are friends, that he doesn't think I can prove anything wrong about him.

But here is something I cannot explain. This fellow, who I think is a communist, who I don't want to see my sister, I know that I can trust him. I don't know why. I began to tell him that I am about to leave and I am afraid to cross the border. I had heard that many other people are caught, sent to Siberia, or sent back (which is the best thing), or simply never heard of again. But I know I cannot stay in Bialystok, in Poland. But I will have to cross the border, and to find a guide who will take me across. And this fellow, whom I didn't like and didn't want to see my sister, he said that he would go with me, and even help me find a man who will take me over and who will be watching me on the other side, when I cross over.

So I prepared to leave. I quickly sorted through my papers and got rid of things so there would be no trace of me in my parents' house. I was sure the Gestapo was coming—and they did come looking for me, after I had left. But as I was removing my papers, I found a little booklet, a little folded thing, that had been given to me by the sports club that I belonged to. Everyone belonged to little clubs, and this group with whom I played soccer, the Maccabis, was a well-known secular group interested only in sports. It had no political connection. And here was this little folder, with the name of the organization printed on it, and also my photograph.

I can't believe I kept it, it was such a small thing, but it was suddenly very important because when they gave it to me, the place where the name was written was left blank, and I had written my name with my own hand. So, I took a pen, and because my name ended with a "y" I added a "cki" which made my name Lithuanian. And I now had a tiny bit of identification with the name "Iwrycki" on it, and that was all I needed to enter Lithuania.

The night I left, I said goodbye to my family whom I have never seen since. They said they felt that I am going away in such a providential way. They cried, my sisters cried. My father and my mother saw to it that I had everything that I needed personally, they even sewed into my coat a couple of hundreds of dollars, American dollars, which was the only money that counted.

That night, I left with my sister's boyfriend, about midnight. We started making our way. And so it started. I started a life of ten years, painful years, which took away from me anything that made me happy and that I looked forward to. I knew I was going into a very dark tunnel and this tunnel, the further in I would go, the darker it would be. And truly it was during these ten years when I saw death, persecution, camps, and later I found out that my parents, my sisters, their husbands, and their children were all slaughtered.

THREE

The Japanese Diplomat in Lithuania

From the start of World War II until May 1941, Vilna and Kaunas were uneasy and dangerous refuges for those fleeing the Nazis. When the news came that Vilna was to be given back to Lithuania in October 1939, individuals as well as groups streamed into the city. The call went out to the various organizations to gather and relocate to Vilna. The Betar movement (a group focused on pioneering in Palestine with a military emphasis), the HeChalutz (which trained would-be emigrants in the trades and agriculture), the leaders of the Bund (a political party of mostly poor Yiddish-speaking Polish Jews), the Mizrachi (a faction of religious Zionists), and others all set up operations in Vilna. Vilna became a microcosm of Polish Jewry, maintaining communications with other centers of Jewish life abroad. Sam was in good company.

As someone who spoke Hebrew and Yiddish as well as Russian, and who was a Zionist and also had a yeshiva education, besides his engaging personality, Sam was welcomed in the many groups and was one of the leaders among the refugees in Vilna.

After the USSR took over Lithuania in June 1940, refugees were still allowed to leave until May 1941, when the issuance of exit visas ended. In June 1941, those Jewish refugees and all the other "anti-Soviet elements" still left in Vilna and Kaunas were deported to Siberia. About 30,000 people, including up to 6,000 Jews (many refugees from Poland) were taken to Western Siberia, Kazakhstan, and other remote regions.

My plan was to return to Vilna, as a fellow who looks for temporary refuge, like many of my other friends who were in the public eye. The reason for so many of us—thousands and thousands—going to Vilna was that at the beginning of the war, before Lithuania fell to Russia, its two cities of Vilna and Kaunas, which was the capital of Lithuania, were the only cities in eastern Europe that were neither Soviet or Nazi. You could still communicate by telephone and be smuggled out to the countries in the world that were still free of Nazis because these two cities were major train stops, and even had airports, the last two open airports in all eastern Europe, perhaps all Asia. Refugees could hope to escape to perhaps Scandinavia, and then go on to Palestine, from Kaunas or Vilna.

It happened like this. Earlier in 1939, in August, Germany and Russia had made another agreement, in addition to their nonaggression pact. This was called the Ribbentrop-Molotov Agreement, and it was made because Russia and Germany had not yet decided what to do with these little countries on the Baltic—Lithuania, Latvia, and Estonia. They left them alone for the time being. Except that the Bolsheviks, who didn't like Poland, found it necessary to correct General Pilsudski's grab and they took Vilna, my city of learning, my city of growing up, away from Poland and gave it back to Lithuania. They made this little gift to Lithuania in exchange for the privilege of moving the Soviet army into Lithuania. Only two days after the Soviets invaded Poland, the Red Army marched into Vilna and took it away from the Polish authorities. So for a short time, Vilna was—like the eastern half of Poland—part of the Soviet Union.

Just as in Poland, the Soviets then began plundering Vilna, confiscating what they wanted, including the Strashun Library. But then came the great news on October 10th that Russia and Lithuania had made a mutual assistance pact. And part of this pact was that in exchange for letting the Red Army occupy Lithuania, Vilna would be taken away from Poland (after the Soviets had finished their plundering) and given back to Lithuania. Now, when it became known that Vilna was to be given back to Lithuania, everyone looking to escape tried to find a way to be in Vilna when this handing over came about.

In particular, the Jewish organizations, like the HeChalutz Central Committee of Poland, the Betar, and the Zionist Organization, sent word to all their members to gather in Vilna. And thousands did go. The trains moving between Soviet-occupied Poland and Soviet-occupied Vilna were crowded with Jews trying to escape the Nazis and hoping to also escape the Soviets. Vilna was filling up with refugees. It was my plan as well, to go, but the city was given over to Lithuania before I could make my way out. The Soviets spent a month emptying Vilna of its treasures, and then on October

28, Vilna was given to the Lithuanians. There was now a border between Poland and Vilna, the Soviet border. I had to cross illegally, and dangerously, and I thought, alone.

It was December 1939 when I said goodbye to my family and left my home. Vilna was about 150 miles away if I could have traveled in a straight line. But there were no more straight lines in my world. My sister's boyfriend and I traveled some on foot, hitched rides, and took taxis and trains when we could. We went to a little village that is near the border. This town was so small that everybody who came there was recognized as a stranger. What we told them was that we came to buy some leather goods, for which they were known. And I am his partner, he is really a connoisseur, and he went to one shop and another shop, and as he went, he found out who are the peasants outside the village who are smuggling refugees across the border, and about the local Polish underground. Every Polish town, no matter how small, had already an organized branch of the underground.

Anyway, a peasant was found who was taking people across. He could do it because the border had been drawn right in the middle of his property. And on the other side of the border, on the other half of the property, lived his brother. This gave them the opportunity to become smugglers. And this was what they did: For a substantial sum of money a person would be taken across the farmlands and be handed to his brother. And after he passed across, anyone who remained behind would be given a note that the person was safe on the other side and would be required to make the payment.

My sister's boyfriend would wait there until he got back the little note that I would sign, with my own hand, that I had crossed and I am safe at the brother's place. This was a good thing, of course, because they could not falsify it, it had to be in my writing.

When I made arrangements and came to this farmer, he hid me in his barn, and I found there another young man, whom I quickly learned to know, because his brother was a good friend of mine. His name was Velvel Nochimowsky. And at the same barn I found also two Polish officers, also waiting to be smuggled across the border to safety. The Soviets were going through their lists and the first list was the Polish military. They were gathering up what was left of the Polish military and executing them.

This peasant brought us to his barn and he told us that we must wait for a fortunate moment. Perhaps it will be an especially cold snowy night so the guards will stay near their fire and drink vodka, or it will be a moonless night and we will be difficult to see. Then, going around and through the woods to avoid the guards, he will bring us to the other side of the border.

We went to the woods three nights in a row. Once we saw with our own eyes the Russian soldiers, covered and wrapped, walking around with their *revolskas,* their rifles, and we were about 50 yards from them. The first night he couldn't lead us across, and the second night he took the officers. But the third time, he took Velvel and me through.

The waiting was as dangerous as the crossing itself. The first night the two officers, who were drinking vodka all the time, wanted unquestionably to kill us. They took out their knives, and decided to kill these "Zhiddies." We started to scream for help, and the farmer came to the barn and he warned them that if they do this one time more, he will not take them across. They cursed us and pushed us, and they threw things at us, but their fear that the farmer may really refuse to take them across the border kept them at bay.

The second night, after we were rid of the Polish officers and we were alone, I and my friend, we heard another discussion about us. There began some screaming between the farmer and his wife. The wife is yelling, "You are not going to do it! They killed our Lord! These are Zhiddies, and you are going to endanger your life and my life for these!" And he yells, "Well I took the officers first." She says, "They are Christian, you honored them. But nobody should save these!" And again and again, the same thing. "We didn't ask for the border! We are now very poor because our fields are far away and we will not have the same livelihood as we could, and the Bolsheviks are going to take away from us the fields anyway. They will make of us old dogs!" She kept on all night, screaming and making a scandal.

Nevertheless, he brought us food and he talked to us. He knew that we could hear because the barn was part of the house. He told us, "This is the way she talks always. Don't listen. I will take you. Only have patience, and I will come at night, it may be at three o'clock, two o'clock, at night, when I will feel that it is possible. Then I will take you." And on the third try, we passed across the border. Finally, we got to his brother's home, and he was waiting for us. I signed a little note to be taken back to my sister's boyfriend. The brother led us from his barn in the morning, and took us to the nearest bus, which was going to the nearest town.

When we arrived in this little town, the local Lithuanian police stopped us. But we were not afraid. They stopped us with a smile. They knew who we were. Hundreds of refugees were entering these little towns near the border. We knew they would not do anything to us, they will not send us back across the border. To me they only said one thing, "Your name cannot be Iwrycki, it must be Iwryckis, because it is more Lithuanian." So they registered me as Iwryckis. I was only afraid however, that when I will arrive in Vilna, there they will register—they register everyone—they will make from Iwryckis, Iwryckisis! But later on I didn't need it, my little sports club identification card with my name as Iwrycki. When I arrived in Vilna, I took out my real identification, which I had hidden in the sole of my shoe.

But this little folder helped me when I first crossed the border, and the local police already were asking for identification. I showed them my sport organization folder, which is a neutral kind of identification.

From this small town inside Lithuania, Velvel and I took another bus, to Vilna. We were now illegal persons, making our way in foreign territory, and it was sometimes quite terrifying. We could be caught any time, sent to a local prison, or sent back across the border, to face the guards, with their dogs and their rifles, or just vanish from this life.

When the bus arrived early in the morning, the city was covered in a thick winter fog and nothing looked familiar or encouraging to me and I was dismayed. After all, this was the city where I spent some three to four years as a happy-go-lucky student who had known all the ordinary and not-so-ordinary places in that city.

At that moment I had no ideas about what to do, nor any prepared place. When the fog cleared and I could make my way, I knew of only one place where I could go, and I could go there even with closed eyes—the house where I lived as a boarder in my student years. But before this, I needed to see myself, change a little bit my appearance, after endless traveling, spending night after night in a stable and trudging around soldiers through deep snow and dirty places. To accomplish this spruce-up, the only place I knew to go was the center of the Jewish community, one of the yeshivas. In one of these, I succeeded in opening the door, in a very early hour when there are very few people. There I took some of my so-called garments, turned them inside out, and by some miracle, I also found in one of the service rooms, a mirror. I didn't like what I saw.

In spite of this spruce-up, when I came at noon to the place where I'd lived, my former houselady recognized me only by my voice. This was good enough for her to agree to let me stay for a while in the room that I had occupied in those past good days. So started a new phase in my life: a refugee, torn away from my home, my family, and wondering, "Now what?"

Vilna was in disorder—stores with broken windows and bolted doors in the midst of the commercial sector. I was told by my houselady that I was lucky, being somewhere else in the past months, because there had been a riot against the Jews in the city. When Vilna was handed over to the Lithuanians at the end of October, the Polish population as well as the communist sympathizers resented the fact that the city was given away to Lithuania by the Bolsheviks. Besides this, prices were rising and bread was disappearing from the shelves, and rumors were flying about. Crowds formed in the streets and for three days, they let the Jews have it![1] Finally, some Soviet tanks and the Lithuanian police restored order.

For a couple of months, the city looked like a no-man's land. Shops and synagogues had been vandalized along the narrow cobblestone streets of the Jewish part of the city, and some of the synagogues had even been bombed. And at certain street corners and road crossings you could see the newly arrived Lithuanian policemen, looking, as they said at that time, like Napoleonic soldiers, with golden epaulets and blue top cylinders, looking more like plastic men than real people. Nobody talked to them nor could they make themselves understood. They spoke only Lithuanian, which nobody in Vilna knew. In Vilna you could speak Russian or Yiddish or Polish and get along very well, but Lithuanian was seldom spoken.

At the time I reached Vilna, my wife Nina, whom I did not yet know, happened to escape to Kaunas, the capital of Lithuania. She had just begun her career as a journalist, serving on the Polish government radio and newspaper team. She left Poland as part of the government exodus in late September 1939, which took journalists and others along, and went to Romania. When they reached the border, looking for refuge in Romania, which was also conquered by the Soviets, President Ignacy Moscicki was taken into custody and what was left of the Polish government later reorganized in Paris. Nina and some other journalists turned north and came in an official or semi-official capacity to Kaunas.

Nina managed to acquire a necessary vocabulary in Lithuanian, in addition to her own kind of Yiddish, which she could produce for the daily paper of the local Jewish population in Kaunas. Those of us in Vilna, however, continued to speak Polish, whether the Lithuanian authorities liked it or not. Only we had to pay attention, or pretend to pay attention, to the unintelligible policemen.

I was not the only refugee. There were thousands. Later, it was estimated that 14,000 Jewish refugees had escaped Poland and entered Vilna in those few months that Vilna was a Lithuanian city. I frequented all the places open to the refugees, the little refugee clubs and cafes and gatherings of refugees at certain restaurants where I was a very active participant, because perhaps of my knowledge and connections that others didn't have.

I could be part of many of these gatherings because I was a Zionist, but I had also attended yeshiva and knew many different members of the different groups.

Now, we were not helpless. Like me, these refugees were mostly very educated fellows. And we collected together by our former professions or political groupings both in Vilna and even before, when some had made themselves into a network to help move large groups across the border into Lithuania to escape both the Bolsheviks and the Nazis.

Some of the refugees were stultified and numb. They came to the gatherings at the appointed hour, they would take their seats like disciplined students, and listen to what others who were not as numb had to tell them. Most of us just looked always for a solution to our dilemma, individually and in groups. And we had very organized, very skillful groups.

The *HeChalutz* were there—the word means pioneers—and this group organized training centers in Russia and eastern Europe to learn agriculture and other trades, to go to Palestine. There were also in Vilna the leaders of the Bundists, and members of the Betar movement, who prepared themselves for agricultural work in Palestine, but they had a military emphasis and also trained as soldiers. There were also entire yeshivas, such as the Mir Yeshiva, as well as the leaders of the Zionist Organization, of which I was a participant. They had all escaped and organized themselves in Vilna. And all of these groups asked for recognition by the Lithuanian government. There was even a council, where representatives of all these different Jewish groups met and collaborated. Or tried to collaborate, because these groups seldom talked to each other even when they had been in Poland, and even now when they were all refugees together, trying to get to Palestine, they still mostly argued between themselves.

I settled myself in a group who like me considered themselves Zionists. We occupied socially a whole floor of a large building, an abandoned schoolhouse, on Trakai Street, downtown. (This street was named for the village where I visited the Karaites as a student.) It became a cultural center for the refugees. There were movies, lectures. The Joint Distribution Committee, an American Jewish philanthropy, was at work there, and some of the small comforts were possible because like me, people had come with as much money as they could smuggle out. Those who had fled with only their clothing on their backs could survive because the "Joint" as it was called, operated soup kitchens and distributed clothing. The Vilna Jewish community helped too, as it could. Trade schools opened, and some of the refugees found jobs that enabled them to survive in some dignified manner.

And we sometimes got news of home from other newcomers. One of the refugees who came later from my hometown told me that my sister's boyfriend, who had helped me cross the border, had married her and was now my brother-in-law. But new refugees stopped coming after the new year. The Soviets were tightening the border between Poland and Lithuania, and after January 1940, very few refugees were added to the city. Many still tried to cross, but did not make it. When Spring came and the deep snow thawed, many frozen bodies were found in the woods along the border. Many had bullet holes in them, others were just frozen.

Many who became Zionist leaders around the world knew each other from their refugee days in Vilna, and even from Trakai Five, as this old schoolhouse was known. I came to know Menachem Begin, who was a *Betar* commander, and also Zorach Warhaftig, who was a leader in the *Mizrachi*. The *Mizrachi* were Zionists, but religious rather than secular Zionists. Warhaftig became later Minister of Religion in Israel. Another was my good friend Leon Ilutowicz, who lived in New York with his wife until he died in March 1997. He had crossed the border by hiding and dodging the soldiers in the woods as I had. He was an outstanding Zionist, trained as a lawyer. There was also my friend Moshe Polackevicz, who was a great gift because he was a doctor. He used to make fun of me—only me—because I was nearly bald. He himself had lots of red hair. One day, I told him that I once had as much hair as anyone, but my hair was red, like his. And I told him that of course nothing could be worse than having red hair and one day God heard me complaining and I became bald.

We Zionists looked at our situation and the situation of the Jewish people in Europe historically, and not just religiously. No one tried to deny the religious aspect. Rather Zionism sought to harness the potential of this Jewish hope that suffering will sometime come to an end, and the Jews will again exist as a nation. To traditional Jews, Zionism was a political movement.

Zionism began in earnest with Theodor Herzl, a journalist who covered the Alfred Dreyfus court-martial. Dreyfus was a Jewish captain in the French army who was falsely arrested in 1894, and later convicted, for treason. It was the great and highly publicized proceeding of France versus the Jewish traitor. Herzl, even though he was a journalist from a very assimilated background, from Hungary, living in Vienna, he understood that such things [as the Dreyfus trial] cannot go on. He thought the French were wrong. The whole affair of a false trial was because another ethnic group was living in France and the French didn't want them there.

So although Moses Hess wrote about Jewish Nationalism in the mid-1800s, it was Herzl who started things moving. Herzl wrote a book on the Jewish state in 1896, and he described why and how it should start. And he became the first "diplomat" of a state-to-be. He saw the kaiser, and he went to see the sultan of Turkey, who ruled Palestine. But he did not talk to the Arabs, because the Arabs were, none of them, an independent state. Turkey covered the whole Middle East. The sultan ruled, so you talked to Turkey.

And it wasn't so bad. The results were not fruitful, but not bad. And the Turks seemed as if they did not notice that whole families—family after family—began coming to Palestine. Jews had been going there before, but they were older people and went to die, to be buried in holy soil. But now families began to come. Later, the League of Nations recognized these Zionists in Palestine as the Jewish Agency to give them a voice in the international debate. But this is a digression.

The one question discussed day and night around the little tables and coffee bars in Vilna, the only question that mattered, was "and what now? Where to?" Because we could not stay in Lithuania even if we had wanted to.

Lithuania, like all the other countries in Europe, soon after the beginning of the war began its policies of "Lithuania for the Lithuanians." And even though Vilna was crowded with refugees, and Poles had been living there for 20 years, the Lithuanian government decided that it would only grant citizenship to those who could prove that they had lived in Vilna before the Poles had taken Vilna in 1919. So it was not only the Jewish refugees who were not welcome, they didn't want any more Poles in Lithuania, either.

In January, soon after I arrived, the Lithuanian government gave an order that all the refugees were to leave Vilna and scatter into the little towns of Lithuania. A few went, but most stayed, as we knew we would be trapped, and we did not trust the Lithuanian government to protect us. Why would they prevent us from being killed by those residents who didn't want us there, either? All my life, I had been a Zionist and had wanted to go to Palestine. I had even been accepted at Hebrew University. I would not go and disappear into a little village of Lithuania. So I stayed in Vilna, a refugee, trying to get to Palestine like all the other Zionist refugees.

Besides, there was a standstill. The fighting had stopped in November, before I had crossed the border, and there were those who were calling this time the "phony war." A phony war! It was unbelievable, but it gave us perhaps a little boldness, that we could succeed in an escape. And we had a small sense of reprieve. Jewish culture was reviving in our little island, surrounded by the Soviets, as there were talented and accomplished refugees in Vilna who did not want to be idle. Plays and concerts were organized. The yeshivas continued their study of Torah. So what did I do? I taught classes in Hebrew. They all studied Hebrew with me in preparation for going to Palestine.

I should say that not all the refugees were determined to go to Palestine. There were many in Vilna who were not Zionists, who listened to men like Rabbi Hayyim Ozer Grodzenski, a great spiritual leader of Vilna. Grodzenski insisted—and insisted very loudly—that we Jews should follow the principle of *shev ve'al taase,* which means to stay put, to be still. That is, don't run around in useless confusion, but be quiet and just let this wordly craziness pass by. This notion of a phony war seemed to prove him right and many gave up trying to get out of Lithuania. Grodzenski died in early August 1940, so he did not see what came later.

But we Zionists did not follow such advice. We prepared any way we could, always planning, always talking of ways that the trip could be made. Most thought the first step to the Middle East was to get to Paris, and the way to Paris would be made through Sweden. The problem was how to get permission to enter Palestine. Moshe Kleinbaum, Zorach Warhaftig, and some others had come up with the idea of establishing a Palestine Office in Vilna in November 1939. And, unbelievably, they did it! And this office was officially recognized by the Jewish Agency in Jerusalem. This was a great achievement, and we were very enthusiastic. The people in my group of Zionists, which counted almost 200, being very careful not to have any spies penetrating, were planning to get certificates for emigration through this office, and then go through Sweden. From Sweden, we would find our way either directly to Palestine, or go to Palestine from Paris or even perhaps through London instead of Paris, if necessary. But they gave to this Lithuanian office only about 400 certificates for immigration. It was a bitter thing.

The few who got a certificate also mostly managed to make a flight to Sweden from Lithuania's only airport, which was still independent, with a transit visa granted by the Swedish consulate in Kaunas. The Swedish would grant a transit visa if you had an entrance visa somewhere. They would not accept refugees, but they would allow them to pass through. And passage through Sweden was still safe. From there it was easy to avoid the German Luftwaffe. Those who had papers but no money were helped by the Joint Distribution Committee with their transportation.

When there were no more certificates, the plan was to find a better place to go until another way into Palestine could be found. Everyone hoped and planned to somehow get a transit visa through Sweden, but there was no clear plan as to where to go from there, as the British were keeping the door to Palestine shut tight. Some thought of joining the Polish army, which was organizing under General Wladyslaw Sikorsky in Paris, where the Polish government-in-exile had formed.[2] Sikorsky had the blessing of the Allies, and an army of his native compatriots were fighting together with the Allies against Hitler. The French embassy in Kaunas was allowing the Polish government-in-exile to operate through their offices and some obtained passage to Paris to join the army.

The Joint Distribution Committee representative in Kaunas was a man named Moe Beckelman, and this man tried to convince all his supporters outside Lithuania that emigration was the only solution for the refugees, but no one would listen. He could not even get the U.S. Embassy to help. The U.S. Embassy would not give out the visas it already had, because they claimed no one was applying for them. But they made many impossible conditions. One of these conditions was a certificate of good moral conduct from the police. An illegal Jewish, Polish refugee could get no such certificate from a Lithuanian policeman, no matter how big the bribe. And this was only one of the conditions.

But in April, when the bitter cold winter had gone and a little warmth was finally making Vilna livable again, the "phony war" ended. Hitler invaded Denmark and Norway. The radio reported every day worse and worse news. After taking these two little countries, which could not begin to defend themselves against Germany, Hitler also invaded Belgium and the Netherlands. And then, the worst news, in May 1940. Sweden closed its doors and refused to grant more transit visas to Jewish refugees.

I and the other members of my group could not even apply for a visa. Our Polish passports were no good. We had to get another kind of a passport. And our plan was this. The League of Nations had once designed, at the end of World War I, a refugee passport. They called this passport the *sauf conduit,* which means a safe conduct, for refugees. It was also called the Nansen Passport because it was invented by a Norwegian called Fridtjof Nansen, who was the commissioner for Refugees at the League of Nations in the 1920s. He made this passport for people who had been thrown away by their own countries. Its purpose was that it does not matter whether you are a Jew or a Pole, only that you are a refugee who is now in danger. It was a great success at the time because there was a labor shortage in many countries after the first World War and refugees at that time were welcomed by many countries.

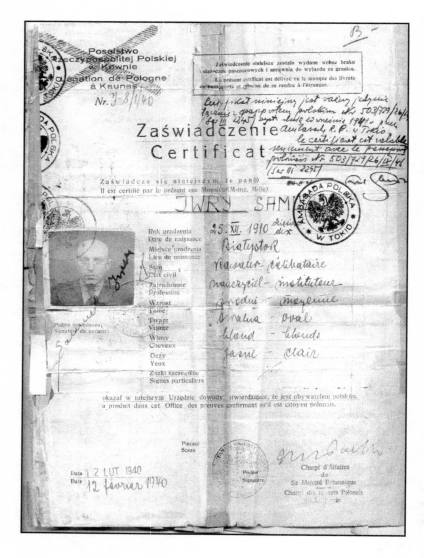

Iwry and his activist colleagues in the underground in Europe put their many talents to life-saving use: this is a very professional forgery of a sauf conduit (safe conduct), or Nansen Passport, identifying Iwry as a citizen of Poland. It is dated February 12, 1940. To escape Soviet-occupied Poland, Iwry hired smugglers to help him cross into Lithuania, carrying as identification only a nonincriminating sports club card. When the Soviets invaded Lithuania in June 1940, these forged passports served as replacements for Polish passports, which the Soviets had declared void. The photo expresses the desperate state of the Jewish refugees under the Soviets.

So we sent two people—a young man and a young woman—who were supposed to find their way to a representative of the League of Nations in Kaunas, to insistently say that a great number of stateless persons were in Vilna, and they would like to have granted to them this *sauf conduit*.

It was our only ray of light, our only hope. But times had changed, and no one wanted any refugees. All the nations were busy trying to keep refugees out and the League of Nations had quit giving out these passports. The two people were not successful in getting the League of Nations to grant everyone a *sauf conduit* but they did get a copy of one. And from this one, we made hundreds of copies.

Now, we did not dare submit copied *sauf conduits* to the Swedish authorities, because it is too risky to submit a copied passport to its own country.[3] So we could not go through Sweden to Paris or London. But there was a way of escape still open and possible to pursue. We could try to get a Turkish visa to Constantinople, and from there go to Israel. However, the nearest Turkish Consulate was in Moscow. This meant undertaking a trip to Moscow, without a permit, without anyone asking you to come there, and then you are a man without a name, without identification—a white bear. It was at the time our only hope. So we copied these two *sauf conduits* with the names of those who wanted to take the insane risk of travel through Russia.

So I got myself a copy of a *sauf conduit*. I have this forged refugee passport even now. And with it, I have my other visas, which led me through, for better or for worse, the chaos and dangers that lurked in every corner. I look at it often, not with nostalgia but as a document that really saved my life and the lives of many others, my friends. It enabled us in this world of bleak despair under the Nazis and Soviets to still be able to plan an escape and knock at the door of any consulate, if the door is still open.

But before we could begin the dangerous trip to Moscow, things started moving, and in a very foreboding manner. In June 1940, France fell to Hitler. For us, the fall of Paris, when the Nazis marched in on June 14, was the decisive fact. Now we are trapped. Not only were we refugees, thrown out on our own and away from our families, but we were also Jews and couldn't be absorbed in any of the new places for any permanent length of time. After Paris fell all of Europe was under Nazi rule. And even worse, it all meant that Hitler is going to win, and win big.

However, we did not have much time to mourn Paris because the very next day, the Soviets took over in Lithuania. Moscow came to us. Their "nonaggression pact" with Lithuania, like all the other agreements made by the Russians, was a joke. They grabbed Lithuania and the other Baltic countries as well. Somewhere in a sewer was found the body, or perhaps two bodies, of Russian soldiers. They were killed by a Lithuanian, supposedly, but more likely it was set up by the Kremlin people. It was set up. The Soviets claimed Lithuania had violated their agreement, so they had rushed in to defend themselves. Defend themselves against Lithuania! And in one day—June 15, 1940—all of tiny Lithuania was taken over by the Red Army. It was done in a matter of hours. They had clearly made ready for this a long time ago. So the Baltic countries were now occupied by the Soviet Union, in violation of their own pact with Germany, the Ribbentrop-Molotov agreement, to keep these little countries free as buffer states.

Stores closed immediately, cafes were closed, and free movement began to be curtailed. The heavy hand of "No, No and No" and the heavy hand of scarcity, fear, despair, suspicion and propaganda settled over Vilna. We were again in a big trap in which nobody, nobody, could dream of getting out. Every organization except the Communist Party was outlawed, and even the smallest businesses were claimed to belong to the Communists. All our Jewish organizations immediately went underground. The Palestine Office was dismantled and the lists and papers they had were quickly destroyed.

There was a song they played, about how they had come to "liberate." We had heard this song already in the occupied cities of Poland. And now in Vilna, we heard it again. And again we saw the trucks, with soldiers holding on to their rifles and standing on the platform of the truck. Again we heard the assurances "We are Soviets, we have everything," which is what they were told, these poor soldiers whose rifles on their shoulders were not even hanging on a piece of leather, but on a torn rope! The soldiers, anyone, who found a leather strap on a rifle would take it off and use it to mend their shoes or make sandals. A leather strap was valuable, and an old rope held a rifle just as well. And they were always hungry, holding a piece of bread in their pocket which they saved, and bit off in small portions, making it last. We could see that they were even picking up wrapping paper. They would see the people who bought some little bit of food and throw away the wrapping paper, and they would pick it up the discarded paper and fold it and put it in their pocket. They would try to get something for it because paper was valuable. In Soviet Russia, when I came there, they wrapped everything, including food, in old newspaper. Other paper was saved to sell to foreigners, for foreign currency. The Soviet Union was bankrupt from the beginning.

Now, as much as all of us there in Vilna detested and were frightened by the Nazis, we were equally unhappy knowing what our future is going to be under the Soviets. Eastern Europeans, whether they were from Poland, Germany, or the Baltic countries, were at least brought up in an open society. But now a great part of the globe was ruled by a regime that day and night told lies, even to each other, to make believe that we lived in this rich and happy country that abounds with everything that humans need. We heard always the slogan, "To everyone according to his needs, and from everyone according to his abilities."

But everyone knew the truth, right away. We had already watched the Soviets take over in Poland. They were doing the same in Lithuania. There are no more of the usual government positions if you are not a Communist. The Lithuanian government had already fled to Germany. The businesses are no more. Every business becomes a Soviet-run entity and if you are not a Communist then your job is given to someone else. But if you are someone like my sister Fanya's husband, he was a lawyer, and he wanted to do some work, normal work in any enterprise, he cannot get a salaried position. So he had to offer his services in any way for pay, in any way an educated person can offer. And somehow you survive.

It is not a situation where there are a lot of alternatives. You immediately know that there is nothing you can do unless you take risks, and if you don't take risks, you are waiting in line like millions of people, not knowing what will come, to know even where bread, more bread, will be gotten tomorrow. Because in these transition times, the bakers may not bake, the delivery may not take place, so all effort and energy is spent on getting some daily bread— in the very elementary meaning of this word, the daily bread to eat.

Even then, in Russia there was a joke. The Soviets promised everyone cars, but the response was, "I don't need a car! I need an airplane! Suppose you heard on the radio that a thousand miles away in Irkutsk there is a line for bread. If you have a plane, there is a chance you can stand in that line."

And then, comes the other things, a place to live. If your apartment was liked by somebody else, you will be told to be gone in 24 hours. It is very good, you are very lucky, when they allow you to stay in one room, and they take over the rest of the place!

So this big lie, which made us shudder, to imagine that these are not the words of some deluded soldiers, but of a powerful group of ruling officials who repeat impossible, unbelievable lies. And under the lies, beyond the lies, is the big threat.

One threat is that you will become a white bear, like many of my friends, my richer relatives or the parents of my friends, who were taken out of their apartments and sent away to the unknown, which means

Siberia. Another threat was called *stenka*, which means to revolve against the wall. If a Soviet decides you are an enemy of the people—and everyone fit this category—then you turn to face the wall and one-two-three you are executed, shot in the back. This would be anybody who made any attempt not to comply with the security rules of this country. He will have it, *stenka*.

The difference between the Soviets and the Nazis was, the Nazis—in the beginning—sent their enemies to Buchenwald or elsewhere and their shoes were sent back to the wife and children, according to the German group order. But with the Bolsheviks, the persons and families who were sent to Siberia were kept together. After the war, many of these people returned to their villages. Sometimes they had frozen limbs and other impairments, but they were alive. There were no alternatives between these two regimes.

So we just endured, stayed out of the way, and tried to make new plans in those days after the Soviets took Lithuania. The Jewish groups went underground. We organized ourselves into "cells" of five or six people and set meeting places, such as a certain park bench, to quietly spread news and keep things moving.

The Soviets carried on with their pretenses. On July 14, 1940, they held elections among the members of the Communist Party—the only legal party—and it was voted that Lithuania should become a Soviet Republic. So the new Lithuanian rulers "applied" to the Soviet Union to join their utopian paradise, and on August 3, the Supreme Soviet "approved" their application.

And then immediately came the announcement of an "independent"—meaning "independent" only in quotation marks—government of the Lithuanian Soviet Republic. All the refugees like me, who filled out the streets and other little places, whether they had run to Vilna to escape the Nazis or the Soviets, were told that either you willingly and enthusiastically declare yourselves a ready citizen of this U.S.S.R., or we will take you to the place of the white bear—Siberia.

We knew that, ready citizen or not, anybody who had been somebody in the Jewish community or in the public life of Poland would be scrutinized and be accused of collaborating with the Polish government or the Polish underground. This meant being driven out from your home or apartment, and handed over to the Soviet military for expulsion to Siberia, without the opportunity to move one piece of furniture. You could only carry a few personal belongings. And this was all.

At this same time, all the remaining embassies in Kaunas and the other Baltic countries were told to pack their suitcases and go home. So not only was there no more Jewish Agency office in Kaunas and no hope for more certificates, there were no more representatives of any foreign countries at all.

Now, we still did not give up on getting out of the new Soviet Lithuania for one reason: the Russians made a pact with the Baltic countries, that they could be ruled by their own Communist parties. And the people who ruled this new republic, being interested in showing a little independence, decided that simply allowing these refugees to leave was a reasonable and easy way to get rid of them. The next route to Israel, then, was to seek a Russian transit visa. A Russian visa! This was ridiculous! In Russia, a Zionist equals an enemy of the people. But inside Russia, it could be possible to go to Odessa, a port on the Black Sea and from there to Constantinople, and if possible, directly to Haifa.

However, there was an even better reason to allow us to leave than just getting rid of us, and that was money. The Soviets needed hard currency and could be persuaded to many things in exchange for hard currency. Very serious discussions were held at that time in Russian with the ambassador in Kaunas, who related it to his higher authorities in Moscow. It was in July, soon after the Soviets had settled in. Warhaftig led a delegation to talk to the authorities in Kaunas, explaining to them that there were refugees who had fled the Nazis—he couldn't say they ran from the Soviets!—and who already had valid emigration papers, but now only needed transit visas through Russia. And I too was mixed in with these talks. Eventually, in September, the German refugees with emigration papers were allowed to go through Russia.

Now, there were some difficulties. Both the Russian and Lithuanian authorities tried to persuade us that in Russia itself we, the Polish refugees, would find our best solution. "Why not go to Odessa and stay there? It is the country of the free, the country of the free." Odessa is in the Ukraine, on the Black Sea. But this was a big joke, a big lie, because our Polish passports were useless, not recognized. And, truly, if we went anywhere outside of Lithuania, if we entered the Soviet Union, we would be immediately arrested as a person without a passport. This is in Russia a very grave thing, since the time of the tsars. If you don't have a passport, an official identity, then you are either a spy or at the best thing, a thief. And if neither, then you are a white bear, and a white bear belongs in Siberia.

However, eventually money won the argument. It was like this. Moe Beckelman, the Joint representative, managed to convince the Soviet authorities to open an Intourist office in Kaunas, because, he reminded them, those with papers for emigration would be paying for their transportation, and food and lodging as well. So Intourist opened an office, and the Lithuanian NKVD[4] [secret police] began issuing travel permits for a very steep price.

Permission was given only for travel through Russia and across Asia, to the town of Vladivostok, on the Pacific Ocean. It was not permission to live in Russia. In other words, Russia is not a destination, they told us. But it is a way, yes, for getting out. Transporting refugees was to them a source of currency. But, we were told, after this was hammered out somehow, before you will be granted a transit visa you must have a country that is a destination, and a visa to this country that agrees to receive you. And there came a night in which we all put our heads together and we discussed a yeshiva student that we had heard of, his name was Nathan Gutwirth, and tried to find a way to do what he had done.

That spring and early summer of 1940, before the Soviets grabbed Lithuania, the name of Nathan Gutwirth was the subject of every discussion by all the refugees around every cafe table in Vilna. This Gutwirth was a Dutchman, a student at one of Vilna's yeshivas. There were very few Dutchmen in Lithuania, so Gutwirth had gone out of his way to become acquainted with another Dutchman, a fellow named Zwartendijk, who was a representative for Phillips Electronics. They shared the newspapers from home, with the soccer scores and other news. When the war broke out, the Dutch ambassador in Kaunas was sent packing because he was a Nazi sympathizer, and this Zwartendijk, even though he was not a diplomat, was asked to run the consulate in Kaunas. Gutwirth wanted to get out of Lithuania, but Hitler owned the Netherlands, so there was no point in going home. So he went to Zwartendijk and asked if he could go to an island that was part of the Dutch West Indies, called Curacao. A remote island was much better than being trapped between the Nazis, Soviets, and Lithuanians.

Now, this Gutwirth, when he had asked to go to Curacao, had been very clever. When he asked for a visa, Zwartendijk discussed this request with his Dutch authorities and was told that a visa was not needed to enter Curacao, only the permission of the governor. Gutwirth asked Zwartendijk to stamp his passport only with the statement that no visa was required, but leave the part about the governor's permission off, and the Dutch authorities agreed. So Gutwirth was able to find a country to receive him, and this would allow him to go looking for a transit visa.

But this was not all. Gutwirth had been turned down by the United States and other embassies, of course, but now he did another amazing thing. He went to the Japanese, to a man named Chiune Sugihara, and got permission to go through Japan.

I will tell you about this man Sugihara, who became famous recently for what he did. After the Russians invaded Poland and were moving their armies about in Lithuania—the privilege they purchased in exchange for Vilna—Japan sent a spy to Lithuania to keep an eye on the Russians. The Japanese were joining up with Germany, and were enemies of the Soviet Union. As a cover for this spy, the Japanese opened a consulate in Kaunas. Before this, the Japanese had never done business with Lithuania. But in January 1939, a Japanese consulate appeared in Kaunas and a man named Sugihara ran it. In the early summer of 1940, Gutwirth went to Sugihara and asked for a transit visa through Japan, and Sugihara wrote on his papers that he had permission to go through Japan.

This was momentous news. Gutwirth knew a rabbi, Eliezer Portnoy, who was with the Mir yeshiva, and after much encouragement from other prominent Jewish leaders, the Japanese consul also gave permission for all 300 or so students of this yeshiva! The news spread and people began lining up outside the Japanese consulate, and Sugihara had a stamp made because he could not write fast enough.

We were amazed at this plan, but before we could take advantage of it, the Soviets took Lithuania. Now, we wondered, how do we also get this stamp to enter Curacao on our copied passports, and get a transit visa through Japan, and eventually enter Curacao as such a large group? If this country doesn't require a visa, at least there must be some authority, which would state that our group was welcome and we don't need a visa. Our quick and very efficient researchers found out what was needed. We found out that in Vilna, as well as in Lodz, there were before the war some wine and liquor stores, whose owner or owners were from Curacao.

We sent two of our fellows to an old Jew who used to operate one of these stores. They came to him after midnight, and asked him to sign a document. The text of the document said, "To the best of my knowledge and according to the instructions of the government of Curacao, there is no need to have an entrance visa in advance for people who would like to visit our island." They wanted the old wine seller to sign his name to the document.[5]

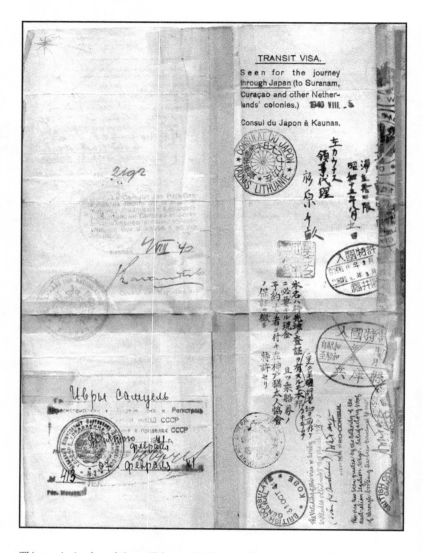

This transit visa through Japan (February 1940), ostensibly to the island of Curacao, together with the forged sauf conduit and an exit visa from the Soviets, enabled Iwry and other leaders of the underground to get many people, including themselves, out of occupied Lithuania, to cross Russia and enter Japan. Nearly 2,000 Polish Jews escaped to Kobe, Japan, through either original or copied transit visas issued by the Japanese diplomat Chiune Sugihara, who has been dubbed "the Japanese Schindler."

The Jew, the poor old man, had no other way but to sign the document, because they would have, I am afraid to say, either beaten him up or broken up everything he had or done other peculiar things. After all, this was a matter of life and death.

The possibility of applying for Japanese transit visas, since Japan had not yet closed its consulate in Kaunas, seemed unrealistic and even inappropriate because none of us had ever had a face-to-face conversation with a Japanese. But Japan was also planning to enter the war and needed foreign currency. They did not stop Sugihara from granting ten-day transit visas, because the refugees would need transportation on Japanese ships, to get from Japan to other countries by way of the Pacific, which was quite a distance. And this would bring thousands upon thousands of dollars.

But anyway, it was a fearful thing just to go to Kaunas. It was only 50 or so miles away, not a long train ride, but a train station was a place where you could be easily arrested. And the Soviets were busy in Kaunas. It was known that there were bodies hanging from all the trees. But my friend Leon Ilutovicz did it. He went to Kaunas, to the Japanese Consul, and stood in the long line outside the consulate from the very early hours of the morning. And he got his *sauf conduit* stamped with permission to enter and go through Japan. He did it! And we copied this stamp, as there were talented forgers among us. [One of them was Josef Simkin, who was Moe Beckelman's assistant.] Ilutovicz got his stamp on August 2, 1940. And the next day, Lithuania was "admitted" into the Union of Soviet Republics and all the foreign embassies were ordered to close and leave the country.

It turned out that Sugihara did not stop stamping passports. For purely humanitarian reasons, he kept on giving out transit visas. Even after the Japanese government ordered him to stop, he continued to write out visas. He even handed out visas from the train station as he was leaving the country.

So, I got a transit visa, and there was on this visa permission to go through Japan to Curacao. The night I got this visa, I couldn't sleep. I visualized myself coming to Curacao, a little country of island people milling around like mosquitoes. I still laugh at myself for these thoughts. Although I read, I knew in my knowledge of geography and knowledge of anthropology that these fears were unfounded, it did not prevent me from thinking differently, because suddenly I am to be thrown in this strange place. However, my strange ideas of Curacao were only part of the problem.

The next problem was how to get an exit visa from Lithuania, which is now under the Soviet Union, and to get an assured means of transportation from Vilna to the port city of Vladivostok, which is more than 4,000 miles away on the Pacific Ocean. Getting permission to leave Russia was not only an administrative difficulty, it was an unbelievable achievement. It was very dangerous to just apply, simply because your name is being sent to places where you would not normally like to be known. And you may instead get a permit to Siberia.

As a matter of fact, the NKVD acting in Poland had, through this same Intourist agency, announced that anybody who had a foreign visa anywhere, and intends to leave, can apply through this agency. Many people had been in possession of visas that they had gotten before the war, visas to foreign countries. They immediately applied, from all over, and paid whatever they were told. When the list was ready, they were all loaded on a train. And the train took them straight to Siberia. This is a fact that was told at that time, friends of my friends experienced this. So getting out wasn't so easy.

At that time, all the trains of these countries also were under Soviet authority. So you have to convince them that you are not a spy, not an enemy of the people. If you succeed, you can ask for a Soviet permit to leave the place where you live, and buy a ticket from the Intourist and traverse Soviet Russia as a passenger. We were unbelievably lucky. We were able to speak to a Soviet representative and to get through the first steps in dealing with the NKVD.

How did this happen? These Lithuanian Communists, even though they were part of the Soviet Union, wanted to assert their independence and didn't revert to such tricks as sending people to Siberia. It was Lithuanian, not Russian, Communists who interrogated us and decided our fate. Of course, they operated with the knowledge of the authorities in Moscow. But these Lithuanians just wanted to get rid of the strange refugees in their midst as fast as possible.

So in this moment of Lithuania's history, the Lithuanian Communists handled the applications somewhat like things used to be in any country. I say somewhat because they knew they were being given phony papers, forged passports with forged stamps, but if you had the money they did not care. And every day there appeared a little piece of paper listing the names of people, seven or ten or twelve a day, who were given permission to leave. And these people could come and get their visas.

Until one day came the final *nyet!* A similar piece of paper, as usual torn out from a book or from written letters but had the names written on the blank side, was put on a door with a little nail. But the message was "No more applications will be accepted." It so happened that the majority of people never got back their passports, and they would every day get back the answer, which is used in America, "Don't call us, we'll call you." You know what it means, that "they'll call you."

But I got my permission before it was too late. It took some time, but the answer was positive. The only thing was that Intourist wanted to be paid for the whole journey—including passports, hotels, even for places where you will have to stay if the 11-day journey is interrupted—all this has to be paid in advance, in cash. Not only in cash, but in American dollars. They wanted over two hundred American dollars! The joke is that dealing in foreign currency is a punishable crime in the Soviet Union. Some of my friends experienced this—before entering or after leaving the Intourist, people are searched and arrested for possessing foreign currency. But this did not happen often. They wanted the money, and if they arrested too many, they would lose too much currency.

Getting our money exchanged was not difficult. We went to the black market for the dollars, and paid a very high rate, almost 30 *lit* to the dollar. The official exchange rate was only about five *lit* to the dollar, but this was another fiction. So we got our dollars. And then we managed to pay Intourist without getting arrested.

When Nina applied to leave Lithuania, she left like the rest of us, her passport in the hands of the NKVD. And she persisted, coming nevertheless to see if she could at least retrieve her passport and be safe. The head of the office in Kaunas was a woman, also named Nina. And the only thing my Nina could do to make this horrible woman smile, was to say "You and I have the same name." And this woman smiled, and it was the saving moment. She told Nina, "Go in here and find your passport." And there was on a table a whole mountain of passports. But Nina, thanks to her habits, had her passport in a red folder. When she came in, the door was open, and the woman at the desk let Nina look through the mountain. She found her passport, she got it. And when she got her passport, she also got permission to leave.

Nina was able to pay for her ticket through a friend named Hanya who was in Switzerland. And this friend wired the money from Switzerland to the Intourist, so Nina could leave the country. This happened without my knowledge at the time. I was with another group altogether.

I barely received my passport in time before another danger presented itself. At the end of November, the Lithuanian government issued an order stating that all "unreliable elements" were to be put on a list, and everyone knew what that meant. If your name is on a list, you will be sent to Siberia.

And we were all unreliable elements five times over—Jewish, Zionists, Polish, not Communists, and possessing papers showing we wanted to leave the "workers' paradise." So we had to use these papers before they started to deport people to Siberia.

Now, one day, somewhere in the wintry month of March, I got my ticket to take the long trip across the vast territory of Russia, from the Baltic Sea to the Pacific, which would normally take—in the conditions of Russia—some 11 days. In our case, however, it was more, and full of unexpected surprises. Of course, there was a limit as to how much luggage you could take, but I didn't have any luggage. I had only a handbag—a little satchel. But I was dressed warmly and ready for anything that can happen.

I made my last call home. I sent a letter, which could now be mailed from there to my home, because eastern Poland and Lithuania were now both under Soviet Russia, and then I made a call to say that I am leaving Vilna. I wanted my oldest sister and her husband to come over and perhaps she could join me on this unknown trip. Her answer was no, she could not leave our parents alone, she felt a terrible obligation to stay with them, no matter what. My other two sisters had left, and endured whatever risk. I think my parents and she were more concerned about me than about themselves, and my luck with dealing with the Communist regime, and entrusting them with my well-being. But somehow, nothing happened to me.

Well, now about the day I began my next escape. In the morning I went to the railway station and the trains went hour by hour, pulling out. I made the journey with my friend Ilutovicz and others—there were about a dozen of us who stuck together. We boarded our train and it started off. We were group after group of shabby Polish refugees, like hundreds of others that had already made this journey, and we were not at all sure that our plan could be carried out.

I say Polish refugees, because the Lithuanian Jews did not try to leave. They were mostly very comfortable, middle-class people in Lithuania, and they stayed. But in 1941, after we had made our way through Russia, Hitler got hold of Lithuania. Germany declared war on the Soviet Union and marched through eastern Poland and into the Baltic countries and then into Russia itself. And decades later, I read a single line in a newspaper article: Of close to 220,000 Jews who lived in Lithuania before World War II, 94 percent were killed by the Nazis.

Across Russia to Japan

The Jewish refugees fleeing Lithuania across Russia were swept along in a tide of forces between Japan, Germany, Russia, Great Britain, and even the United States. Great Britain and the United States were focused on stopping Hitler and did not want an influx of refugees. Germany and Russia both wanted to be rid of the Jews: The Nazis simply invented death camps, while Russia saw an opportunity to collect foreign currency and deliver the Jews to the Japanese. Japan was as deeply anti-Semitic as Russia, but ultimately adopted a uniquely practical policy.

Simply, the Japanese believed that behind every major government was a shadow Jewish government that was the real power. They considered Germany's murderous stance to be a wasted opportunity. Japan instead sought to influence the Jews and make use of them to preserve and promote Japanese business and political interests. And because Japan was not yet ready to go to war with Russia, Great Britain, or the United States, who they believed to be Jewish powers, the Japanese were very careful to appear tolerant. Jews who could be useful to Japan were treated well, and the Japanese broke their policy of decency toward the Jewish refugees only under severe pressure from their partners, the Nazis.[1]

Our first stop after we left Lithuania was Minsk, the capital of the Soviet Republic of Belarus. It was a shabby, poor, gray, unpromising city, although many fine cultural institutions, including Jewish institutions, had once been quite prolific in Minsk. But cultural institutions die quickly when the Soviets take over.

The passengers getting on and off were very drab. In the other countries you would call such people beggars, but they were not beggars. These people were traveling to work either for a government institution or for a factory, or for some agency. It was cold and they could not throw away a single garment because there were no more to be had. If there are no buttons, you wear it without buttons. Nothing else can be substituted. One sleeve may be shorter, the other is longer, who cares! The sorry shoes—something that they buy on the flea market. That's the only place where most of the people go to shop now.

You can read everything on their face. Their poverty, their hopelessness was so great that no one could even acknowledge a joke. Hardly did I see anybody smiling. Even if there is a little accident, or if someone missed something, or if the door didn't open and it grabbed him, normally people are after that smiling to each other and saying to each other, "He made a little mistake, you see, it didn't open." Even that, no smile. You didn't even see passengers reading the paper, because there were no papers to buy.

Our train went slowly but surely, stop by stop. We were told it would eventually arrive in Moscow. And there we will have to wait, after a new inspection of our papers, of course, for another train, which would take us, as we hoped, across all of Russia, across the enormous Asian continent, to the other side of the globe, to Vladivostok. And our luck stayed with us. We finally arrived in Moscow.

By the time I arrived in Moscow, in late March 1941, the fate of the Jews was already sealed, for death. Because those in control of Europe already looked at us as people who could be disposed of. So even though a few of us, I and my friends and some others who had fled to Lithuania, were able to get a visa, to escape, this was in a way a small thing. What worked stronger in us was the feeling that we were sentenced to something terrible. We would, in these last moments, despite the NKVD, despite Hitler, despite everything, we would do anything to save ourselves. The only thing is, we felt—every one of us—that we had all left behind somebody who would finally have to pay the price.

Many of us hoped that something will happen, that Hitler will not have the last word. We put all our hopes on the British and even the French, because at the time the war was still a European war. The Soviets and the United States were still not getting involved. Japan was fighting in China and treating Germany like an old friend, but the Pacific was still quiet. England was being bombed but Hitler was not winning there, and we could hope that the British would make Hitler back down. But once we were in

Russia, we knew that this is only the beginning. We saw that Russia was getting ready, really, for a lasting effort. All along the train tracks, we saw the soldiers and the war machines.

And even in Moscow, far from the border and any other country, the Russians were all taken by some mirage, some idea that everyone who is not a Russian is a spy. The fear of spies overruled all other suspicions, all other concerns. They looked at every person that even stepped across the street, and imagined that he is to deliver some message, that he has in his pocket some critical information. So therefore, when they saw us, foreigners who were not diplomats or people from well-known European industrial firms that are going to buy or sell, but rather who arrived with our satchels and with our old great mantels covering everything up to our foreheads not to get frozen—they knew that we were refugees, people who escaped and who did not belong in Russia. But refugee or not, simply being a foreigner is enough.

So we came into this land that is full of spies. We had been refugees for nearly a year and a half, and looked it, too. Yet despite our looks, we looked still ten times better than they! And they willingly placed us in their czarist hotels. They made room for us not only because we can pay money, but so they can have a better look at us, and to be sure we don't go wherever we wanted.

The hotel was an old but dignified Russian czarist hotel, still used by foreigners or by high dignitaries. All the chairs and sofas were of red velvet, many of them roughed up or worn through, but the rooms were cleaned more or less every day. The corridors were crowded with valises and people who had no place to sleep. One could hardly pass. We were expected to behave like foreigners, like the other foreigners who came on business, such as the Dutch, Belgians, or Italians.

We could mostly communicate with the hotel staff. We would speak Polish, and they would somewhat understand. But this understanding was not so great. German wasn't so popular in Russia. French was understood by some, some of us could use a little Russian. I was different. I was fluent in Russian, but for my own sake, I thought it not wise to go around and show off with my Russian conversation. I tried to make myself understood in whatever way I found it possible without speaking Russian, but of course I understood everything I heard. And so I was a moving ear to know whether they paid any attention to us, and to listen to everything that was said about us. It was the same thing in the street, and wherever the need was—I listened.

There was no reason to read the few newspapers posted on the wall although I could easily read Russian. They contained only lies. The only thing audible were some spoiled radio stations. They would occasionally tell you about two or three things that were of interest to you, but mostly it was the same thing, you hear about "our sun," S-U-N, Stalin, never otherwise! He is the sun! Our sun! And the diminutive "Our lovely sun, Stalin," "Our great communist" and "successful communist Stalin" and again, "our wise man, Molotov." Every one mentioned had superlatives before his name.

Their music was not bad, but it was always the same, either marches or their standard communist songs. These were the same songs played by soldiers on the big trucks as they entered Poland and Lithuania, and this is what you heard normally on the public radio.

The several hundred dollars which this honeymoon journey cost us, mostly in dollars and the rest in local currency, at a very high rate, was supposed to provide us with our hotel in Moscow and breakfast and dinners every day, until we would move on and continue our journey. Days passed and we were not yet called or told that our train is ready. Apparently all the passengers had to be checked anew, papers inspected, and somebody had to order a train to be made ready, or determine whether the train will have seats for us, so we will be able to go.

In the meantime, I had a distant cousin, a doctor, in Moscow. His mother and my father were first cousins. I heard his name mentioned when I was a youngster, and I remembered that he lived in Moscow and practiced medicine. Well, I tried to get in touch with him. I had to use many tricks and find people who would help me. It is not as easy as picking up a phone book, finding his name and dropping in a coin.

But after several attempts, I got him at home, on the phone. He was terribly surprised. I told him who I am and he very barely remembered me, except that when I told him his mother's name and that she is a cousin of my father, this made a recollection come to mind, of course. And he says, "Did you see her?" I said, well a couple of years ago, she lived in another city, not far from Bialystok, but I had seen some other cousins of his, who lived in our town. Anyway, he told me that I cannot myself come to him, he lives with many other people in the same apartment. Although he is a doctor, here he must share an apartment with others.

I told him the name of my hotel. He didn't want to come to my hotel because there are spies and he cannot come to a hotel. But he told me that if I go right and left and turn again, there is a post office, a big post office not far from the Kremlin. So he told me I should have certain letters in my hand, so he will recognize me. This is nothing, people come to a post office with letters, and he, too will hold letters, white envelopes of some kind.

We met very carefully. We didn't, either of us, show any signs of surprise or any emotion of greetings, nothing. It was as if I asked him, what is the time now. We stayed there for a while, in this tremendous place, a lot of people came and went, and none of them paid any particular attention to me. Except he told me that my coat and my winter hat looked too much of a foreign make, that some people might notice. Well, if it had not been so cold, I would have taken it off. But I couldn't. I knew that my appearance made him uncomfortable. So what I did was, I remember, I turned my coat inside out. I did it! It had a woolen lining and this too was gray. It looked very bad, some bits stuck out. It wasn't right, especially the sleeves. But I looked a little bit less foreign—not normal to a Russian, but less foreign.

He took me on the underground, the famous Russian subway. Yes, the subway was very nice. It was built like it really was the greatest achievement of Soviet Russia. It was finished already by then. A lot of space, a lot of marble in it, a lot of pictures, pictures, and pictures, and you could not help but see that this is part of the Communist propaganda machine.

When we came out into the sunlight, he led me through the streets, which were very shabby. Well, I saw boys and girls going around and laughing. He showed me a library. And we went into his apartment. I will not describe how it looked, but in the kitchen were names and hours, for whenever each family can use the kitchen. And as to the bathroom, better not to talk about it. Of all the people who lived there—several families in one apartment—only a young girl was home. He then called his wife, to tell her she should come home and visit me.

And he told me then, how to live in Moscow. You go and you mind your business, and you don't go where you are not permitted. And you do not go in the company of people who are under suspicion. If you do this, you can have some life for yourself. And if you are lucky, you do not get sick or otherwise, you can go on like this. Anyway, it is a living. This he told me! A doctor!

After this meeting, I made a decision. I said to myself, I will not live that way. I will escape from this "paradise" and if I do not survive the dangerous journey I am on, then so be it. And if it will not end the way I hope, at least I can still claim that I lived as my own person and nobody took that one decision, that little bit of freedom away from me. I thought a lot about it. I saw the people in the streets, I knew how they were living, and I understood that they paid some price for their small comfort. But this was not for me.

After about eight days we were finally permitted to continue our journey. I was very happy. I knew also of some people who came on the same train, and they had British visas to Palestine. They too, were trying to see the Turkish consul, which was still in Moscow, and a number of them, maybe five, maybe ten, got permission to go to Turkey. They were going to Odessa, on the Black sea, and from there, by ship, they would go to Constantinople. In Turkey, there was still an office of the Jewish Agency, and they were hoping to get permission to go to Palestine.

Had we known when we were in Vilna that it was so easy to secure a Turkish transit visa, we would have done this. These visas could have been duplicated, using the same technology that we used to copy the *sauf conduit* and the stamps of Sugihara. Because of lack of communication between countries—the Turks did not ask the British if a visa was issued on this day to this person—it could have been done. In wartime, when these matters are a question of real life and death, everything was tried. And a few did get through. But then Turkey sided with Hitler, and these Jewish refugees became an embarrassment to the Turkish government, and the door closed.

My transit visa, however, was for Japan. And it is a long, long 11-day train trip across Russia to the Pacific Ocean. The train left Moscow in the middle of the night, sometime around two o'clock. The train had once been a trans-European train. But after using it so much and never making any repairs, it looked like a poor-house on wheels. The Siberian Railroad had been built in the 1890s, and they were probably the original train cars. There were seven or eight people in a "cabin," so to speak, so there was enough room to sit, and if some were willing to sit on the floor, another, perhaps a sick person, could even stretch out and lie on the bench.

The food was like in a cafeteria—when it was supposed to be warm it was cold. However, you didn't have to worry about whether anything had been in the refrigerator because it was icy everywhere. We did not dare to get off the train to buy food or even stretch our legs when the train stopped moving, even if it was only for wood for the locomotive. We understood that we were on no excellent terms, even as paying passengers, and the train ran on no definite schedule.

At some stations, too often, we saw very tragic things. Children would run out, and come as close as they could to the train, and ask us to throw them sugar or a piece of bread. Some places the train stopped right at the gate to the station, and we saw the guards holding back masses of half naked—half naked!—people. The line of guards would break, the people pushed so hard to come close to the train to beg. When the train stopped in a field, or didn't quite reach the station, and there were no guards to keep them at a distance, then people came and if you opened the door—you couldn't open the windows, Russian trains do not have such windows—you heard their voices, and they would implore you for things, anything.

They were hungry. They had nothing, and many people threw out to them things that they owned. You wouldn't think that they would, and I was surprised to see people giving away their scarves, as if they thought that they would be always on the train. Maybe the train will indeed reach Japan, and they will get another scarf. But these Russian peasants were half naked. They didn't have anything but bare threads on them, not even sweaters.

And they asked for sugar because even in this place, they had sugar, sugar enough for our tea. One thing that you get on a Russian train is tea and tea and more tea. And Russian tea is thick with sugar.

One time, after I returned to my seat after walking a bit and washing myself, I got a note from somebody, a note that they wanted to see me. And it was specifically to me, it had my name. The note was left because I was not in my seat. And I began to shiver. When I met the person who had left the note, he asked me if I am Sam Iwry. "Yes," I answered him. He tells me, "It is written on your passport that you are a teacher." "All right," I say. "You are from Poland?" "Yes." "Would you like to stop, to step down and we will take you to Birobidzhan?"

Birobidzhan is a place where Soviet Russia claimed in the late 1920s it would build an independent Jewish republic, on the Amur river at the border of Manchuria. I had wondered many times, what kind of a Zionist state is there going to be? "And how do you know of Birobidzhan?" I asked. He told me that he is from there, and that he is also a person who knows everything. So when they went over the passports, he decided that I could be of some use. And then he said, if you would only want to stay there shortly, for a short time, and to give some instruction to the teachers, it would be nice.

Well, this Birobidzhan is another Soviet joke. There was never a Jewish state there, but they settled it with some Jews because they were afraid of the Japanese. The Japanese had Manchuria and the Soviets thought, if the Japanese want some of Russia, too, then they can first fight these Jews.

I knew that he was a fellow that worked in the NKVD, and his business was to spy on Jewish people, people who had some kind of profession and an education. He wanted to see if he could remove me from the train without causing suspicion. It could have been that if I said that I am a medical doctor, maybe he would have asked me to take care of someone. These people accompanied the passengers, they were always sitting on the trains. Of course, you never knew who they were.

I almost was taken off the train, and I know if I had stepped off, I would have never returned. One night, as I remember, we reached the town of Irkutsk, which is in the high frozen Asian plateau over a hundred miles north of the border of Mongolia. And he then "invited" me to step off the train in Irkutsk and from there he said maybe we could find some connections to Birobidzhan. He spoke very nice to me, he spoke first Russian, then Yiddish. But I decided to leave my things on the train, because if he wanted to take me by force, at least I could tell him I had left my satchel and could get back on to retrieve it.

When we headed for the platform, and I was almost there, I thought I was going to be a prisoner. And then I heard, when we stepped down from the train, that the temperature was 72 degrees below zero. The train was not leaving for another hour, and I remembered what people had told me about Irkutsk, that if you stay outside as long as two minutes, you will never have your ears back. They will freeze this fast. So I stepped right back on the train. I went back to my seat, and I didn't see him after that. I never knew if he was still on the train when it left Irkutsk.

Now, this was my Birobidzhan nightmare. The rest of the trip, the rest of the journey, was terrible. I felt that I was in danger, and every time the train stopped, I was afraid that somebody would come and ask me to step off. I remember well every day of those tense and fearful days until we finally arrived in Vladivostok, on the far eastern coast of Asia, which was our destination.

Vladivostok was the last stop on the vast Asiatic continent. It was a huge place on the Sea of Japan, built on a tremendous dimension to illustrate the weight of Russia. But even then, it showed signs of neglect and mismanagement. There were people of all kinds and nationalities—Chinese, Japanese, French, and high Russian officials who were sharply dressed. But on the other faces, the local faces, there was poverty.

The unbelievable thing was that the railway station was equipped with telephones, telegrams, and all other means of communication and without great difficulty, I made a telephone call. Imagine it! I called New York City! And I even reversed the charge. How they paid for the call, I don't know. But I think, if I remember correctly, just for starting the call, I put every bit of money I had left into the telephone. Well, it was as easy to get this connection as it was for me to call from the Royal Hotel in Tokyo, because the territory was almost neutral. We were far, far, away from Moscow.

I called the offices of the Jewish Agency in New York, to tell them that a group of Jewish refugees had made it across Russia and were about to enter Japan. I knew the names of the people in the Jewish Agency, especially Dr. Nahum Goldmann, who monitored the coming and going of Jewish refugees. Goldmann was trying to help us, to save all of us, and make it possible for us to leave Japan.

The Intourist had done its job and a small Japanese ship was waiting for us. We were met by some Japanese official who knew who we were and that we were going to Japan in a sanctioned capacity. They told us that in three days, our ship will leave port, and we must remember the name of the ship and be ready. It would take us to Tsuruga, a small port on the bay of Wakasa Wan, on the western coast of Japan. These were old and familiar arrangements to the Japanese officials. They never even checked our papers! Thousands had come before us, thanks to Sugihara, from Lithuania through Russia to Japan. The dozen or so friends that I was traveling with would soon be joining all the others of the larger group who had left Vilna ahead of us. Even so, we were somewhat anxious.

We should have felt relief to be escaping Russia, but now all of a sudden this new discomfort came over us. Who would we deal with in Japan? What would we do now? It was really a difficult time. I had been a refugee for nearly a year and a half and I had no money left. Nearly all my companions were in the same condition.

When we finally boarded the little Japanese steamer, which did not look as if it would survive the journey, we found there were only a few cabins for several hundred refugees. In better times, it had been used to transport cattle or other livestock, and seemed barely able to go to sea. But it was somehow "refurbished" to carry people—refugees. This same boat had been used to transport all the refugees that had been given a visa by Sugihara.[2] We slept on the floor in our own blankets. The conditions on the ship were unspeakable, but the journey did not last long, only about a day and a half. We were lucky to be making this crossing at the end of winter. Earlier in the season, storms had made the trip difficult and it had taken nearly three days.

So, we left this continent, on which such terrible things were happening. When the ship neared Tsuruga, I was lucky to be one of many standing on deck, even though it was still cold, and we saw something that is impossible to imagine. Near the port were big heaps of coal, mountains of coal the texture of sand. It was used for ships and for industry. And there were Japanese workers in white socks and white shirts—white!—and something like a kerchief on their heads, standing with shovels and moving coal with little wagons on four wheels. They were using people to move these big heaps of coal. And always their shirts and socks stayed white.

Little radios were playing the same music that we heard in Moscow, but here it sounded like a child's song, to put somebody to sleep. Around us were very normal things. We saw wagons, horses, we saw also automobiles. The skies were very high, and around the sea everything was blue. It was a sudden paradise after all of the slush and dirtiness and the fear and terror of the world we had just left. All of a sudden we were looking at a different world, a different existence.

Not long afterward, we docked in Tsuruga. Very politely, we were helped by Japanese officials, to come down from the ship, holding on to the rail. They asked us if we wanted to rest, if we want to walk, if we would like some tea, all of these things spoken in English. They also spoke Russian, if we had preferred. We were also politely informed that Japanese trains were very clean, and we were asked if we wanted a bath. We were taken to the bath at the station, and we found showers with hot water, places to change, and a large Japanese bath where you walked down three steps into the water. It was like a Jewish *mikvah,* or ritual bath. The women's bath was to the left and the men's to the right, and they were separated by only a linen screen.

The bath gave us our first strong impression that we were not just in another country, but had entered an entirely different culture, with a very different mindset. And for a moment we were finally able to relax. We could stay in Japan for the rest of the war! We had only one question: where are they going to take us? We were told, "Kobe."

From Tsuruga we rode on a train. It was clean and fine. The conductor was a young girl who said always something that means, thank you, we are welcome, thank you, we are welcome. We slept on the train, and the movement, the rhythm of the train, is so even, we really felt at home. When day came, we could see the landscape, we could see factories, the yards, and the schools. We no longer felt afraid.

Foreigners were welcomed in Japan only as tourists, but there was a Jewish community in Kobe, and they took care of us. These were Russian Jews. They had escaped to Manchuria from the Bolshevik pogroms in 1903, then migrated to Japan after the Japanese invaded Manchuria in 1904. It was a vibrant community, of 50 or so families. When the refugees from Europe began to arrive, this community formed a committee to help.

Now, there were too many of us for them. The first refugees to arrive from Europe were German Jews who left when Hitler was only beginning to be a threat. They were older than me, and remembered perhaps more clearly the first world war. They came as families, traveling with their possessions and some money and were more like tourists. So the Kobe committee helped them with hotels and such matters. But later, when the war had begun and Sugihara was writing transit visas for thousands like me, it was a different thing. I and many others in my group were more or less young men who had left behind our families, and we had nothing. I had spent my small fortune that my parents had sewn into my coat in getting in and out of Russia. So the Joint Distribution Committee and other organizations had also come to Kobe, to help this committee, because there were too many refugees for them to take care of alone. So when we got off the train in Kobe, we were greeted by one of these committee members, and there was a place prepared for us. We were well taken care of. It was not at all like my escape to Vilna.

The head of this committee was a fellow named Gerechter, and his team of 13 or so was very busy.[3] They arranged for houses and even a hotel for the many thousands of us that were arriving in Japan. I shared a small Japanese house with many others—there was barely room for all the refugees crowding this little community—that was made of thin wood and paper, with fabric hangings and paintings on the walls. The floor was not just to walk on but to sleep on as well. The chairs were outside. In the house was a pot with coals for a little warmth. We were given about ten yen a week for food, and we shopped and cooked as best as we could with these strange Oriental ingredients. They arranged for medical care for those who needed it. And on a few occasions I was given a chance to earn a few yen, sweeping a floor in a factory.

The yeshiva students were particularly well taken care of. Many organizations, in New York and other places, were looking out for this group of refugees, and they were able to keep their daily routine intact. They even found a place to continue their traditional day of studies. So there in the middle of this Japanese town you could hear their humming and singing as they learned Torah.

But the most important help was perhaps with our visa problem. We still had no place to go. Curacao was not a real solution,[4] it only got us a transit visa from Sugihara, and we were supposed to be in Japan for only ten or maybe fifteen days. But the Kobe committee and the Japanese officials that they were friendly with allowed us somehow to stay for months and months, as we needed. Somehow the necessary bribes were paid. The Kobe committee was also able to help a few get visas from the embassies in Tokyo. And we could communicate with relatives and others by mail and even telephone if they were outside the reach of the Nazis and Soviets.

All communications with the outside world were handled through an embassy. There was even a Polish embassy still in Tokyo although of course it was not formally recognized. So it was through the American embassy in Tokyo that I communicated with Goldmann at the Jewish Agency in New York. I went often to the post office, to send telegrams to the American embassy, which would forward them to Goldmann. And it was a fortunate thing that I had to go there often, to do Jewish Agency business. Because it was there in the Kobe Post Office, as she was waiting and waiting in line behind me—I had very many telegrams to send that day—that I met Nina.

Nina had come to Japan before me and, at that time, worked for the Joint Distribution Committee, which operated for the sake of the refugees. She helped the Kobe Jewish community take care of the refugees and with their interviews with the Japanese government. She was much appreciated and a favorite in the Committee office, and a wonderful worker. Nina was the only European girl with a university degree to come to Japan. Most of the refugees were men. The few other women had never had the opportunity to study and work as a journalist as she did. We became acquainted, in Kobe.

From Kobe, I often took the night train to Tokyo, to do business with the embassies there. Like the Russians, the Japanese do not associate with foreigners, and I would be watched and monitored. None of the other passengers would come near me, except that immediately after I sat down on the train, a security person would also sit down, and it was to ask questions—Who are you? What is your profession? Why are you traveling in Japan? These were called *kempeitai,* the thought control police. Nina, too, was treated in this manner. All foreigners were.

Even though Japan was not like Germany or the Soviet Union, it was not a free society as we think of a free society. They were on a crusade to build a New World Order, Japanese style. I was told that the radio was under the control of the government and everything had to do with the latest campaign by the National Spiritual Mobilization Movement. This was a government commission to make sure the population supported the war in China and in the Pacific. They had endless campaigns to conserve electricity and gasoline, and even had neighborhood officials who made sure everyone had the proper "moral attitudes." These were called the *tonarigumi.* I could not understand Japanese, so I do not know what was on the radio, but I know that the authorities kept an eye on us. The *tonarigumi* were especially curious about the yeshiva students and their endless humming and singing. But eventually these officials decided the students were "religious fanatics" and were harmless, and left them alone.

Soon after I arrived in Japan, Goldmann had an affidavit waiting for me at the American Embassy in Tokyo. It happened like this. I had an uncle in America, my father's brother. And he knew that I was in Japan, because they sent an affidavit on my behalf, through Goldmann. When I arrived in Japan, I found out that, yes, there was a telegram at the American consulate and the affidavit had been sent out, that I had relatives in America who would receive me. They told me, we will let you know.

And really, it was not long before they sent for me. I went to the U.S. consulate in Tokyo. I was a terrified refugee, and this was my first encounter with an American institution. And I met with the people there, "This is the affidavit and this is me." There was no question, as I understood, of any quotas, because those countries where a quota was in force were occupied by the enemy. So the possibility of immigration was open. Okay! So I filled out whatever forms, answered whatever questions they asked me, and I answered truthfully. What did I have to hide there?

But U.S. government policy prevented most of the refugees from leaving.[5] It was not like in Kaunas, where there were many impossible conditions to meet. We were not asked to get a statement of our moral character from the Japanese police. But they had their own ways. The answer from the consulate was no. When I returned a week later, they said, "Your visa was refused." Why? Here comes the little story. The woman who told me this didn't make a mystery of it. She was a very nice, respectable, young blonde lady, like all the others at the embassy. She spoke nicely, with a smile. She said, since you told us in your declaration here that you left your parents and sisters in Poland, we cannot have you come to America. So I asked, "What, you are afraid I will bring them? You don't want more refugees?"

No. The reason was—she said it honestly—in order to keep some people out, to limit the numbers that come, we have to make a difficulty. The difficulty clearly said, your parents may be tortured by the enemy, by the Nazis, to force you to spy for the Nazis. That means, I, with my great knowledge about America, I am such a slick fellow with my Polish accent, I will go and spy! Right away, I will go down to the Pentagon or wherever and I will want information because I want to save my parents. What would not a son do for parents who will be tortured? Therefore, says the nice fine respectable blonde American foreign service woman, you cannot come to America.

Spring 1941: After escaping Europe and crossing Russia, Iwry was appointed by David Ben-Gurion (soon to become Israel's first Prime Minister) to serve as the Jewish Agency's Far East Representative, working to rescue Jews and enable them to emigrate to Palestine. Iwry enjoyed a brief, happier interlude in what he called the "fairyland" of Japan, where he met Nina Rochman. Nina also worked for an

As a matter of fact, not all the Jews were turned away. Some who could not write English, who were the same age as me and looked more or less like me, couldn't fill out the application. Hardly could they write their own name in English, but they gave them a visa. And also people who were there with family members, perhaps a wife or children, received visas. But all the others, who knew a little English as I did, and who filled out everything to the last speck, like me, they remained in Japan.

The Japanese were fair to us, even though we were foreigners. It was the spring and early summer of 1941. It was just before Hitler, after his army and his fighter planes had failed to bomb the British into defeat, turned around and attacked the Soviet Union. So I was in Japan when, on June 22,

arm of the Jewish Agency—the Joint Distribution Committee—which helped the refugees together with the local volunteer Kobe Jewish Committee. The characters on the sign depicted here read "Okifu Photography Studio."

1941, the Germans marched across eastern Poland, into Lithuania, and set about grabbing Russia. So the Soviets were now at war as well, and at least Britain was no longer fighting alone. But the Russians were not well prepared, and Hitler seemed to be unstoppable still. When the Germans took Lithuania, that was the end of all escape for the refugees as well as the Lithuanian Jews. The Nazis set up a ghetto and began mass executions in Vilna and Kaunas, like everywhere else. We did not know about these mass murders then. We only knew that no more refugees arrived in Kobe after Hitler invaded Lithuania.

The Japanese, too, were preparing for war. They were already fighting in China, and they were preparing for a much greater effort in the Pacific. They already had rations on everything, and it was a real wonder that we, who came only half-legally to Japan, received the same rations as everybody. We even had special permission to buy two eggs per week. I also remember that one day, it must have been a Jewish holiday—either Rosh Hashanah or perhaps some other holiday—a delegation of Japanese came over, to our place where we lived, in the little street in Kobe. There came a group of people carrying little blue and white flags with a Star of David, and they brought us food, saying the two Hebrew words, very clearly, *b'ruchim, haba'im* which means "welcome." We were often brought food and gifts. The Japanese people were very generous and gracious. They felt sorry for us, I believe.

Never, never was anybody mistreated there, or heard even a loud voice, while I was in Japan. I never felt any enmity from the Japanese during those days. In fact, the Japanese, despite their alliance with the Germans, had a peculiar appreciation for the Jews. It began when the Japanese were at war with Russia in 1904. They needed money to engage in this conflict but the banks all over Europe would not take them seriously and they could not get any loans, until the Japanese ambassador in the United States met a fellow named Jacob Schiff. This Schiff was a Jew who was born in Germany, and he was also an official in a New York bank. He gave the Japanese several loans, before they had won even a single battle, because he hated Russia. The Japanese won the war and took Manchuria away from the Russians, and so this one Jewish man made a big impression on the Japanese. They knew that this man had made the loans because he was a Jew and so he had reasons to hate the Russians, and the loans had nothing to do with America. Schiff was treated like a hero in Japan, and he became the first foreigner to be granted the Order of the Rising Sun by the Emperor. After the war, the Japanese found that the Jews in Manchuria were a very practical people. They were capitalists and engineers and other things the Japanese needed.

But the Jews were leaving Manchuria because conditions had become very bad for them there. The Japanese police had not protected the Jews from the White Russians who hated them—they liked to kidnap Jews and hold them for ransom as it was the easiest way to get rich in Manchuria— and the Jews were moving to Shanghai and other places in China where they would not be harassed. So the Japanese developed the Fugu Plan in the late 1930s. It was an idea that some Japanese officials had several years before the outbreak of the war when Japan, for all kinds of reasons, wanted to keep the Jews in Manchuria and even bring more who wanted to escape Germany.

Now this name, the Fugu Plan, was never official, because it was a kind of joke. The *fugu* is a fish that is very delicious, but if it is not cooked in exactly the right way, it will kill you because it is also poisonous.

The Japanese were divided over the question of the Jews, but were not willing to miss what they considered an opportunity. They considered the Jews a useful people and thought that if they promised the Jews religious freedom, the Jews would not only develop all the resources of Manchuria, which Japan desperately needed, but would also get the capital investment Japan needed from the West. The Japanese, who knew about the financial power of certain Jews, thought they could tap into this great world power for their own gain. The Japanese really believed the stories going about like "Roosevelt is not Roosevelt. Roosevelt is Rosenberg. Rosenberg is a typical Jewish name. The Jews rule there, in America."

But the Japanese also believed the Germans and Russians, who thought the Jews were trying to take over the world. They had translated and read a little book that was actually written by the Russian secret police, called *The Protocols of the Elders of Zion*. According to this ridiculous book, the Jews held secret meetings to plot to take over all the governments of the world. So the Japanese were afraid that if they invited the Jews to Manchuria, these Jews would join with those in Birobidzhan, across the border, and turn around and conquer Japan. So they proceeded very carefully.

The Japanese invited the Jews in Harbin, the largest city on the Russian-Manchurian border, to form an official council called the Far Eastern Jewish Council, which could be recognized and do business with the Japanese. And in 1937, they held a conference, the overall Jewish conference in the Far East in Harbin. The Japanese organized it, although they did not want it to be widely known. They did not want to embarrass themselves with the Germans and Italians over the Jews. But they needed to influence the Jewish community there, because they thought, well, these Jews have connections all over the world, and the Japanese wanted the world to know that they were tolerant and civilized. The Japanese saw Germany and other countries mistreating the Jews, and they thought that they will treat the Jews well and prove that they are more far more culturally advanced and morally superior than these decadent, arrogant, racist Western countries.

So there was a conference of Jews in the Far East. And a Japanese official, who was a biblical scholar, came to speak at the conference. His name was Dr. Setsuzo Kotsuji, and he delivered his speech in Hebrew! There were a number of Japanese like this. I was told that they were Christians, but as Christians they felt some great respect for the people of the Old Testament, and they included Hebrew in their education. And I also learned that this Dr. Kotsuji, who was a Hebrew scholar, was also a wealthy man and he paid some of the necessary bribes from his own pocket, to extend the visas of the refugees.

As Hitler came to power, another matter made a great impression on the Japanese—the Jewish importers and exporters around the world organized a boycott of German goods to protest Germany's treatment of the Jews. The Japanese found their businesses booming because many people were refusing to buy from Germany. This too made a big impression on the Japanese.

So even though Japan began to cozy up to Nazi Germany, and they knew the Nazis blamed the problems of the world on the Jews, and wanted to get rid of the Jews, the Japanese didn't adopt the anti-Semitism of the Germans the way the Nazis wanted. They really believed that the Jews indeed controlled the politics and economy of the world—they thought that the Jews were behind the scenes and making the big decisions in Great Britain, the United States, and even China. They believed this. But they didn't understand why the Nazis wanted to get rid of all the Jews. The Japanese thought that it would be better to befriend the Jews and use them to influence the world on behalf of Japan. (Besides, the Japanese knew a little about Zionism and thought of the Jews as Easterners, like themselves, who wanted to come home to the Middle East.)

In the short time I spent in Japan, I had many fine experiences. I had known someone in Kaunas, in Lithuania, who is now also living in the United States, whose family was in trade and he gave me the name and address of a businessman he knew in Japan. When I arrived in Japan I got in touch with him. He lived in Yokohama, which is between Kobe and Tokyo. When I called him, he said to me on the phone, I want you to be my guest for lunch, at home. Now very few of the men I know ever saw the inside of a Japanese home. They meet in the Japanese downtown. Even officers, even those who had lived there 20 years.

But I had the real distinction that he came for me in his automobile, drove me back to a most beautiful neighborhood. I saw the Japanese trees and the gardens. They lived in houses amidst little gardens, very well equipped with everything that a European could desire. I came to his home, which was in a Japanese style, a very rich home. There, of course, I took off my shoes. I was prepared for it.

He took me first into a study-like room, very European. And at the door between the study and dining room, I saw his wife with her beautiful kimono, coming into the room, saying something in Japanese and in English. And she herself served the lunch for us. This was a great distinction because they didn't use any servants.

Later on, in the door only, appeared his beautiful daughter. She had just graduated from the Japan Women's University, of which, as I learned later, only daughters of the rich, upper-class people attend.

She asked me a couple of questions in German, and I understood and she understood and I tried to answer her. I was so amazed that she spoke German without any difficulties. She also, at the same time, translated to her father what was said. And she told me that Japan should not be seen only outwardly. Japan, as I understand what she said, has its own mystique, and if I will be in Japan long enough, she will perhaps help me in a way to pick up some readings that will put me on the right track to understanding.

It was a very nice, very nice visit and I was happy that I was given the chance, the occasion to really see at least one segment of Japan. He took me to one of Tokyo's fine traditional theaters, which was called Kabukiza. I sat in a box, and the explanation that my host gave me, before every act, was so unusual, because he knew from traveling in Europe how to explain it in European terms. After that I took some of my friends, and also Nina, to this theater, and if I was not as good a guide as he was, I at least shared with them some of the peculiarities of Japan.

I stayed in Japan for several months. The reason why I left Japan in 1941, while Nina and others were still captivated by the charm of pre-war Japan, was because I got a telegram from David Ben-Gurion, who was in Palestine. Ben-Gurion later became the first Prime Minister of the state of Israel. But in 1941, he was head of the World Zionist Organization, and he asked me if I would organize a delegation representing the Jewish Agency to talk to the British authorities in the Far East about certificates of immigration to Palestine. This was possible because the British were in Shanghai.[6] So I agreed to leave Japan and go to Shanghai.

Shanghai was nearly the last open international city in the world. It had a French concession, and the English-American concession, as well as a large population of Russians and also Jews who had come to Shanghai from Iraq in the late 1800s. I knew that as a consequence of the latest White Paper, which the British authorities issued, immigration was strictly limited. A very few certificates were allotted as a last alternative. But the Jewish Agency could not distribute even these few certificates through their European offices because all Europe was under the Germans. In Europe, there was nobody to deal with.

However, in Shanghai, there were not only embassies, there were also many thousands of Jewish refugees. It is not well known, but enormous numbers of European Jews escaped Hitler and Stalin and ended up in

Shanghai. It was very cheap to survive in Shanghai, and those who ran out of money or could not find a place in the economy of Shanghai found themselves living in old schools, warehouses, and other places that were rented and turned into "homes" and dormitories by the Joint Distribution Committee. So there were thousands of Jews in the big old buildings of Shanghai. They were living in these places for two reasons. Some of these buildings had been bombed in the battles between the Japanese and Chinese and they could be rented very cheaply. In addition, there were no imports from Europe going to China, so there were also warehouses that stayed empty. So there were refugees, and a way to get in and out of China, but no certificates for immigration to Palestine. Ben-Gurion needed someone to represent the Agency in Shanghai and give these few certificates to the refugees who were there.

I gathered a delegation from my friends and we arranged for tickets on a ship that went to Nagasaki, and from there, after stopping over for a night or two, to Shanghai. The waters were very stormy, and we were very happy to reach the protected haven called Nagasaki, which would be so devastated a few years later by the atomic bomb.

When we arrived in Nagasaki, a person was waiting for us and the other few passengers, especially those who didn't know Japanese, and took us to a lovely hotel. And life seemed fine. Around six o'clock, dinner was ready, a typical Japanese dinner, rice and flounder without any sauce and two pieces of some plastic vegetables, some soda water. The service was beautiful—the waitress in the kimono always bowing.

Also sitting at our table at this hotel was another foreigner. After we introduced ourselves, he told us that he is a Swedish engineer representing his company in Japan. Now, his company tells him it is time to come home, and hurry. He hoped to stay a while in Shanghai. After dinner, I went up to my room to read the only paper that was there in English, and he knocks at my door and asks me if I would like to go out for a cup of coffee to one of the local all-night coffee houses that were popular at that time in Japan.

The guide at the desk gave us directions where to go. The narrow little streets were getting dark, and we held on to each other so as not to stumble. Finally we saw paper lanterns lighting up a little house, and we entered a very noisy place with a lot of young people, mostly students sitting there. And we are happy to be here among young people. And it is noisy, but to our liking. The music was loud, as you expect in a place like this. We ordered something to drink. And this Swedish engineer told me his impressions of Japan. But then in an abrupt moment a young man came straight to our table and he left a napkin, with something written on it. When he read the napkin, the engineer, who could read Japanese, said, "This is English!" And it was for a moment very funny because everything was badly misspelled. The engineer read it, reciting all the misspellings. But the message was not funny. The message said, "You are foreigners. We are now in a time which might bring war. You are our enemies. Bad enemies. Would you please get lost and leave this place"—and then there was a very long, misspelled, word—"immediately."

I couldn't care less, so I said to him, let's pay and go. He said, nothing doing. I'm not impressed by these Japs. I came here representing my government, and they cannot do anything to me. To my misfortune, I couldn't repeat this kind of a litany. I didn't represent anybody. I was a refugee! And I said to him, listen friend, I don't know you. You may be intending to play a hero here, but I would like you to leave and come with me to the hotel.

While we were discussing this, a second napkin was served to us, this time with a dirty rock in it. Not a little stone, a rock. A rock that could break your head. Which means business. Even my engineer understood. And I reminded him that, after all, he was the one who talked me into coming with him and I will not find my way to the hotel alone, I'm sure! He, with a heavy sigh, got up very slowly, called the waitress to the table and waited in a nonchalant way for the small change that she brought back. He took away all his change, but I left her something. And he got mad at me. So we left, we left. The next day we were happy to board the ship.

But even before this, there were signs that things were changing in Japan. While I was still in Kobe and making plans to leave, I received a phone call from the Japanese businessman who had invited me to his home. He told me that he regrets that I am leaving Japan, and he also wanted me also to know that he cannot continue with this friendship with me. He told me that I should not mention his name to anybody and not try to contact him, because the times are going to be very delicate. And he explained that Japan is entering a new phase of existence and foreigners cannot share with them either friendship or information. None of us.

Nina also felt this, later on, when I had already left Japan. She stayed as long as she could, being so charmed by the fairy tale of the country. Nina, too, when she saw and experienced parts of Japan, felt like, in her own words, she was in a fairy tale dream. She couldn't believe that this little hotel is really in a city. That the theater and the music is like from another world. However, the Japanese are not sentimental. As their plans progressed towards the December attack on Pearl Harbor, their attitudes toward the refugees also changed.

Nina had been taken in by a German Jewish family in Kobe and stayed in Kobe after all the other refugees in my group had left for Shanghai. Eventually, however, she made arrangements to leave for Australia, and had already sent her luggage to a ship that was supposed to take her to Sydney. Before she left, she remembered to go and see her dentist, her Japanese dentist. And this dentist, whom she had seen several times before, was now wearing an officer's uniform under his white coat.

She told him she was leaving for Australia. And then he said, well your teeth are all right, but you cannot go to Australia because there will be war in the Pacific. This was on December 4, only three days before Pearl Harbor. He said, I know that you are a nice person and nothing will happen to you here in Japan. But even though there is to be war, don't judge us by our behavior during the war, because we can be tough. Remember, you lived in Japan in peacetime, and can remember us for good. This was true. So she did not board the liner for Australia. Her possessions went to Australia, but she remained in Japan, like a prisoner.

All the refugees who like Nina had stayed in Japan came immediately under the supervision of the authorities when the war on the Pacific began. They weren't rounded up immediately, but later on, of course, they were. They had had to stay in Japan even though their transit visas had long since expired because they had nowhere else to go. So when the war in the Pacific began, the Japanese authorities collected these refugees and took them to Shanghai. Nina, too, was brought to Shanghai.

So I arrived in China earlier than the other Polish refugees, in the early summer of 1941. The Germans were about to go marching into Russia. Bombs were dropping and blood was flowing all across Europe. The Japanese and the Chinese armies were fighting somewhere to the west and north. The respite I had enjoyed, after escaping Russia and living in a crowded but charming little Japanese house, surrounded by a lovely Japanese town, was now far away. I stepped off the charming little Japanese ship into the thick air of China and looked up at the enormous, glittering *Bund,* the tremendous wall of skyscrapers that faced the harbor. I picked up my little satchel and I made my way through the crowds and crowds of Chinese. And then began my peculiar life, my most strange situation, a Jewish refugee from Poland, in China. And I took up my residence in the unusual Babylon called Shanghai.

Shanghai Ghetto

Iwry went to Shanghai as the representative of the Jewish Agency, appointed by David Ben-Gurion. He took some close friends with him, and they were a formidable committee. He did not identify his other coworkers, beyond the red-headed doctor, Moshe Polackevicz. However, the complementary activities of Iwry and Leon Ilutowitz, perhaps the heart of the committee, can be distinguished. For instance, it was Ilutowitz who braved the trip to Kaunas to get a transit visa that was then copied by the other members of the group. The records of the Joint Distribution Committee mention the Warsaw-trained lawyer as a flamboyant advocate of the Polish refugees. It was Ilutowitz who led the argument against being moved to the refugee ghetto, which the Japanese created later in the war, by claiming the Polish refugees were not stateless.

Iwry, for his part, had a gift for making advantageous connections and spoke a number of languages. He instinctively knew whom to ask when he needed help crossing the border into Lithuania, and moved freely through the refugee groups in Vilna, gathering news and assisting in negotiations. It was Iwry who kept the World Zionist Organization informed of the refugees' status, worked to help refugees escape, and handled Jewish Agency business. In Shanghai, he contacted Boris Topas and got office space for the group. He also made friends with Mendel Brown, got a dinner invitation from Sir Elly Kadoorie, and acted as diplomat with the British. We do not know who else contributed, but it is clear that this little committee was a powerful force on behalf of their fellow refugees.

Now, terrifyingly and enormously big, is this Shanghai. And so unbelievably teeming with masses upon masses upon masses of people, that the first thing a man loses there, is the notion that he is created in the image of God.

You could stand in the midst of the millions of Shanghai, this enormous city of Chinese, and see human beings passing by, passing by. And every one of them leaves on you one speck of impression, and this becomes dust, becomes a layer. And you feel it so well, without ever entering into discussion with them.

I could see the imprint of an old and enduring culture in the dignity of the older people making their way in life, despite their poverty. Also in their everyday life with their families, as they ate from one great steaming pot of rice and vegetables, with little bowls. All of the young people show respect for the elders, which is not just artificial or learned. It apparently goes very well with their outlook, their personality, their behavior.

The younger people in China always looked sad to me. There would be a grin, but it would be sad. They very seldom gave way to an emotion, even smiling or laughing freely like we do. They were also very, very far from being affectionate in public. Hardly would you guess that all these people were born because of sex!

But I do not say that humor is lacking. Once I was hanging on a tram, and I do mean hanging! The trams rolled along the lines, always filled with the hundred million Chinese, some sitting, some standing, some hanging on the outside. And the hanging riders are like a shield around the tram. At the beginning, in Japan, I learned some words, something like, "keep to yourself, don't push." In China, this wouldn't help. Nobody would listen to you.

But one time I saw two trams that found themselves opposite each other. Apparently, somebody failed to pull a switch to put one on the left line. And here we were, two cars, full with each of their million people, and one cannot go further unless the other is pushed backward. But nobody is in a hurry to do it. The two conductors stepped out, and they faced each other, and all the rest, all the passengers formed a big circle. Like two roosters, the conductors stood face to face, and started pouring words on each other.

A friend of mine who was with me—I never went alone—explained that there is a very important kind of dispute going on between these two. One of them says that "while you were still in infancy, my grandfather was one with the great people of China. He was a member of the people who served the emperor Chu Yuan-chang. He helped drive out the Mongols

Shanghai in the 1940s was an enormous, international city and the last open port receiving refugees from the war in Europe. Behind the Bund, this façade of great architecture facing the harbor, was Shanghai's peculiar mix of obscene wealth, decadence, and poverty. It was also overflowing with refugees, both from Europe and from China's interior, where the Japanese were at war with the Chinese. In 1941, Iwry was directed by Ben-Gurion to leave Japan and go to Shanghai to negotiate with the British on behalf of the thousands of Jewish refugees in Asia. His work was halted by the war on the Pacific, when the Japanese confined the refugees in Shanghai's Jewish ghetto. Credit: Library of Congress, LC-USZ62-27782

from Peking, and you are empty grass. You came from the rabble. You have never seen the right. The other one listens, then it is his turn. And he of course says the same thing, apparently, in another way. And the long recitations of these two conductors, who mixed their speeches with some beautiful—I was told—phrases and historical references, turned into a theater, a great entertainment, and people forgot where they had to go and enjoyed themselves.

This was Shanghai before the war—an enormous waterfront of sky-scrapers called the *Bund*, facing out to the Whangpoo River. Behind it, Shanghai was divided into many different districts, different ethnic centers, and each was its own city. Shanghai was a British colony, or rather, was partly a British colony. The French concession was owned by the French, of course, and the British and Americans lived in a big section called the

International Settlement.[1] The Chinese mostly lived in the district of Nantao. So as a whole, Shanghai was even too big to get one ticket for a tram and travel all over. At the boundary of one district, you had to get off your tram and buy another ticket to cross another district.

Now, I should explain that in the time before World War II, Shanghai became famous for corruption, for the place where anything and everything was for sale. It was sometimes called the Paris of the East, but mostly it was also known as the whore of Asia. It was a city of opium dens, gang lords, fancy hotels, and even an amusement park called the Great World. There were alleyway factories where children were worked to death, there were Rolls Royces and rickshaws, a thoroughbred racetrack, prostitutes, drunken corrupt police, and those hundreds of bars where foreign sailors got "shanghaied."

All of the important industries in Shanghai were owned by foreigners, and there were rich foreigners everywhere. The British, of course, ran everything. The French were there as well, and a lot of Jews. The Chinese called these rich and powerful foreigners who ran their industries *taipans*. There were Japanese at Hongkew Gardens, a part of the city behind the International Settlement. Even before the Japanese invaded China, the biggest group of foreigners in Shanghai were the Japanese. But Nantao, the largest section of the city, was very poor and occupied only by Chinese. Foreigners almost never set foot in Nantao.

Not all the foreigners were rich as we think of rich, but to the Chinese they must have seemed unbelievably wealthy. Most had managed to become a sort of middle class, except for maybe the Russians. There was a population of Russians—there were almost as many Russians as Japanese in Shanghai—who had been loyal to the tsar, and who had fled to Shanghai when the Communists took over. They had no official place in Shanghai, and many were even worse off than the poorest Chinese. They brought their decadent tsarist nightlife culture to Shanghai and the luckier ones opened nightclubs. Mostly they were reduced to the lowest existence, as servants and prostitutes. These white Russians were "citizens of nowhere" and even the poorest Chinese showed them not the least regard. Such was the decadence of Shanghai that there was a famous quote by a missionary who had come there, "If God lets Shanghai endure, He owes an apology to Sodom and Gomorrah."

But this Shanghai that was so famous for its corrupt life was not my Shanghai. That Shanghai was mostly gone four years before I came there from Japan. Even while Shanghai partied, the Japanese were chopping up the rest of China. Japan had been trying to take over China since the end of World War I, and by the 1930s all but controlled Manchuria. Then, in 1931, they took over in a big way and started swallowing chunks of China bit by bit. China was poor, and itself divided by the growing number of Communists that were also trying to take over, and never managed to kick out the Japanese. By 1937, the Japanese had also taken the Chinese sections of Shanghai, and many parts of the city were a wasteland.

There had been a series of battles in the late summer and fall of 1937, when the Japanese military marched into Shanghai. I was told that the British had stood on the balconies with champagne glasses in their hands and watched the battles between the Chinese and Japanese. In places— mostly in Nantao and in Hongkew districts, which were occupied by Chinese and Japanese—the city looked like there had been an earthquake. The defending Chinese troops had even bombed their own city—their planes dropped bombs along Nanking road in the middle of a Saturday afternoon. They had also bombed an amusement park in the International Settlement. The day came to be called Bloody Saturday. Thousands and thousands of ordinary people died. It was said to be an accident, but some said it was intended to provoke the British and Americans into joining the war with China against Japan. Later, after the Japanese had taken Shanghai, they moved on and captured Nanking, and committed the atrocities that were made famous as "the rape of Nanking."

So the Japanese were slashing away at China, as the Germans were setting fire to Europe and Russia. Later that same year, when the Japanese sent their planes around the Pacific and attacked Pearl Harbor, the war in the East and the war in the West became a world war. However, when I arrived in Shanghai, the Japanese were not yet ready to take on the British and the Americans, so the International Settlement was still left alone by the Japanese.

In the summer of 1941, Shanghai was nearly the only remaining free port.[2] You didn't need a visa to come to Shanghai, to the International Settlement. And because the Japanese also occupied the Chinese territory of Shanghai, I could enter the International Settlement from Japan. So I found myself in Shanghai.

As unbelievable as this place was to me, I myself, a Jewish refugee, was nothing new to Shanghai. Jewish refugees from Europe had been arriving in Shanghai ever since *Kristallnacht.* At first certain very wealthy members of the Iraqi Jewish community in Shanghai had welcomed them and taken good care of them, but soon there were far too many, and they were overwhelmed. The Shanghai authorities didn't want these refugees, of course, and tried to stop them from coming. But there was no other place for them to go. All Europe had shut the doors on the Jews. So ship after ship full of refugees kept arriving in Shanghai harbor. Eventually, the Joint Distribution Committee sent someone to Shanghai. Her name was Laura Margolies. She had a budget and arranged the placement of the refugees in *heimes*, which I will tell of later.

The refugees from Poland, who like me had escaped to Vilna and across Russia were the last to arrive, and the situation was not favorable. We had nothing left and depended on the goodwill of those who were trying to help. There were already thousands and thousands of refugees in Shanghai, and not much goodwill left. But we had our education and determination and we mostly did very well for ourselves.

Now, I was at that time still very energetic. When I arrived in Shanghai in 1941, I was 30 years old and full of purpose, and as I have already mentioned, the purpose was this: The Jewish Agency thought that as long as transportation to the Near East is still possible by way of the Pacific, then we could try this way of getting the refugees to Palestine. If our ships were not allowed passage through the Suez Canal, we would send them around the Cape of Good Hope to approach Palestine through the Mediterranean from Gibraltar. The ships were to be arranged by the Joint Distribution Committee. The refugees were my task. It was up to me and my little delegation to try to deal with the British, to arrange for certificates, and choose the people to go to Palestine.

I got in touch with some of the people who were already there, who left Japan before me, and I was also in the possession of two or three telephone numbers of some European businessmen who had lived there for a long time. This was my good fortune right away, because I didn't have to go to the "refugee processing center." This particular nightmare was in the Embankment building donated by Sir Victor Sassoon, and if you had no place else to go, and were a refugee who needed to be taken care of, then you had to go there and fill out form after form for the committees who would eventually take care of you. They would assign you a corner or a shelf to sleep in, and tell you how to get your meals at the free kitchens that were operating in Shanghai for the refugees.

I had names and a card that read, "Samuel Iwry, Representative of the Jewish Agency for Palestine in the Far East, Chairman." This card and the telegram from Ben-Gurion in Jerusalem worked wonders. The Russian Jewish community in Shanghai took care of me. They found me a tiny room in the French concession where they all lived. They understood that I had a mission and they were all ready to help me. Boris Topas was one of them. Boris Topas was then the president of the Russian Jewish community, which was officially called the Shanghai Ashkenazi Communal Association, and as a Russian Jew, he was also a Zionist, and was ready to help. He put at my disposal a desk in his office, some secretarial assistance if necessary, and a Chinese servant who would make telephone calls if needed.

One thing that I needed to do was to get in touch with the British consular authorities, to work out the passage of refugees to Palestine. My contact with the British came through one of the Jewish *taipans* of Shanghai, Sir Elly Kadoorie.

Now, I must say something about the Jewish *taipans* in Shanghai. They were originally from Iraq, Sephardic Jews, who had escaped persecution under the Turks in the late 1800s. There were a number of these *taipans,* and I will tell you about four. Sir Elly Kadoorie had come from Baghdad and also England, as he was a British citizen and had even been knighted. He made his fortune in Shanghai in banking, real estate, and rubber. He had built a mansion on Bubbling Well Road in the International Settlement that amazed even the wealthiest foreigner. It was the first house in Shanghai to have air conditioning. It had a ballroom with chandeliers that were 18 feet wide. It was called Marble Hall because it had so much marble in it, and it is still standing. It is now a school for gifted children, called the Childrens' Palace.

The second Jewish *taipan* was Silas Hardoon. He had also come from Baghdad, and started out as a rent collector. He eventually made millions in his tenement buildings and utility companies. However, Hardoon was not as impressed with the British as they thought he should be. He adored Chinese culture. Hardoon was also civic-minded, as they say, and had built the Beth Aharon synagogue that once stood on Museum Road. During the war, the ever-tolerant Japanese, mostly on the advice of their newly acquired advisors, the Germans, turned this synagogue into a stable for horses.

Another of these Jewish *taipans* was Sir Victor Sassoon. His grandfather, David Sassoon, had come to England from Iraq and had made a fortune in international trade, mostly in drugs. Sir Victor was educated at Cambridge and had been in the Royal Navy, but was crippled by a plane crash and always used two walking sticks. He came to Shanghai in 1931 to run the family business there. The Sassoon family was very devout, and Victor's grandfather left instructions for a lavish synagogue in his will. The synagogue was built and named the Ohel Rachel, after Sir Victor's grandmother. Sir Victor built the famous Cathay Hotel and gave fabulous parties. He always had a camera with him, and loved to take pictures of his stuffy British guests as they were drunk and acting absurd. This is what I heard.

Sir Victor did much to help the refugees when they began arriving in Shanghai, and gave his Embankment building to the people helping the refugees. This building had no bathrooms, but it did have a swimming pool! Sassoon left Shanghai just before I arrived. The war destroyed much of what he had in Shanghai. However, when the Communists took over, he went to the Bahamas and built another bank and made a new fortune.

There was another Jewish *taipan* from Iraq, Isaac Ezra, who reportedly became wealthy in the opium trade. Eventually he came to own a lot of the international houses, and even big chunks of China's industry—electrification, shipping, and other basic and very important economic possessions. His sons were very fond of the races and spent a lot of money on thoroughbred horses.

These economic giants would never, I'm sure, talk to the average Sephardic pauper or one of their little echelon of managers who worked in their shipping or other industries. But Sassoon and Kadoorie did help the refugees. They were very wealthy, and it was very much expected that they would do this. The Russian Jewish community got less involved in helping the refugees. That was because these early refugees were German Jews, and the Russian Jews disliked them, as they hated anything that had to do with Germany. However, later, the Japanese forced the job of caring for the refugees on these Russian Shanghai Jews.

Let me tell you how there came to be a Russian Jewish community in Shanghai. When after 1918 all of Russia became communist, with their pronounced hatred of *kulaks*—anyone the communists decided was too rich—many of these Jews decided not to become citizens of the communist "paradise" but made their way into China, to Manchuria. In Manchuria, especially in the cities of Tianjin and Harbin, many of these Jews found opportunities in the construction of the Manchurian-Russian railways and all the exporting and importing that was going on. There grew in Tianjin and Harbin a sizable Jewish community. They were also religious, but not so terribly orthodox. They led, as I said, a middle-class, comfortable life. When Manchuria was taken over by the Japanese, a large portion of the Jewish population moved to Shanghai, and also to Kobe.

Well, from the beginning of my stay, it was the Russian Jewish community who took care of me, as they more or less willingly took care of most of us Polish Jews. Russian Jews and Polish Jews have much in common, and they took me in. They could not boast of any potentate. But they were not poor, either. They had their own synagogue, the Ashkenazi Oihel Moishe, and they had little to do with the Sephardic community in Shanghai, rich or poor. They were all of them middle class. The Japanese occupation had disrupted their businesses, and many of them were having financial troubles (though some were enjoying a nice profit from the war). But as for me, I had been a refugee for nearly two years, and they seemed to be living a life of great peace and comfort. And I felt at home with them, as my Russian was very good.

The French concession was a very well-conducted municipality, not much different from any city in France—except for the hundreds of Chinese begging and dying in the streets. The French had little regard for the Chinese or the Japanese (or the English). The courts, the police, all were French. And they fared very well, thinking that this corner of Shanghai was theirs forever, and they would not allow anything, ever, to disturb their tranquil life, their tennis at the Cercle Sportif Francais, their good humor, and even better wine.

I remember seeing the security patrol in the French Concession. You would see them any time of day or night, walking. The patrol consisted of a French officer with a flat red or blue hat, and a small, very well-kept mustache, and his little baton under his arm. He walked first, and alone. Behind him came two Russian Eurasians, descendants of Russian generals or immigrants who lost their high positions in Russia. They had revolvers in special leather holsters, and in their hands they held two billy clubs. They never used their revolvers. Behind them, walked a group of six tall Sikhs with their turbans on their heads, and they had rifles hanging from their shoulders, in case they needed them. These six walked as a group, day and night. A little bit after the foot patrol came a jeep with Chinese policemen and a machine gun. That was the standard unit of security in the French Concession. This you could see any time.

Chinese would come and go freely. The exhausted, the very poor, the hungry would come to find a little piece of bread, whether outside the stores or in the garbage. The French were very strict with them and so there were fewer in the French Concession. However, in the much larger International Settlement they were found in the thousands, because the English and American establishments there relied on Chinese help, in the offices or for other jobs. But the entire city was overwhelmed with Chinese refugees from the countryside. They came to Shanghai after the Japanese and Chinese soldiers had destroyed their villages and crops. In the International Settlement, and everywhere else in Shanghai, you could see, to your bitter disappointment, Chinese lying and dying in the streets, hundreds and hundreds at a time.

They explained it to me, like to every European who asks, why don't you give them some help, why don't you take them to a hospital? They say if you do it, at this same place, where you saw today two people, there tomorrow will be lying in the same place two dozen. They are "taken care of" early in the morning. They are dying, and during the bitter cold fall and winter nights they freeze to death. The next morning workers come in big trucks and shovel them up. If someone meets tragedy, that is where they die—under the sky, in the streets. And the trucks collect the bodies every morning.

They told me a story about a rich Jew—they always speak these words together, "rich Jew"—who came to Shanghai like I did for the first time, and saw them, and he asked, "They are going to die, why don't you do anything?" They didn't answer. Why should they explain it again and again? He said "How much will it cost to take them to a hospital? Take them. I will pay." The Jew took four people, and they loaded them in a rickshaw, he followed, in another rickshaw of course, and went to the hospital and paid them—this is true—for one month in advance. But this man, the local people told me, was one big sucker, because he didn't understand there are 12 million Chinese waiting in line!

However, the Chinese are a very motivated people, and they still wanted to do things on their own, like the little Chinese boy I knew, who spread out a little towel, and made and sold lucky statues, that was his business. There was also the fellow who goes around in the streets of Shanghai, with a long bamboo on his shoulders and his portable kitchen cabinets hanging from both sides. On the one side is also a shelf with a big container of soup, and on the other side are hanging the serving pieces. Not only is he carrying it, but it is ringing with little bells and he, with his own way of singing, invites people to buy from him. There was one Chinese who invented a potion that was supposed to sharpen the wits. It had a picture of a Jew on the label and it was very successful.

Well, I had to tell all these little stories at the beginning. Now, I will tell about the job I had to do. Because it was the summer of 1941, the Germans were winning in Russia and the war in the Pacific may break out any time, so it was necessary for me to act quickly. One obstacle was that the different Jewish communities never talked to each other. Once a year, some locals met only for one purpose—how much matzos and where, will they make this year? That is the thing that united them—they all ate matzos—on Passover and other holidays.

Boris Topas gave me and my delegation an office and some assistance. As a next step, I needed to be introduced to the English ambassador in China or at least to his first secretary. However, my Russian friends did not talk to the English—it was the Sephardic Jews who knew the English officials. So while Mr. Topas gave me an office, I had to contact the Sephardic Jews and make acquaintance with their rabbi on my own. I found out that this rabbi was not the official rabbi, but really the principal of their school, the Shanghai Jewish School that belonged to the Ohel Rachel synagogue. His name was Mendel Brown, a very fine man.

So, somebody gave a message to this Mendel Brown that among the new Polish refugees there is a young scholar, and he is here with some mission and he would like to meet you. He called me on the telephone and then came to see me. He was pleased to find that I am a man with an advanced education, which was not common among the teachers with whom he normally came into contact. His first question was, did I want to help him out with his school, because they teach Jewish subjects and the people they hired are not equipped to teach the more advanced classes.

Anyway, I told him, this we will leave for later. And I explained my situation and my request. He told me that in order to meet the English authorities, he would have to relay my message to Sir Elly Kadoorie. Not more than three or four days later, I was informed by the rabbi that he and I would be a guest at the palatial Kadoorie home, the famous Marble Hall, and also the first secretary of the English Embassy and the consul would be there.

When I came to this home, to Marble Hall, which really was an English castle in the middle of Shanghai, I met the "potentate" and my friend Mendel Brown said that it is good that I could come along and speak for myself because he barely is acquainted with the old man. Sir Elly Kadoorie was wearing a hearing aid and sitting in a big chair, like on a throne. On regular chairs around him were his sons. This was an anniversary or birthday of someone in the family, which made them gather together, and to which the old man also invited the English officials.

He himself, the old man, was wearing the same head cover as I. He thought it would be nice to receive me and the rabbi like this, and he greeted me in very good Hebrew! He said to me, *barukh ha-ba,* which is "welcome visitor," or literally, "blessed be he who comes." He asked me to make the *hamotzi*—the blessing—over the bread. And after that, the dinner was served in a different room, in an entirely different wing of the palace. And there were some 20 or 30 Chinese servants bringing all the traditional dishes. After the dinner, we moved to the study, yet another room, and there Sir Kadoorie told the English consul that I had some matter to tell him of.

As it happened, the consul already knew my name and my business. He said that five days earlier, he had received a letter from Ben-Gurion, and it said that the Jewish Agency would like to make it possible for more immigrants to enter Palestine and to arrange for them a number of certificates. And they would approve a local representative from among the people who want to go to Palestine, a certain man called Samuel Iwry. He agreed that yes, I will select people, present a list, with doctors' certificates and other documents, and the Consular staff will issue to every one of them a visa to go to Palestine. Fine! After this conversation, and after drinking a little bit of wine, the first secretary told me that he will be very happy to see me in his office next week, on Monday if possible, at ten o'clock.

It was true, the secretary and the consul worked out the procedure: I should bring the first time five to ten people. This first group should come in person. They will see the people, they will verify that these are true refugees, that they cannot go home and they want to leave Shanghai. We also decided that I can use a doctor from our own people to sign the health certificate. The doctor will come and introduce himself to the secretary. After this first group, they will rely on the doctor and inspect only the documents.

All this worked out very well, and the authorities wished me every success, they even told me, you can come whenever you want, feel at home, and they introduced to me the general manager, as I would describe him, of the consulate. This manager was a certain Chinese called Young Wan, and he gave all the instructions that were necessary for a smoothly running post. Young Wan knew everything that went on in the embassy. He knew how many certificates were being sent, what the text should be, and how to write out the visa. Some high official of the embassy signed them after they were written, and they would allow the owner to go through any country and enter Palestine.

Our next job was to actually select the first group and to go with them to the embassy. The next day I got two other men to help me, and we started interviewing people who could be candidates for emigration. Then, I had to see to transportation.

The arrangements for ships came from the United States. I had a conversation with Goldmann at the Jewish Agency in New York, and he made the arrangements with the Joint Distribution Committee, who paid for them. And the operation really started moving. We didn't know who should go first, the young people, or those with families. There were always little crowds of people who wanted to be considered or given a certificate to emigrate to Palestine. However, we didn't have any disturbances around the offices that Mr. Topas gave to us. Things were going well, and I was sure that after one or two groups were sent off, and the committee was operating smoothly, then I myself would be one of the passengers, making my own exit from Shanghai.

But as things started moving, it was very difficult to tell people, you wait, because we have other candidates. It was very difficult. All these refugees shared a Zionist ideal, wanting to bring about the day when Jewish children were born into their own country, speaking the Hebrew language, educated in a Jewish school, and living in a place where they could be safe.

These refugees didn't have any money, none of us had any money. The Jewish Federation, through the Joint Distribution Committee, paid for it, they leased ships from Japan. And ships were still moving on the Pacific. We succeeded in sending out the first group of refugees, 30 passengers on their way to Haifa, in Palestine, which is not a small journey. We began to make preparations for a still larger group, and I myself planned to be among them.

During this entire time, as we were all trying yet again another route to emigrate to Palestine, the news on the radio and in the English daily papers became very ominous. Because while I was still in Japan and just before I arrived in Shanghai, the worst thing that could happen did happen—the outbreak of the Russian-German war, on June 22, 1941. The German armies had lashed out in a most terrible and swift *Blitzkrieg,* called Operation Barbarossa, which devastated the Russian army. And now the news that we were able to get in Shanghai made it clear that Stalin's forces were disorganized. The Russians didn't have any sort of an army that could stand up to the Germans and the Soviets were sent packing like schoolboys. The Nazis were moving across Russia toward Moscow and we wondered if they could really reach the Pacific coast. It became clear to us that not only all of Europe, but now even Asia was falling under the beastly swastika.

My friends and I understood Russian very well, and also most of us could understand English. And the news on the radio wasn't good. Every day the Russian radio in Shanghai kept reporting this ominous news, that the German army was rushing toward Moscow, trying to get there before Russia's best ally arrived, meaning winter, Russia's white winter. The forward-moving armies were already demonstrating what would happen later to all the communities of Europe. People were being machine-gunned wholesale by the Nazis.

A terrible paralysis seemed to take over our world. Not one day was I free from thinking of what happened to my family and all those whom I left, now completely at the mercy of the Nazis. It made me bitter to live.

Not long after these things had happened, the other refugees from Lithuania who had escaped to Japan were brought to Shanghai. About half of them, like me, had not been able to get a visa to another country and our transit visas through Japan had expired a long time ago. So the Japanese authorities put them on a ship and brought them to Shanghai. It was August, one of the worst heat waves Shanghai had known, and we were all unprepared for this horrible climate and the living conditions in Shanghai.

I and my friends were busy all that summer and fall just with the refugees, who were already ready to go and waiting for a place on a ship. We considered only whether they had a visa, imprinted on the one *sauf conduit,* or passport, and were strong enough to make the trip. Of course, none of us had anything to tie together, or to take with us. But the voyage would be very difficult. It was becoming winter, and the cold weather in Shanghai is even worse than the heat. It is a penetrating, unpleasant cold. But whether it would be an easy or a difficult journey, these people really wanted to go. Many of them were young people. But the Jewish Agency looked for families with children, who could all go on one certificate.

One bit of bad news for me, was the word from Palestine. I spoke to the foreign secretary of the Jewish Agency in Palestine on the phone. The call got through after two days of difficult arrangements. I was told I should by no means leave, I should stay as long as there is the least possibility to save people.

This was a very difficult time. I really began to feel what the Chinese were feeling, that the Japanese were holding their arms [restraining them]. Because the English newspapers were telling us that there would be war also in Asia, not just in Europe. The Japanese and the Germans were about to mix together the war in China and the war in Europe and the whole Northern hemisphere would be on fire.

And in early December 1941, it came. I remember being awakened by a terrific bombardment. This was the Pearl Harbor of Shanghai, and it happened only a few hours before the attack on the United States, the real Pearl Harbor. No one could believe the Japanese would send planes to bomb the United States. But the attack really happened all around the Pacific Ocean. Pearl Harbor was only the last stop. The Japanese sent planes to strike Singapore, Hong Kong, Shanghai, and the other harbors where the

British and Americans had their Navy ships. It was the beginning of the war in the Pacific.

In Shanghai, I remember hearing a terrific exchange of bombardments, from the ground and from the sky, from both the planes and the ships. Then the British were silent. The Americans resisted a little longer. Then, quiet. The several British and American military ships that were in Shanghai harbor were told to surrender. So they did.

The Japanese were already in Shanghai, of course, so there was no invasion in the usual sense. But they took over the International Settlement and left no question about who was in charge. It took very little time for the United States and Britain to declare war on Japan, so the residents of the International Settlement were now prisoners of war. That day the people were afraid to go out in the street, and around 11 o'clock the first Japanese patrols started to appear in their official places, saying "now you are all under our rule."

I and my two friends knew very well that we had about 150 passports lying on the desk of the Chinese official at the British Embassy. He was supposed to give them back to us in a day or two, after signing them. But all of a sudden, all of this happened, and we felt responsible for the people who without any documents or passports were stranded in the Far East, stranded in an environment where we could not communicate much with the Chinese, let alone reason with the Japanese, who were aligned with the Germans. These passports, these certificates that perhaps could help them to reach freedom, were all they had.

Therefore we did the most impossible thing, Leon Ilutowicz and Moshe Polackevicz and I. From the French concession, we walked along the wall and we entered the grounds of the English Embassy from two blocks away. A soldier saw us—Chinese, or Korean, or Japanese—he was standing with a rifle on his shoulder. He did not understand who we were, or perhaps he thought we were part of the compound, and he didn't ask us any questions. So we went in. One of us remained outside, and I and the other one opened the door and we found the passports were lying exactly where they were supposed to be. We knew, more or less, to two or three, how many had to be there, whether it was 151 or 153, but we knew that we had them! We got a brown bag that was lying there, and we put them in the brown bag, and under the terrible feeling that we were about to be arrested, we came out again.

We still had to go from the British Embassy back to the French concession, and only two blocks from the embassy, there were already

Japanese tanks and patrol vehicles and military encampments in the streets of the International Settlement. And of all the millions of Chinese in Shanghai, there were only one or two, here and there, in the streets. The only other people besides the Japanese soldiers were we three, walking now, carrying a brown bag. But we did it.

And wonder of all wonders, all the passports were already signed! I don't think that the Englishman signed them, he was already long gone when we heard the bombardments. The Chinese official, this day or the day before, signed them. Of course, we couldn't use them anymore. The war now involved nearly the whole world. Europe was Nazified, the Japanese are at war in the Pacific, America had joined the fight. The British were out of business, as they say, and we could get no more certificates. But a useless passport was much better than no identification at all.

Unlike in other places, there was no great panic among the millions of Chinese who lived around Shanghai. The French, of course, didn't feel so *poppy*[3] as the Japanese convoy marched through the streets of their concession. However, they mostly maintained their municipal administration and their way of life. France belonged to the Germans, who were for now partners with the Japanese, so the French were treated differently than the English and the Americans.

The British and American residents who were still in Shanghai were told to pack up all their possessions and were taken away, under arrest by the Japanese military. They ended up in a concentration camp. But us refugees, they did not bother with us at first. But they did send the last very few refugees from Kobe to Shanghai. Nina, too, came to Shanghai.

Once again, we were trapped under a hostile military establishment, though we managed for a while. The hope of getting to Palestine was no more. I was again out of a job with the Jewish Agency, and set about finding other work as a teacher in order to have a little bread or something to eat. But I was not alone, and we did not lose hope. Not yet.

And now I must tell you more about the Jewish refugees in Shanghai. Those of us from Poland were the last refugees from Europe to arrive in Shanghai. We topped off the refugee population. As I already mentioned, the first to come were the Germans. They were mostly older, and brought their families and their possessions. Many of them were professionals, and they were able to earn a living, as doctors or lawyers or teachers, and some were living well in Shanghai. Many were able to support themselves even if they did not live very well. The war meant that Shanghai's import and export businesses were making money, so some were able to get jobs in these businesses. English teachers could earn a living, and so could tailors, bakers, and engineers. But others could not adapt, and were completely dependent on the Shanghai Jews, who had scrambled to form support committees to take care of them. But there were soon too many refugees for this Shanghai committee and that is when the Joint Distribution Committee sent some funds, and Laura Margolies, to help them. Later they sent Margolies an assistant, named Manuel Siegel.

Besides some 10,000 German refugees, there were also perhaps 5,000 Austrian refugees, who came on their own and were living in different, more normal quarters. The refugees grew less and less welcome, and the Shanghailanders tried to get the Japanese to stop the refugees from coming. But Japan let them come. The reason was that during the battles to capture Shanghai, the district of Hongkew had been very much destroyed, but the European Jewish refugees set about cleaning it up and rebuilding it. The refugees did such an incredible job that parts of Hongkew became known as Little Vienna. They even installed some European plumbing. Sassoon, even though he didn't like the Japanese, had set up some construction "loans" that allowed the Jewish refugees to rebuild in Hongkew and go into business for themselves, and it was very successful. There were many European coffee shops in Hongkew. Some of the loans were even repaid.

Then, last of all, came myself and the other Polish Jews. Of all the refugees that had escaped Poland to Lithuania, about 2,000 made it to Kobe, mostly because of Sugihara. Of these, half found a destination—Australia, Canada, America, and other places. The rest of us came to Shanghai. We were a grand mix of Polish Jewry. About half of us were the Orthodox yeshiva students, including of course, the Mir Yeshiva, which had traveled and escaped as one single body. Quite a few were Hasidic Jews, with their long curls in front of their ears and their long black coats. They ignored the war and the Chinese and just kept on studying Torah. The Chinese thought these Hasidic Jews were somewhat like the Sikhs and their turbans on the security unit in the International Settlement, and they called them "little Indians."

Many others were Zionists of some sort, from the Polish underground, like me and my small circle of friends. There were only about a thousand of us Polish refugees, and according to Margolies, we brought the total European refugee population in Shanghai to about 17,000.

The Polish refugees, were, one by one, very interesting. They were nearly all young men, just beginning their profession, and they were lively, interesting, and intellectual. We were not Hasidic, but dressed and looked like any other European. And we were all, almost to the last, doctors—that is, doctors of philosophy. We were all very well educated and from all kinds of professions, including artists, writers, even sinologists, who knew the history of the Chinese. So I had an extraordinary group of people around me, whom I would have never met if we had not all been thrown together in this place.

However, even with our education, not all of us could earn a living in Shanghai. Some were destitute and completely dependent on the refugee committees to keep them alive. They were put in a *heime,* which I will now tell about. The Committee had located some large buildings that were left standing after the battles fought in Shanghai—most of them were in Hongkew—and fixed them up a little to make dormitories for those refugees who could not earn enough to feed themselves or to rent even the poorest room in Shanghai. These crowded and appalling refugee "shelters" were furnished with row after row of beds, just wooden shelves, with no space between, and not even a hook for your personal belongings. The Germans named them *heime,* which means "home" in German, but they meant this word to be an insult. A few of these five or so facilities had only a few sinks for cleaning up, and porcelain bowls instead of plumbing. One or two had showers, and you could get clean for the price of a Shanghai penny. Some had kitchens for those who needed meals for free or at a very low price. Sometimes, the conditions were appalling and there were epidemics of lice. Morale was low, and there was much bitterness and accusations of favoritism among those who both lived in a *heime* and had a job serving food in the kitchens.[4]

The Russian Jews did not like the German Jews, and up to then had not been much involved in helping the refugees. They let Sassoon and Kadoorie do it. But they were more sympathetic toward the Polish Jews, because we had much more in common with these Jews who had fled Russia than with the German refugees. Even though we were the last to arrive, we could not do as the German refugees did. The Germans who had arrived earlier barely knew they were Jews. They had assimilated into German life and were still in shock at what Hitler had done. To make things worse, they insisted on speaking German, which was offensive to Russian and Polish ears. So the Russian community felt little sympathy for these Germans, but they were a little more involved with us, especially as their rabbi, Rabbi Ashkenazi, was a very learned man in Torah and he prodded them to help us a little.

The Iraqi (Sephardic) Jews had done a lot. Besides the several buildings made into the dreadful *heimes,* there was the Shanghai Jewish Hospital, where a number of refugee doctors were employed. Kadoorie had donated X-ray equipment and other supplies. Some of the *heimes* had their own clinics and kitchens. There was even a maternity ward. Surgery was performed at the Shanghai Jewish Hospital.

There were many European doctors practicing medicine in Shanghai. They even managed to inoculate nearly all the refugees against the diseases of Shanghai, which no one had heard of in Europe. But these doctors knew very little about the health problems of the Far East. We were given instructions on how to stay healthy, if possible. We were told to never drink unboiled water or eat uncooked food. The bread had to cut very thin so you could find the worms and take them out before you swallowed one. Shanghai was full of dysentery, stomach worms, cholera, beri beri, and typhus. And heat. Several dozen refugees died in a great heat wave. But considering the conditions we were living in, including the doctors—who had as little food to eat as the rest of us—our health could have been far worse.

Also, besides the kitchens and clinics, the committee had made a reception center for the refugees that kept coming. Most of the refugees had come on ships run by the Lloyd-Tristino company, which charged very high rates. Representatives of the relief committee would meet these ships if they knew about any arrivals, and would take the refugees to a reception center. Then the refugees would fill out endless papers and be assigned a place in a *heime,* if necessary. However, not long after I came to Shanghai, the Mir Yeshiva arrived all at once, and they would not go to a *heime.* So Rabbi Ashkenazi took them to the Beth Aharon Synagogue and they slept on mattresses in the hallways of the synagogue. Eventually they found other places to sleep, but they continued to use the synagogue for their endless days of study. Later, when there was no more work for me to do, there were many days when I joined them and took comfort in this remnant from Eastern Europe.

I was lucky to be taken in by the Russian community and given a place for the Jewish Agency work. When at the end of the summer, the remaining Polish refugees arrived from Kobe, I felt the comfort of familiar people around me, and I must say we had quite an effect on Shanghai, though we were the smallest group of refugees. We were the most Jewish of the Jews. We wanted to do things our own way. We were from Poland and we had never completely assimilated or adopted the ways of the people around us. And we really changed our small corner of Shanghai. When we came to Shanghai there were no Torah schools, the Jewish community of Shanghai had little knowledge of their history, although they were Zionist in their politics.

So, there in the midst of the millions and millions of Chinese, we organized and began a Talmud Torah school, and later, after the Mir Yeshiva students arrived, there was begun a rabbinical college taught by these yeshiva students. However, they taught classes in German and Yiddish rather than Hebrew, which I considered unfortunate.

A radio station in Shanghai even had a program of Yiddish language and music every week. There were many who earned a fine living as a tailor and many tried peddling door to door, as well as opening coffee shops or teaching English, which was the main business language of Shanghai. Plays were written from memory and performed, and there were concerts. There was even a puppet theater, and a few refugees began a small pay library at one of the *heime*. Some of the Polish refugees that I knew tried to start a newspaper, the *News for War Refugees in Shanghai,* but somehow the Japanese authorities did not approve and the refugees burned all of their papers. However, the Russian Jewish community published a newspaper in three languages, called *Unser Leben,* or *Our Life,* and about the time I arrived, they began publishing a supplement in Yiddish.

So, when I arrived in Shanghai, I found there, in the midst of the millions and millions of Chinese, three—not one, but three!—distinct Jewish communities. The Jewish *taipans* from Iraq and their Sephardic community, the Ashkenazi Russian Jews, and the refugees, who were really having an effect. In fact, the refugees, before I came to Shanghai, had already begun to form their own *Kehilla,* or organized Jewish community. I will tell you about this *Kehilla,* which the Germans call a *Gemeinde,* which means "district" in German, but is an organization that covers the Jewish life from the cradle to the grave. It didn't matter whether you were a holy-roller Hasidic or a secular Zionist, the *Kehilla* was the organization that made sure there was a Jewish place to be born, kosher meat to eat, Jewish schools, marriage and death certificates, and all other Jewish community matters.

Well, the first refugees to arrive from Germany had tried to fit in with one or the other Jewish communities that was already in Shanghai. But this was difficult, like a Protestant from Wisconsin, let's say, trying to fit in with a Cuban Catholic community in Florida. They weren't very warmly welcomed. So as more and more refugees came to Shanghai, they decided to have their own *Kehilla,* the Jewish Community of Central European Jews, called the *Jeudishe Gemeinde.* So even though there were not enough rabbis and no money, the *Gemeinde* was begun and eventually had an office on East

Seward Road, with all the departments including an organization for cantors, an arbitration board for settling disputes—and a list of refugee lawyers who could represent you. There was a youth organization, and even a budget for buying cemeteries, which filled up quickly at times.

When the war in the Pacific finally began, there was not any shortage of anything in Shanghai, at first. No speculation or high prices, no dearth of bread or eggs. A few years later, of course, starvation came. Even so, we were seeing now, just as Nina's dentist said, that the war would show the Japanese in a different light. And did it show!

Already in 1940, the Japanese, as would-be conquerors of greater Asia, had become part of the Axis, the alliance of Japan, Germany, and Italy. So the Germans became the friends of the Japanese. And these Germans told them, be aware that in Shanghai, as elsewhere, lives a sizable group of refugees, former German Jews and other Jews. And the Germans started working with the Japanese and explaining to them that "they have to be taken care of because they are our enemies."

Nina not long ago told me this story: Among the Polish Jewish group that found its way to Shanghai from Lithuania was a certain group of Hasidic Jews, and they had a leader, a rebbe. His name was Shimon Kalish, and he was the rebbe of Amshenover, a very respected, authoritative, and courageous man. This rebbe was called one day to the Japanese, and they asked him, "Why do the Germans and others hate so much the Jews?"

He reputedly told them what no one else would tell them. He said, "They hate us because they think that they are of a superior race called the Aryans, with a different history and origin and who continue their superior racial distinctiveness. They look at everyone else who are not Aryans, and especially the Jews, with disgust and hatred." When the Japanese asked more about this, the rebbe had the audacity to tell them, "If you think that they do not hold you with the same disgust and hatred, you are mistaken. It is only now, while you are in a military alignment, that they don't show it. We alone are now their target. But the truth is, you too are not much different from us in their eyes."

The Japanese did not immediately adopt the Nazi policy toward us. They had given up on trying to get the world to do their bidding by influencing the Jews of the world and were more willing to cooperate with the Germans in their treatment of the Jews. But the Japanese still considered the Jews a very useful, practical, and also influential people, and they were afraid that the Jews who—they still thought—controlled the governments of the world would turn against them if they mistreated the refugees.

Before Pearl Harbor and afterward, the Japanese did great business with the Jewish *taipans* in Shanghai. Sir Victor Sassoon was a close friend of the brother-in-law of Chiang Kai-shek, and the Japanese thought that they could influence the Chinese through Sassoon. But Sassoon didn't like the Japanese and this didn't work. They gave up on Sassoon and were happy to take over his Cathay Hotel offices after the war in the Pacific began. Then they thought perhaps the Russian Jews would be more helpful, so they would talk to Boris Topas instead. And when the refugees began to arrive from Europe, they invited them to settle and rebuild the Hongkew section of Shanghai, as I have already mentioned.

So in spite of the Germans, the Japanese didn't treat the refugees badly even after the war in the Pacific began. After Pearl Harbor, the Japanese authorities decided that all the refugees would be represented by our *Kehilla,* the *Juedische Gemeinde,* which was not a political organiza-tion. A Japanese, often Captain Koreshige Inuzuka himself, would come to the meetings and try to interfere, and especially try to get rid of the elected leaders who he knew were anti-Japanese. They also outlawed all the little refugee newspapers that were printed and sold around Shanghai, except for the *Shanghai Jewish Chronicle,* which was in German. Not much else changed immediately. A while later, in January 1942, we were all required to go and register with the Japanese, at the Russian Jewish Club on Mulmain Road.

The larger problems began in the spring of 1942. Margolies was told that with the war, there was no more money coming from the Jewish Agency in New York to help us. Some with friends or relatives in neutral countries managed to still receive some help, but there was no more from the Joint in New York. The Polish government-in-exile set up a committee in Shanghai, and sent a little assistance. They even arranged for a few refugees to leave Shanghai and go to Mozambique. But there was no real substitute for the Joint funds from the United States.

Margolies had to close the refugee hospital, even though there was a typhus outbreak and a number of refugees died of the heat that summer. The kitchens in the *heimes* could serve only one meal a day, a stew of sorts, with beans and more beans. But like on the Russian trains, we could still have hot tea and more hot tea, because of course people could drink only boiled water.

We all tried everything we could to earn a few coins and buy extra food, but this was difficult. I did not do too badly, as many of the teachers at the Shanghai Jewish School were British and they left when the Japanese took over. So the school needed teachers and I was able to work. And I even published an article, about the three Jewish communities in Shanghai, in the Yiddish part of *Unser Leben*. The article was called "Drei Kehillos, Drei Zeitungen," which means "three *Kehillos*, three newspapers," and was printed in May 1942.

I was glad to teach and write a little because once again, there was no more Jewish Agency activity, no more hope of a certificate to Palestine. The war in the Pacific had closed the door. A great paralysis set in, as we waited to see what would happen to us, and to try to make the best of our situation in spite of the news from Europe and the growing influence of the Nazis over the Japanese.

So there began a time of just over a year, when the war in the Pacific and the war in Europe had all the world in dread and turmoil, and we just tried to continue living, as best as we could, in this peculiar corner of China. The children still had their schooling, of course. And even though there was very little food, there was a great deal of culture. I especially was happy that there was theater. A number of refugee theaters formed, including actors I had seen during my romantic college days in Vilna. The actors got together and wrote out the best-known plays from memory, and there were original works performed as well. There were many musicians among the refugees and concerts and recitals of all kinds were available.

Best of all was the sports. There were many professional soccer players among the refugees in Shanghai, and the matches at the soccer field on Chaufoong Road, next to the *heime*, were well attended. Refugee soccer players became the stars of Shanghai soccer, and sports became a way for everyone to enjoy themselves for a while. The children, of course, had their sports activities as well, and this kept them safe from Shanghai's many dangers when they were not in school.

But by the summer of 1942, times were becoming extremely difficult. The price of everything was going up. It was the beginning of the stupendous inflation that crippled all the city over the next few years. And the Nazis were having an effect. There were even articles in the English Shanghai newspapers that blamed the Jewish refugees for the black market and for profiteering. This was in Shanghai! As if this was unknown in Shanghai before the refugees arrived. It was absurd, of course. But the war had made life difficult for everyone, and it was easy to create hard feelings toward the refugees. Worst of all, there began rumors of a pogrom, organized by the Japanese military with the help of the Germans. And it was in fact not a rumor, it was true.

This rage of the Japanese, the military, was hidden from the central government in Tokyo. They were in cahoots with the Germans, and they thought that a thing like this would please their friends, and it would be kind of a service to the future world in which they would remain of course in power along with the Germans. So the military was acting on its own authority, with the government in Tokyo supposedly not knowing anything. But the Japanese vice-consul, who was a very decent man named Shibata, went to the meetings of the Japanese military and when he found out about this plan, the very next day he arranged a meeting with the leaders of the Jewish Community, and warned them.

The people who were at the meeting were all prominent in the Russian Jewish community, and some were acquainted with some prominent Japanese. They decided to try to reach any Japanese they knew, who could talk to Tokyo, and mobilize against these plans. However, this did not work, and even worse, the Japanese found out that that their own Shibata had leaked this information to the Jews. Finally, the Russian Jews just printed it in the newspaper, hoping the Japanese would back down. And they did, but they were also angry because this was bad publicity that embarrassed the Japanese. And then—this was in June 1942—they arrested everyone who had been at this meeting, including Shibata.

One of them was Boris Topas, my very good friend, who received me so warmly in Shanghai; they arrested Mr. Bitker, and other prominent Russian Jews who had lived there since the beginning of the century. And they took them to the Bridge Jail—it was called that because it was near the Garden Bridge. This was not just to confine them. They beat them up so terribly, like they later did to me, but much worse because two of them died right away. Bitker was not released until he confessed to spreading "false rumors" and came out a broken man—I heard that they had dragged him up sets of stairs and then thrown him down again—but even so, after he had recovered he continued to help the refugees.

My friend Boris Topas was released as well, but then he was arrested again only one week later. I heard that he was accused of being a spy but this was absurd. What really happened was this: Some White Russian gangster wanted a pawn shop that Topas owned, and when Topas wouldn't give it to him, this common criminal talked to the Japanese and got Topas arrested. I never saw him again.

There was no pogrom. But the German ambassador in Shanghai kept pressuring the Japanese about these enemies of Hitler, and the rumors continued to be frightening. I learned that three high and mighty Nazis had come to Shanghai to advise the Japanese on the Jews, and one of these was Robert Meisinger, who was called the Executioner of Warsaw.

As the cold Shanghai winter fell on us, we heard more rumors, rumors that all the Jews would all be declared enemies of the state and enemies of greater Asia, and then they would be taken out in groups, as in Europe, and put in little dinghies on the water. The dinghies would be pulled out into the open sea by a guide ship, and then let go on the ocean. There were other rumors that said they are preparing some place in the salt mines, which are some tens of miles from Shanghai. They will let the Jews work there and die there and forget them.

The Sephardic Jews—the Kadoories, Sassoons, and others—had British citizenship and were considered enemy nationals. The Japanese took over their businesses and property. Most of these Jews either left Shanghai or were arrested with the British. Margolies and her assistant, Manuel Siegel, were also eventually arrested. However, in the end, the Russian Jews were not molested because the Japanese were still very much afraid of Russia— they knew that the next ally that would hit them would be the Russians.

But they did finally do something about us, the refugees. In February 1943, more than a year after Pearl Harbor, there came a proclamation from the Japanese authorities. It said that all "stateless elements" were ordered to leave their residences in Shanghai, regardless of where they lived, even in the French concession, and move to a designated area—they called it very carefully a "designated area"—inside Hongkew. They would not use the word "ghetto" or even the word "Jew" because they were still afraid that the powerful Jews who were supposedly in control of Russia would be offended. They even put a date on the meaning of "stateless," which was since 1937, because they did not want to offend the wealthy Iraqi Jews who were not British citizens, and who had been "stateless" since coming to Shanghai. And it went on, that these stateless elements will be placed under the supervision of the Japanese authorities without any right to appeal. Anybody who showed resistance or avoided this proclamation would be punished according to martial law. And nobody would dare not to be registered and moved by the date given, which was by May 18.

These words were much more refined and careful than the words used by the Nazis. Even so, they constituted a complete reversal in the Japanese host-like attitude, and reflected the Nazi philosophy of putting aside people for their own purposes. So an area of about a square mile—a little square for 17,000 people!—was cut out of Hongkew, and made into a ghetto, almost a concentration camp.

Well, I must say this about the Japanese. They did not march or work us to death, which I later learned they did to their American and European prisoners of war, forcing them to build a railroad.[5] They did not torture and slaughter us as they did to millions of Chinese. And they did not do to us as the Germans did, even though the Germans wanted them to. But the Japanese were very clever and managed to cause great difficulty for both the refugees and the Russian Jews of Shanghai. They did it this way. A few days after the proclamation announcing this ghetto, they called a meeting at the club of the Russian Jews and gave them the job of enforcing the relocation of the thousands of refugees to the ghetto. They also made them pay for the cost of fixing the ruins of Hongkew and making them into a place for the refugees to live. And because we would also be unable to support ourselves, the Russian community would have to feed us as well. It was another shock, and made for very bad feelings at times between the refugees and the Russian Jews.

The Russian Jews did not want this job, but they had no choice. The Japanese had sent a man named Tsutomu Kubota to be the director of affairs for the stateless refugees, and he told everyone that if the Russian Jews refused the job, then the Japanese military would do it for them. So the Russian community elected a committee of 18 people to be the relief organization, and to supervise and enforce our move to the ghetto. It was called the Shanghai Ashkenazi Collaborating Relief Association, or SACRA. They put in charge of this unpleasant committee a Dr. A. J. Cohn, a Jew who was raised and educated in Japan. He was very close to the Japanese, and everyone, including the Russian Jews, was suspicious of him.

Besides making us move to the ghetto, SACRA also had to pay for an apartment for Kubota, his salary, as well as the salary of a secretary. Kubota then declared that all Jews who were not refugees were members of SACRA and they had to pay up, to support the refugees and the Japanese officials. Some of these Russian Jews were going broke because of the war, and now they had to pay for us as well. There was great resentment of these mostly German refugees, and many refugees thought of the Russian Jews as traitors.

My acquaintance Mr. Bitker was one of these committee members and he told me they were trying to delay the Japanese as long as they could, and perhaps the war will end before this ghetto would be formed. But the end did not come soon enough.

Among us refugees, the proclamation left us no room for hope. There were many refugees who were managing to support themselves, and others like me who needed some help but I could also earn a little here and there. But now that we had to move to this designated area, most of us would lose our very little income. When the war started, the Joint Distribution Committee could no longer send money and we knew that SACRA could not feed every refugee. It struck us all as a terrible military act that could be the beginning of some far worse things to come. If we did not starve or die of a terrible disease in this ghetto, then they would simply machine gun us like the Nazis wanted.

And there was no hiding, like in Poland. In Poland and in Germany, where they did hide some Jews, it was possible because a Jew could often go unrecognized. But here, it was not possible. There were very few Europeans among the millions of Chinese, so wherever you turned, you stood out. And everyone around me was looking for a legitimate outlet or exemption. Those who were taken in by a Russian Jewish family, as Nina had been, did not have to move to this ghetto. Also, some who were needed for special jobs, like the doctors at the Shanghai General Hospital, were given exemptions. Those with businesses outside the ghetto protested that they would be forced to starve, so the Japanese gave them a little extra time to move their businesses. Everyone was looking for a way to escape this ghetto.

The yeshiva students refused to move because SACRA tried to arrange for them to be together in a *heime,* which was a Salvation Army building that had been converted to a big bunkhouse. They were outraged! They shouted—shouted!—that the yeshiva is the highest of all Jewish cultural institutions, and that made them the cream of the crop and they would not be thrown in with the cast-offs of Shanghai! They insisted that SACRA find them private quarters with their families, and they even broke the furniture and the windows in the SACRA office. So besides finding them housing, the SACRA committee had to turn around and pay the Japanese a big bribe to keep the yeshiva students out of prison.

Some of my Polish friends, too, were furious at being "betrayed" by the helpful Japanese and refused to cooperate with SACRA. They would not even give them any names. They were especially offended by being called "stateless" because the Polish government-in-exile in London had never revoked their citizenship the way the Nazis had taken away the German Jews' citizenship. They demanded an exception from the ghetto because they were not stateless. It was refused, of course, but they then sent a letter to the Japanese authorities insisting that they were Polish, and they would not be declared stateless. The war was not yet over and Poland would exist again. And these Polish Jews insisted they were waiting to be repatriated and returned to Poland.

But I knew that if I tried to find a place or a way that would allow me to escape being put in this "designated area" someone could perhaps find out that even though I had friends in the French concession, I was in a way connected with the British. I had had dealings with the British Embassy, and with Kadoorie, who was later arrested, and with the Jewish Agency in the United States. And I had no intention of returning to Poland.

So I knew that my best chance to survive was to get lost in the masses. After enduring and escaping two years of occupation by the Nazis in Europe, and nearly two years in the Far East as a nearly destitute refugee, I now had to enter this prison camp, and perhaps face an even more terrible fate, the great and terrible fate that met so many. I resigned myself that this was the only thing to do—to pack up my few *shmates* (rags) that I had, for better or for worse, and follow the little wagon to Hongkew.

20,000 Refugees, Two Visas

*The "designated area" of Shanghai—where the Jewish refugees were confined—
was a slightly skewed rectangle, occupying a small section of the city north of
Soochow Creek that had been bombed two years earlier during battles between
the Chinese and Japanese. The boundaries that accompanied the declaration
stated the area to be bordered on the west by the line connecting Chaoufoong,
Muirhead, and Dent roads; on the east by Yangtze Creek; on the south by the
line connecting East Seward, Muirhead, and Wayside roads; and on the north
by the boundary of the International Settlement.*

*It was composed of about 40 blocks of crowded, drab, dirty, haphazard lane
housing and warehouses that had been repaired as cheaply as possible. This area
included the* heimes *and the refugee hospital, but not a single park. On the
whole, it was a dismal place. The city was bombed again by the United States
toward the end of the war, and the continuous rebuilding of the past decades has
left only minute traces of the area that was once the Shanghai ghetto.*

The first few months of our imprisonment, everybody was just trying to get
a corner to sleep. Some of the houses and buildings in the ghetto were empty
and broken. They had been destroyed in the battles fought several years ago
between the Chinese and Japanese in Shanghai. One of these was a
warehouse, a big oval building on—if I remember correctly—Seward Road.
This warehouse was rented by SACRA and patched up into a *heime*. And
this was the shelter that I and a few of my friends were forced to accept.
Then we had to make good whatever little corner we found. And there were
people among us inmates, so to speak, who hired out for pay, to fix or build.

Everyone started to make the best of what they had. Families were taken care of first.

There wasn't any authority to assign resources. The Japanese authorities ordered us to move, and it was up to each person, each family, to find living arrangements in this "designated area" in Hongkew. Many refugees were already living in Hongkew as that was where the most affordable rooms were. And many others were able to find a place for the few coins that they could afford. But there were thousands of us who had lost all means of supporting ourselves, and we had to depend on SACRA to give us a place, a bed in a crowded, demoralizing *heime.*

People fell into groups. I stayed with many of my friends from Vilna who were in my same circumstances. Families who knew each other would share a house, and try to make it livable. Not to furnish it, there were no furnishings, but everyone tried to make their place livable. It was then the Summer 1943, and "livable" was still very uncomfortable. The only "amenity" in some of these houses was running water. Later on, in certain areas there was electricity. This electricity was rationed and it was not on very often. But the water supply was kept on because they were afraid of epidemics and other things.

Everything was crowded. Those who could afford to rent something found a room in a lane house. These lane houses were little rectangular boxes lined up one against the other along the tiny, cluttered, crowded, lanes. These were not quaint European lanes, with their charming stone walls and window boxes. They were dismal, dirty little Shanghai alleys. Each lane house was meant for one family, but the tenants all divided these little houses into more and more rooms, and rented them out. So there were refugee families living in tiny windowless rooms and people even sleeping in the closet that held the electric meter.

Most of these houses did not have toilets. There was only a tub for the entire house, and in the morning, the tubman would come and get the "night soil" and take it away to sell to the farmers. So you never ate anything that was not well cooked.

The Japanese authorities that set up this charming arrangement thought that the Chinese residents would be happy to pack up and move out so the refugees could have their houses. But this did not happen. Most of the Chinese stayed in Hongkew—they did not leave just to do a favor for the Japanese. They all had some little business there and could not move without losing their living as well. And the Chinese will do business even on the roof! In places where you would not set your foot, they will spread out a towel and do business. They will bring you milk or food, or you rented from them even towels and other things. They came and went from all sides. We couldn't leave, but they could. They were not under any supervision. Many of the Chinese not only stayed, but also made some extra income from the extra room in their house they could now rent out.

However, many of the Japanese residents were happy to leave Hongkew. Suddenly their living space was worth much more than they were paying and they were able to trade their place in Hongkew for a much nicer apartment in the French concession and make a profit at the same time. The Japanese military of course praised these Japanese for their "sacrificial attitude" in the German-language newspapers.

Those of us that had no income any more, and were dependent on SACRA to not starve, had to go to a *heime*. These were just big buildings crammed with shelves for beds, and no privacy. Not even a peg to hang anything on. There was little soap, and so lice became a problem. There was no escape from the lice, and everyone was miserable. A bath cost a Shanghai penny, which many did not have, or used only for food, as the kitchens in the *heimes* could now serve only one meal a day—a thin sort of stew. Most refugees, including those in the *heime,* had once been well-educated professional people, and the existence we had been forced into by the Japanese was difficult. But most kept their sanity. Even though alcohol was around, there was very little drinking. A Shanghai nickel would buy a Chinese girl, and the Joint had a ward in one clinic for the few who caught a disease from a prostitute.

The worst was the inactivity. There was no job to do, no daily routine. We felt that we are degenerating. Food is whatever you can get, clean water was the first and most terrible need, the highest priority. In a city of millions of people and inadequate plumbing, you cannot imagine the condition of the water supply. And even to dip a foot in Soochow Creek would be lethal, as you would die of some disease in days. Even though everyone understood that you had to be careful, many got sick. This fear of getting sick was overwhelming. Even though there were a number of fine European doctors in the designated area, they had little or no medicine. So, the story of this time is a very long one. It was very bad to have lived it.

After a while, by the beginning of the second year of imprisonment, those of us who endured, who were not sick and who didn't die, had organized ourselves and were somehow living. That first year, when the war was not going too badly for the Japanese, we had a little breathing room, so to speak.

It was possible to leave the ghetto, if you had a job or permit or some reason to get a pass. But even if you had a permit, you still had to get a pass from one of the two Japanese guards who were in charge of the ghetto, and this was no small matter. These two guards were famous for their ways. They did the ghetto work for Kobuta, and they were formidable.

One was named Okura, and he would give you a pass or not, depending completely on what mood he was in. He could be very mean, and if he caught anyone disobeying even the smallest rule, he would punish them harshly. The worst was that he would simply send you off to the Ward Road jail, which was a death sentence because you would die of typhus. But the other guard was named Ghoya, and he was crazy. There were several psychiatrists among the refugees, and they knew him to be psychotic. He called himself the King of the Jews. This was true! He considered himself a favorite of the children, which was fortunate. The children were always allowed to leave the ghetto to attend school, before the school was moved to Hongkew. It was also fortunate for me and other teachers, because he would always allow the teachers to be in school as well. But others were tormented. After standing in line for hours and hours in the miserable Shanghai weather, these guards would humiliate them, scold them, and make a terrible scene. Then they would refuse a pass, or else hand you one for longer than you even requested. You never knew what would happen to you, after standing and more standing in line, when you finally were face to face with either Okura or Ghoya.

But sometimes people could slip out anyway, because of the *pao chia*.[1] The *pao chia* was a group of refugee men that the Japanese gave the job of being our policemen. Some of these men took their job too seriously, and they were hated for being traitors. But others did what they could, and would let a few slip out of the horrible, crowded, ghetto and scrounge for food, peddle something to earn a few pennies, or just enjoy a park for a few hours.

The yeshiva students had a special arrangement. Kobuta had given them permission to leave every day to go to the synagogue to study and keep their daily routine. The SACRA committee arranged it for them. But this permission lasted only for a while. Later, when the war was going badly and the Japanese allowed very few to leave, they were no longer permitted to go to the synagogue, and had to find rooms in the ghetto to use. Many days and evenings I spent among the refugees from this yeshiva. And I felt comforted, that here is a remnant, perhaps the only one, from the great diaspora in Eastern Europe.

These students were in some ways the envy of all the refugees. They continued their devotion to the Torah and were fed and housed. The head of their school, Rabbi Abraham Kalmanowitz, had somehow made it to New York, and worked continually to send the money and support them.[2] So this rabbi, somehow, and other American Jews, through their unusual channels, cared for them, cared for many of us. We stayed alive. It was the hope and purpose of these students to take the same path I intended—to go to Palestine. As a matter of fact, in Palestine, the members of the Jewish Agency were already preparing a place for them and other refugees, to settle them there. But, like me, they ended up in America.

Well, the Russian Jews remained in their homes, their life went on almost normally. But their school, the Shanghai Hebrew school, needed teachers. Many of their teachers had returned to London just before the Japanese took over, and the administrators of this school demanded, really demanded, to have me assist the remaining teachers, helping them with some of the material that they taught, especially Hebrew. So several times I got a permit to leave the camp, for as long as a month.

Unfortunately, Mendel Brown, the headmaster of the Shanghai Jewish school and the Sephardic rabbi, disappeared. He must have been taken to the camp where all the British residents were taken, because he was English. I remember that a well-known old man named Kakuli died soon after we were all taken to this ghetto. And Mendel Brown must have been with the British prisoners because they couldn't find him and they came looking for me to perform services.

I also had students come to me. Many of these Russian Jews knew that I was there and they got permission from the Japanese authorities to come to visit me in the ghetto. There was one family called Tookachinsky. The parents were originally from Poland, from a place not far from the region where I was born, and they had lived in Shanghai for ten or fifteen years. The senior Tookachinsky was the president of the Jewish Recreation Club, and he was friendly with the Japanese and even kept the soccer and other sports events going after we were sent to the ghetto. The two Tookachinsky children—they were teenagers then—showed up there, in their white automobile, and stayed with me for two hours, three times a week. I taught them all that I considered important and necessary for an educated Jewish person. They were very talented, a boy and a girl. The boy's name was Yosef, and he later changed his last name to Tekoah. He eventually became the president of Ben-Gurion University, but I will tell about this later. There, in a Japanese prison camp, I taught them Hebrew.

Of textbooks, I had only the Bible in Hebrew. All the rest I created myself. Remembering them is a pleasure. They were beautiful, elegant, very well brought up. Their chauffeur was a former Russian officer, an older person who took good care of them, and waited while I was teaching. A lot of people around me knew when the Tookachinsky children came. Of course they brought me a lot of things, which I shared with my friends. Later on, they also got permission for me to leave the ghetto for the day, and I tutored them in their home. The chauffeur would bring me back to the ghetto later in the day. So I felt a little bit privileged compared with a lot of people. But this arrangement had consequences that went much farther than my small comfort, because this boy, my student, later became such an important person in the young nation of Israel.

I make this digression in order to say that not always, not every hour, did we find ourselves in a desperate situation. Of the people that I knew, Nina had it better, by sheer luck, and her great talent. Right after she arrived in Shanghai, on a Japanese military vessel, she found a job that allowed her to live in some acceptable way, and she also contacted a Russian Jewish family who had advertised a room for rent. This family, the Citrins, became a second family to her, but also, Mr. Citrin was a member of the board of the Shanghai General Hospital. And after they saw what a very talented person Nina was, they asked her to take a job in this hospital, even though Nina hated hospitals. She became one of three of the administrators of this hospital who were not doctors and entrusted with the ten or twelve currencies that were circulating in Shanghai and which changed their value daily. She could tell you the value of a stick of gum on the black market every day.

Many rich Chinese were treated at this hospital, and they paid with gold bars, pounds, dollars, Swiss and French francs, or Chinese currencies of different kinds. All these currencies reflected the population of the people who came there. And this hospital and its staff was exempted from the military occupation because the Japanese were preserving it for their own needs, in case the war came closer. So Nina was spared having to move to the designated area.

There were other people exempted from the rules of the occupation, who were people needed by some institution. When their name was submitted, they were told that they can go, under the condition that they leave and return at the designated time and don't try to overstay.

The rules about returning when your permission ended were very strict, and you took these rules very seriously. The Japanese took offense at very little. Okura would throw you in jail, and Ghoya was happy to beat you up. And if you were found doing anything anywhere in Shanghai that a soldier didn't like, you would get a slapping. The Japanese soldiers would give people a slapping for anything, and it was always slapping the face. If a person was not properly polite to the guard at the bridge or perhaps did not understand that the guard was trying to speak to them, that unfortunate person would get slapped about the face until blood poured from the nose and they fell down dizzy with pain. After this correction to their manners, their face would be swollen and bruised for days. This could happen to anyone, inside or outside the designated area.

Another thing. Even though the Japanese were officially in control, the Chinese kept on fighting in terrorist kinds of ways. They had a tactic of killing a prominent person who had helped or cooperated with the Japanese authorities, and then hanging this person's head in a very visible location. And then of course the Japanese would do a similar thing in return.

So the Japanese were a little better than the Nazis. The only good thing to say about them is, they didn't come into the camp, looking for illegal literature, or for illegal radios. Once, soon after Pearl Harbor, they went about confiscating radios, but many were hidden and the Japanese didn't come around again. And that was a good thing, because we lived for good news from the radios.

The first year of our imprisonment there was little good news of course. The Japanese made their famous broadcasts in English. Tokyo Rose taunted the American sailors and the Japanese talked constantly of glorious victory after glorious victory. A year earlier, while we were so busy trying to find a way of avoiding the ghetto, the Japanese had taken the Philippines and considered themselves invincible. They hated the Dutch and the British, and had a very great contempt for the Americans. They thought the Americans were weak and without moral stamina, and would just sit down and let the Japanese take over. We never heard that the Americans had bombed Tokyo in April 1942. It was called Operation Shangri-La, I learned later, because the Japanese could not imagine where the planes had come from, and the U.S. president said they came from Shangri-La. The pilots who flew the planes had to land in China because their carriers were too far away to return to them after they had dropped their bombs. One or two of these pilots ended up in a prison in Shanghai and we heard of them by word of mouth from our many informers. And the Japanese radio never mentioned the word "Midway." But they did loudly declare a great victory at a place they called "Blood Island." This name meant nothing to us, of course, but later I learned that the Americans called this Blood Island of the Japanese by the name Guadalcanal.

It was the Russian radio that was our real source. And in 1942, while we were listening to rumors that the Japanese would follow the Nazi policies, the news from Russia was bad. Hitler was marching across Russia and had taken Kiev and Minsk, and by September, Hitler was attacking Stalingrad. The Germans had swallowed an enormous territory.

We heard only a little about what was happening in Western Europe or the Pacific, however, because our news came from the Russian radio in Shanghai. The Russians considered the war not a world war but their own war, a war between Russia and Germany. They called it the Great Patriotic War and considered the battles on the Western front by the British and the Americans to be insignificant. So mostly we heard about Russia's great war, fought single-handedly, against the Germans. The Russians never declared war on the Japanese until the United States dropped its atomic bombs, when they were already defeated. This was convenient for Russia because all through the time of the war in Europe they could get supplies from the Pacific, from ships that sailed into Vladivostok, and the Japanese did not interfere. Of course it was difficult to get these vital supplies back across the vast Asian continent, but it was better than nothing. But we heard much less from the Russians about the war in the Pacific or in Western Europe.

And through 1942, Russia did poorly. But as 1942 ended and the great Russian winter was setting in, the Germans had at least been halted. Just before we were imprisoned in the spring of 1943, the news started to improve. That winter, the terrible winter of 1942-1943, the Germans near Stalingrad froze to death by the thousands. And it was also reported that the British and Americans began sinking U-boats by the dozens. They had figured out how to fight against the U-boats. Germany was not advancing any more, and all through the spring of 1943, the news gave everyone a real sense that Hitler was losing steam. We were hopeful that the war would end and we would not have to move to this ghetto after all, but this did not happen. Even so, soon after our confinement, in July, we heard that Mussolini had been arrested, and a while later, assassinated.

The only thing that kept us alive in those two years and three months we were in the ghetto was the news that the Allies had landed in Italy, that Rommell is having difficulties in North Africa, and America was now built up, with strong bases in both of these theaters of war. By the summer of 1943, as our imprisonment was just beginning, the Russian radio was becoming very optimistic—reporting every day for the weary Russian people. And telling them of the situation after Stalingrad, when the Germans started retreating. We knew every geographical place. They called it regrouping, but we knew what this regrouping means. The war began to turn around. By the end of the summer, the Russians began pushing the Germans back out of Russia, and in November even Kiev was Soviet again. And all of Europe and Asia had the feeling that after all, there must be a God in heaven, and there must be a stop for the Nazis. By 1944 the situation was ominous for the Germans. The reports of German retreat multiplied. In Russia, the Germans were already facing the possibility of defeat, and together with them, their Japanese partners.

We did not know then that the Americans had sailed across the Pacific and taken island after island away from the Japanese. So things were not going well for them, even though they stuck to their official broadcast of declaring every battle a glorious victory. But the truth was sinking in, perhaps. In November 1943, the Japanese lost the island of Betio. They had made it a fortress, and the military cliché about this fortress of theirs was that a million men could not take it in a hundred years. But it was captured by some 10,000 U.S. Marines in four days.

Perhaps this fueled their rage, because in Shanghai, at the end of 1943 and the beginning of 1944, under the guidance and advice, I suppose, of some German officials who came to Shanghai, conditions in the ghetto became much worse. The Japanese appeared willing to set up "a final solution" for these stateless Jews, especially the German Jews, who were all spies now, because they know German and among them are scientists and whatever, delivering the information and solace to the Western Allies. We were continually terrified that at one moment, soldiers—Nazis or Japanese acting for the Nazis—would simply enter the ghetto and begin firing their guns at us.

The ring around the ghetto was tightened. The dealings with the Chinese, for supplying us food and other things, underwent changes. And people started moving around, hungry, starvation showing on their faces. And after a time, there began arrests and beatings by the strict Japanese gendarmerie. People were not slapped but instead they were badly beaten for violating the rules—leaving without permission, for returning late if you had been given permission to leave for a certain job, for trying to escape. These people were beaten up and thrown into jail.

Being taken to jail was in itself a death sentence. This jail was once an apartment building near the Garden Bridge, but the Japanese converted it into a jail, and it was where the worst criminals were kept. It was a place so bad that when the Japanese authorities could not get prisoners in other jails to cooperate with them, they would threaten to transfer them to this Bridge Jail. Anyone who went there immediately contacted typhus—Far Eastern typhus, a very difficult typhus—and they were there to die. This business of the jail was a very difficult thing.

I learned that Dr. A. J. Cohn himself, who was the president of SACRA, came to see some of the victims in this jail. And it was he who told them, his fellow Jews, that there was little hope to get out once the Japanese had decided you belonged there, nor to be cured of the typhus. Simply, people who were taken to the jail were not supposed to come back.

The situation in this jail was so bad that one day, several of my acquaintances, Polish refugees who the Japanese considered troublesome, disobeyed a rule and were arrested and taken to the jail. After a few days, they were released. But the only thing that the Japanese released were six corpses. And these dead were brought back to the ghetto, to bury them. But even to bury them, everyone was afraid to touch them. And a great number of the inhabitants, mostly the Polish and the Viennese, erupted in a demonstration, at the funeral that was held for them. The funeral crowd began to grow in numbers, and they screamed out so loudly, "we don't want to die, we don't want to die" that the Japanese decided they had to be silenced, and the soldiers surrounded them on all sides, beating and hammering and arresting the protesters. And among them also was me.

I was taken in for interrogation by Ghoya. He first screamed and frightened me, then he picked up his telephone and threw it into my face. And I was beaten, my teeth knocked out and kicked until I became unconscious. But I was not taken to the jail. Ghoya just had me thrown out of his office after I was beaten. Somehow, Nina heard of it and she sent a couple of Chinese to get me. They came there at night, and stole me out from the place where I was lying and brought me to the hospital. Nobody knew exactly how, but they brought me to the hospital and I was there in this hospital when I awoke.

The only thing was that I lost my badge. They told me, don't worry, we have at least a couple of people die during this time, and they found me a badge. They didn't have the names written on them, so I could have any badge. I was for a long time in this hospital. But eventually I was made to go back to the camp, the designated area.

By January 1944, the Russians had driven the Nazis out of Russia and were forcing them back across Poland. So now the Russians owned Poland again. It was better than Hitler, but not much. As the bitter Shanghai winter faded and warm weather returned, the radio reports grew more and more optimistic. The reports came of the landing of the British and Americans in Normandy, the famous D-Day of June 6, 1944, and then the Warsaw Uprising.

The Soviets had pushed the Germans back across Poland until they were packing up to leave Warsaw. The Polish underground thought the Soviets would enter the city any minute, so they attacked the Germans all by themselves. But the Soviet army just sat outside Warsaw, waiting until the Polish underground had completely sacrificed themselves fighting the Germans. After the Polish fighters had died and the Germans gone, then the Russians marched in and "liberated" Warsaw—what was left of Warsaw—from the Nazis.

And there was some relief in the Shanghai Ghetto as sometime early in 1944, the Joint Distribution Committee was again able to send money to help the refugees. So we were saved from starving. It was a great thing and gave us a great hope. The refugee hospital even was opened again, which was needed as more than a hundred refugees had died of cold and malnutrition over the bitter cold winter.[3]

But even though the war in Europe was going badly for Hitler, the Japanese were convinced they were winning, and they couldn't even think of surrendering to the Allies, even though as we found out later, only a few weeks after the Warsaw Uprising, the Japanese had been defeated in a very big way in a battle over the Marianas Islands. They called it a grand victory, of course. The Emperor, as well as Tojo, and all other leaders of the war machine, were telling all of Asia that they were going to stay there, like Hitler said, another thousand years, and perhaps forever. So the war, for us, continued on.

But the Japanese illusion was fading. In July, they lost Saipan to the Americans, and then Premier Tojo was forced to resign. Near the end of the summer, the Russian radio was full of talk about the coming German collapse, and the great Russian victory in their Great Patriotic War. And then there was news—even if the Russians could not take credit—that Paris had been liberated. And later, in October, the Americans got back the Philippines and chased the Japanese out.

Winter came again and Hitler was still fighting. My 34th birthday passed as we listened to the reports of the fighting in the Ardennes in December 1944 and into January 1945. The Allies had crossed France and were in the mountains of Belgium and the border lands, making a march directly toward Berlin, which was being bombed day and night. That fighting was Hitler's last gasp. By spring, the German soldiers were surrendering to the Allies by the hundreds!

The Japanese were suffering the same fate. In February, the fighting on the Island of Iwo Jima began. This island was part of Japan. It was some kind of fortress, no Japanese civilians actually lived on it, but now the Japanese were defending their own territory. And a few weeks later, the Americans began bombing Tokyo just like they were bombing Germany.

Finally, in the beginning of May 1945, there came the news of Hitler's suicide and the end of the war in Europe. The Russian radio announced happily and with great celebration that the Germans had surrendered to the Soviets on May 8. I learned later that the Nazis had surrendered to the Allies the day before, on May 7.

Then the news came about the tremendous annihilation of the Jewish population in Europe, and it was just unbelievably horrendous. Until then we did not know of Hitler's annihilation plan set in place specifically for the Jews. And we told ourselves we didn't believe it. It is always like this, of course, war brings great destruction, and everybody was still hoping that maybe his family is safe. However, I had even at that time the feeling that all the rumors that now came through the Russian radio, the rumors that were everywhere about this fate of the Jews in Europe, must be true. I was very grieved and had many sleepless nights worrying about my family and friends at home in Poland.

And later on, the situation became bad for the Japanese. The Americans were bombarding the different islands in the Pacific, and also later on reached Shanghai. A sizable part of the Japanese army and fleet was in Shanghai. So as the end of the war drew close, the bombing of Shanghai began, just as Berlin and London and Tokyo were bombed by the planes and more planes that flew overhead. And the bombing didn't stop, until the two great atomic bombs were dropped, the two that destroyed Nagasaki and Hiroshima and brought the Japanese to their knees.

Near the end of the war, even the ghetto itself was bombed. General Albert C. Wedemeyer as we remember, representing the Allies, found it necessary to attack also this corner of Shanghai, where we were. The Japanese at that time put out some red cross signs. The red crosses were supposed to mark places where the refugees and others lived. But the Japanese used them for deceptive purposes. They put their military supplies in and around the ghetto, their stocks of dynamite, bombs, heavy artillery, and other military equipment that the Japanese had stored in Shanghai.

So the ghetto paid its price. One day in July, the 17th, by mistake or by necessity, when people were sitting in the kitchen of the *heime* that was made from the old Salvation Army building, hundreds of them eating, they were suddenly attacked by incoming squadrons of the air force and literally a rain fell upon us. Many people died—Chinese as well as refugees.

Well, in Shanghai, numbers don't mean a thing. It can be 25 people, or 130; it can be 540 dead and wounded, this doesn't mean a thing. Whatever the number, the Chinese cleaned it up to be ready for the next emergency. And what an emergency it was. Nobody could communicate and tell the fighting forces that here are peaceful people.

There were refugees and Chinese both in this disaster, and everyone helped. The last little scraps of blankets and clothing were made into bandages, and those who knew how gave first aid and treatment to whoever needed it. And everyone stayed put to guard the little houses and living quarters that were damaged, so there would be no looting. There wasn't much to loot among most of the refugees and Chinese living in this designated area. But to lose your very last piece of clothing or scrap of food would have been a disaster as well. So things were cleaned up and new shelter was somehow found for those who needed it. And later, the Chinese brought bits of food for the refugees, to thank them for their help. Because the refugees had helped anyone who needed it, whether they were Chinese or Jew, which is not the Chinese way. The Chinese way is to assist your family, and anyone else is not your responsibility. But the refugees had not done this, and there were great warm feelings between the refugees and the Chinese after this crisis was over.

But despite this disaster, things began getting better when it was clear the war would end soon. One of the changes was that Ghoya, the lunatic ghetto guard, disappeared. This must have been arranged by the authorities because he was replaced by a sensible, kind man who handed out passes as they were needed and allowed us to come and go. And this small thing made life more bearable, even hopeful. Well, I must say that Ghoya did not leave Shanghai, even though he no longer ruled the ghetto. I know this because soon after the war ended, Ghoya was seen in the street by some refugees, and when they saw this man, who had tormented them and called himself the King of the Jews, they jumped on him and beat him and beat him.

When the war ended for us, all things were dramatic. Dramatic because one night, at one o'clock or whatever, we heard that the Japanese Emperor Hirohito was on the radio. Hirohito himself! It was the first time ordinary people were permitted to hear his voice. He was supposed to be descended from a god and not a mere mortal. So it was a historic thing that when I got up one night, I heard Hirohito talk, as well as the news he gave. It was only a few days after the bombing at Nagasaki and Hiroshima, and it was translated, and he said that he decided to end the war, and he said it in a very dignified fashion. And he said that, as he called them, the other party will take over all possessions in the Far East that we have conquered and I want everybody and his forces to cooperate with them. And then started the wild dancing in Shanghai.

It was a night of great joy. The millions of Chinese were very happy, of course—jubilant, even—but their promise that they will hang every Japanese soldier on a pole—this never came. I didn't walk around Shanghai looking for dead Japanese. I was only so happy that I forgot about this threat they had made. And then we found some bottles—unopened bottles of vodka!—which were somehow "popoloved."[4] And we drank them in a great celebration. Later, we heard on the radio of the ceremony on the ship, the signing of the surrender on the USS *Missouri* in Tokyo Bay. And six days later, the marines landed in Shanghai.

Well, these 30,000 marines, which landed in Shanghai in a single day, almost took over the city. And they were running wild as nobody who had not seen it could imagine. There are stories and stories about these, shall we say, eccentricities that they showed.

For instance, some of these marines took over the rickshaws. Instead of sitting in the rickshaw, and letting the rickshaw man drive them, they stopped in the middle of the street—on the main Shanghai roads that are always so clogged with people—they stopped and told the rickshaw man to sit in the rickshaw, to his amazement. Otherwise he would beat him up. So the rickshaw man had to sit in the rickshaw and the marine took over, and he said where are we going? He doesn't know where! Another marine who got off a rickshaw and found that he had no money in his pocket, and the rickshaw man wouldn't let him go. To pay nothing, is not a joke. The drivers do not let this happen. The marine looked at the people gathered around and said, since you will not step away from me, here is what I am going to do. He raised the rickshaw in the air and turned it over. It stayed there all day.

One went into a little restaurant, and said "I want a one-pound steak, and it should be made well-done, as I tell you. And I want to have six glasses of milk, lined up, lined up." Well, the kitchen wasn't prepared for such an order, in quantity or in quality. Steak! But they must have had some milk or a similar thing because they lined up the glasses. And another marine, his friend, was there and these two had made a bet. So this second marine took out his pistol, his rifle, and he put them down on the little table and he began drinking each glass of milk.

Well, while they were going crazy, the army called for a celebration in the largest park in Shanghai. The commanders had a lot to say. The main speech, however, was given by a young Jewish chaplain, who I was told was called the Hollywood rabbi. He had performed weddings, so he told me, for a lot of known personalities. And he gave a marvelous, ringing speech: half humor, half victory, half drinking a little bit too much.

In addition, several hundred or more Jewish American GIs cleaned up in one day the beautiful Beth Aharon synagogue on Museum Road, which the Japanese had used as a stable for horses. And the same evening, they had a Friday night service by the famous Jewish scholar Harry Gordis. The synagogue was full of soldiers, some of them had already girlfriends accompanying them. After the service, I introduced myself to Harry Gordis, and we quickly became friends.

Gordis after that asked me to come over to his hotel. I was in the best suit that I could find at that time, which was a joke: it was full of holes. We had a very long conversation. I then felt the price, personally, of the war. Gordis told me that most probably my parents were not alive. He described how the Nazis destroyed Jewish communities and the Jews themselves by the millions. I learned to my great bitterness that the rumors of the death camps were not rumors. The Germans had been exterminating the Jews. My family had most certainly perished.

My brother Benjamin had fought in Europe with the British, and when the war ended there, he went to Poland to see what was left of our home. But there was nothing there, no trace of our parents and our sisters. It was not for another ten years before I found out from a former neighbor what had happened to them.

After our conversation, when we said goodbye, he asked me to remember him, to write to him, and if I should want to come to America and to teach, he would introduce me to the dean of the Jewish Theological Seminary.

But at the moment, I had other work to do. The Jewish Agency, which I represented there, began again to send parties to Palestine. And the thousand Polish refugees, the many thousands of Germans, and the several thousand Austrians, all of them wanted to go. But the Jewish Agency in Jerusalem got from the British only 1,500 certificates for the whole world. To us in Shanghai, they sent 50. Fifty certificates for 20,000 refugees! So what!

I and my friends, we never wanted this job. The screaming! People wanted to kill us. And this was the time when I was told by my friends to act. The English consul already knew me, and now he came to me and said, the war is ended and we want to send people.[5] And he asked his Chinese secretary, and he told him, in our presence, "Here is a letter that we can give fifty certificates. They have to have the certificate for entry." And then he went to play golf.

Fine. From these 50, we made 500. With the assistance of the good Chinese secretary, who didn't care to report to the consul, who also didn't ask, we did a great thing. When we told them there in Israel that we had an opportunity to send as many as we want, they said, do it! Only the three of us knew, I and my two friends. And so we sent people out.

And eventually, I planned also to make the trip. My story is that Nina, whom I loved, wanted also to go to Palestine. Her original plan was to go to Australia, which did not beckon to me. And since Nina worked in the hospital, as administrator and was also entrusted as cashier of the several kinds of currencies, all the refugees used to come to her, this is where they got medical help. And among them were many fine, well-educated fellows. So I had more than 150 competitors. Now, after the war and after her plans to go to Australia were long finished, I told her, "For you, it is very difficult, because they wouldn't raise a certificate for only one little girl, unless you marry me." She says even now that I blackmailed her. It was a joke.

Our first group was 400 people in one ship, then 200 in another. The United Jewish Appeal covered the cost of the ships. However, a difficulty developed. To get to Palestine, they had to go around India. And England, at that time after the war, was sticking to the White Paper, which set a limit on how many Jews were allowed to emigrate to Palestine. Even after all that had happened with Hitler and the Nazis, they expected us to go back to Europe. To Germany and Poland! This was insane.

When our first two transports reached India, the foreign minister of England, [Ernest] Bevin, gave orders to intercept these two transports and put the refugees under a quarantine in India, some of them in New Delhi, some in Calcutta. He considered them illegal immigrants. He stated that small numbers can go, only small numbers, between 30 and 50. And until they received from the High Commissioner in Palestine permission to come, these two groups had to stay in India. And they were not permitted to leave until 1948, after the state of Israel had been established.

So, suddenly, again—again!—we were out of business. We could no longer do our work in Shanghai, forming new groups of refugees to transport to Palestine. So there was no reason for me to stay in Shanghai any longer. Then started the time of, "What will happen to us?"

My idea was unquestionably that after all that has happened to me, to my family, my place is only in Palestine. There were already a large number of Jews, 600,000 or more who had already migrated, including my brother Benjamin, who were prepared as I was to strive for a place to just live, to be, for ourselves and all generations to come. Not with any apocalyptic hopes of a coming Messiah who will save us, but a clear-cut political answer to the centuries of persecution. To show that the Jewish people cannot be slaughtered any more, in any country, and especially in Europe, where all the nations during the last 200 years began to identify their national boundaries according to their ethnic composition, such that a "Pole" and "the Polish country" is the same. We looked at ourselves no more as victims but as people who for right now had to face a new world with very mixed feelings.

Therefore, after the war ended, my plan was to go to Palestine. I didn't have any money, yet I felt I could find a way, with what I had experienced, with what I knew. And this is what I strove for. We were already free people, of course—in China we were more free perhaps than we had been in any other country. The Chinese didn't take any interest in us. However, time was becoming very, very critical. Almost every day brought new surprises and whether we wanted or not, we had to start packing, start preparing to leave, just living from day to day because the Communists were moving in.

The Japanese were gone, but China was not at peace. The conflict that had been brewing all along, between the official Chinese government, or the Nationalists, and the Communists led by Mao Tse-tung, was simply resumed. Japan had been fighting in China and gaining territory since 1931. By the time war began in the Pacific, China was roughly divided into three territories: areas controlled by the Japanese, those occupied by the Communists (backed by Moscow), and those still under the corrupt but legitimate Chungking government (supported by the United States). As Japan's defeat drew near, the two Chinese armies left the war with Japan to the United States and instead focused on their conflict with each other.

When Japan's surrender came, the two Chinese armies raced to grab as much territory as possible, each claiming the right to accept the surrender of Japan in whatever district they could. The United States airlifted Nationalist troops to Shanghai to accept Japanese surrender there, in order to keep Shanghai from the Communists. However, in 1946, about a year after Japan's surrender, the fighting between the Communists and the Nationalists began in earnest. The Communists got to about 20 to 30 miles away from Shanghai. They did not enter the city because there were still a lot of American forces there. But the situation was becoming very bad. The inflation, like in Europe after the war, made any amount of currency worthless. A big bag of money barely bought a handful of rice. Starvation had come and all the Chinese inside and outside Shanghai were desperate and dying. The Joint Distribution Committee was still helping us, or we would have starved along with the Chinese, even though World War II was over.

We were very lucky. We had people looking out for us and were not in immediate danger. And I at least had opportunities to consider. Gordis had returned to America, and he really was interested in placing me in one of the institutions of learning, which needed young—I was young once—scholars. The reserve of young scholars was very meager and the hiatus during the war caused these scholarly institutions to be in search of new talent. I had three places in the United States from which to choose, and these were the Jewish Theological Seminary in New York, the Boston Hebrew Teachers College, and the Baltimore Hebrew College. All of them were apparently interested in having me come and be interviewed.

Well, to those in America, all this can sound very encouraging. However, in Shanghai, when you come to the U.S. Consulate, it became a matter of bureaucracy. They tell you, leave your name and address, we will call you, don't bother us.

So these plans were put to wait. I knew that it would take some time until the American Consulate would wake up and call me. We were all in a position, as time went on, to take any opportunity to leave Shanghai, and we would find a way to fulfill our dreams when we said goodbye to China.

In the meantime, to strike a more optimistic chord, Nina and I decided to get married. Well, she still considered going to Australia, as many of her friends were there. I really wanted to go to Israel, but I considered Australia as it was a way to get out of Shanghai. So here came the time when we had also to answer our question, Nina and I. We didn't want to be quarantined in Calcutta. But we didn't want to stay in Shanghai, because the Communists were knocking on the door. And there came a day when we thought, we must go soon. We will have to accept any visa and just go. But we decided first to get married and look for a little place to live. Because it can take months, and really, while the war ended in September 1945 in the Far East, it took a year until people began go into the pipeline and were somehow registered and brought to the attention of the international authorities and were allowed to go.

In the meantime, the new rabbi of the community, who took over when Mendel Brown was gone, introduced me to other members of his synagogue and asked me to have another look at the Shanghai Jewish School, which was in a very fine new building. The children were mostly of Sephardic origin, but there were others, children of Russian Jews, whose parents paid for their education. And there were, to my wonder, also a number, maybe 10 or 12 percent, of Chinese children. Their parents were business associates or minor officials in this empire of the Kadoories, who had decided that they wanted their children educated in this Jewish school.

The greatest surprise, however, was when I found out that the headmaster was a Chinese Jew. He claimed that he knew the Chinese Jews of Kaifeng, and one day he will really introduce me to some of them. I had always thought that these Chinese Jews were a legend. But this man told me that he is a long distant cousin of these Chinese Jews. At that time I didn't take this story seriously. But he assured me that there really are Chinese Jews.

Well, it seemed to me that this Chinese headmaster is a very fine fellow, and I liked him. However, except for the couple of words about his being a distant cousin of the Kaifeng Jews, I couldn't get more out of him. But one day, a young man who introduced himself as Rosen, and another, a GI, came to see me. They were also interested in the question of the Chinese Jews, the ancient Chinese Jews. In this time of war, and without libraries, it was difficult for them to search in a scholarly or even a journalistic way for information about these people. However, someone told them that there is a man named Sam Iwry and maybe he knows something. So they came to us one day. Nina and I were sitting in the garden surrounding the hospital where Nina lived and worked, and they made an acquaintance with us. The GI looked very interesting, like any American. He was unobtrusive, but held himself well.

I no longer remember the name of this GI, and I regret this. He was from New York, a regular GI, he is just interested in the Chinese Jews, he says. A couple of times, we went out with him. We took a liking to him, and we found that he was interested in many things. He wanted to learn more from us than he could have from reading. This GI insisted that he wanted to meet my headmaster, that this is the only living contact with these Jews. So one day I arranged it and I brought him to the school. And then the headmaster started to talk.

He told us that the only thing that remained until today is the description of those people who he thinks were Jews, because they were called the "People of the Sinew," the people who didn't eat the meat with the sinew, because it was where the angel touched Jacob, and crippled him, after their wrestling match. So they were called the Sinew-people, something like this. Then the GI asked him how far away they were. He told him about Kaifeng, and he also mentioned that there is another group of Chinese Jews who are no longer in Kaifeng but they moved near to Shanghai to work and this would not be more than 40 or 50 miles. But this meant going into Communist territory. The GI told the headmaster that he will arrange for a couple of jeeps and some friends to go along for the ride, and he didn't think that it will be very dangerous. I thought that they were crazy. How could he say it is not that dangerous? Everyone knew that only 50 miles from Shanghai, the territory was under dispute, and the Communists were fighting there.

But he was so insistent that we agreed to go with him. He didn't want to let me out of it. And finally, we arrived and we met some people, three men, two women, and a couple of youngsters. They talked with the headmaster and this GI. They told the headmaster that they were originally from Kaifeng, and because of economic reasons, they moved to where they are now, to eke out a living. One thing impressed me more than anything else, that these Chinese were very eager to have us understand that they really were Jews. They insisted that they were the "people of the sinew," and they were eager to tell us what they could.

To them, 30 years and 300 years and 3,000 are almost the same. They operated not in history, rather they operated in memory. They remembered what their father or grandfather remembered. The headmaster could only tell us that sometime around 1840 or 1850, there was a great community in Kaifeng. But their synagogue no longer exists, and there was nothing left. I learned that early in the 1900s, some of the wealthy Iraqi Jews of Shanghai, Ezra and others, had sent a delegation to Kaifeng, to help these fellow Jews rediscover their history and tradition, but it was too late. They had forgotten everything Jewish except the idea that they do not eat a certain portion of meat and are called the "people of the Sinew." This is all.

But this is a diversion. Finally, Nina and I set the day for the wedding. It was the end of 1945, the war was over but times were very difficult because of inflation and the threat of the Communists. So it wasn't anything grand, not at all like the usual preparation for a wedding. The Citrins, the family that adopted Nina after she arrived in Shanghai, helped. They offered to have the little ceremony in their spacious apartment in Shanghai. And it was the

Rabbi Meir Ashkenazi, who had been so dedicated to the welfare of the refugees who came and performed the service.

The wedding was attended by some 40 or 50 people, our friends and acquaintances from the years that we spent in Shanghai, and a few of the friends of the Citrins. We also invited this GI friend, of course, to the banquet. And shortly before the ceremony, the GI came. In he hurried, and like always, talking with special energy, he told me he was unable, on this day, Sunday, to get to any European store, let's say to get a bouquet of flowers. And he is very much ashamed to come without anything. This, he says, could only happen to him, who didn't think of anything two days ahead of time. But, he says, while I don't have a bouquet, I have brought you one little gift, which you will forgive me for putting in this little envelope.

I didn't like this. Nina understood that this is the American way, putting a check of some amount in an envelope and giving it to the young people. In Europe we didn't do this, ever. Besides, we didn't need it. At the time, we had some very small income, we had made our way through the war, and we knew we would continue to manage. But when we opened it later, it was not a check. It was a little note from the consulate. "Come, Monday, 10:00 A.M., to get your visa for immigration to America."

SEVEN

Coming to America

Sam and Nina Iwry arrive in the United States as two great events are unfolding—the discovery of the Dead Sea Scrolls, which had a great impact on Dr. Iwry's career, and also the debate in the United Nations over a new state of Israel. In addition, with the end of the war, a great mass of soldiers were returning from service overseas and going to college. The U.S. government had created the GI Bill of Rights in the Summer of 1944, and among other provisions, it allowed the soldiers returning from the war to get a college education. All the colleges in the country were filling up with soldiers and the need for teachers of all kinds had grown exponentially. These three things allowed the Iwrys to start a new life on the best possible terms. Having set out for the United States with (now) two offers of teaching positions and the hope of resuming his studies with the world-famous scholar William F. Albright, Iwry was in a very providential position. He was soon exactly where he wanted to be.

This GI had never told us his position nor his purpose for being in Shanghai. We only knew he was a government official, and he knew that we were waiting for whatever opportunity would come first. We never told him about our plans for the future or where we wanted to go, and so he had casually thought we wanted to go to the United States.

The path to Palestine was still blocked by the British in India, so of course, the next day we went, and we brought ten dollars with us. We arrived at 10:00 A.M., at the consulate in the center of Shanghai, which was really new at that time. There were some other people there, U.S. citizens, but the first person to receive us, to examine our papers, was a Chinese. He, like at the English consulate with whom I had business, was the secretary for the American official. And he asked us, are you these people? Yes. Can you show me your documents? Yes. Do you have the ten dollar fee? Yes. And then he told us that for now, until he took care of all the formalities, to simply relax and you will be presented to the consul for the final step.

We still don't know why or what got us this visa. Of course, to have this visa right now would allow us to leave, so we took it. Then the door opened and who of all people came out? It was our GI. He worked there and he said that he had my papers. He said, here they are, the papers. They were sent from the Baltimore Hebrew Teachers College, by the offices in Washington, and there is Dr. Louis Kaplan's signature, president of the college. They arranged it, and stated that the college will assume all the responsibility.

We laughed a lot, and then he said now I will introduce you to the consul. And he opened the door to another room. There was sitting an older, very dignified higher official. And our GI said to him, here are the people whose wedding I attended yesterday. The consul congratulated us, and then said, "I really shouldn't give you a visa now, because you did not invite me to your wedding." So we exchanged some silly conversation of this sort for a couple of minutes. And he asked us, "Do you really want to go to Baltimore or to some other city?" And he told us a little about Baltimore, to show us it was not a picturesque place. "If you had a choice," he said, "I would go to Boston." Well, all this was very nice. Then the GI took us out to lunch, very nice. And that was the last time we saw him.

There were still days of preparations, we waited maybe more than a month or two. During the days and nights of the end of 1946, we learned very little. But soon after the new year, at the beginning of 1947, after surviving five and a half years in Shanghai, we were passengers on a liberty ship that was packed to the hilt and on its way. And it was a long way across the Pacific. There were storms, winds, and it was uncomfortable. But nothing caused us great distress. We knew that this was the ideal, leaving Shanghai. We were not going to Palestine as I had dreamed. Instead we were on our way to America. But we finally said goodbye to Shanghai.

This was a very important time in my history for another reason, although I did not know this at the time. It was about this time, in early 1947 perhaps, that in Palestine a Bedouin boy who was looking for one of his goats went into a cave, and discovered that this cave was filled with clay pots, and in these pots were ancient scrolls. This cave of course was in the cliffs high above the Dead Sea, and these scrolls in the years to come became known as the Dead Sea Scrolls. They were to be very important to me as a scholar, though I could not even dream of such a thing at this time, when Nina and I were finally getting on a boat and leaving Shanghai.

The trip was on a liberty ship—it was used to transport soldiers and tanks and other military equipment, and not to carry passengers, so there were few comforts available. And the seas were stormy, very stormy. My wife somehow survived these storms by playing bingo or whatever it is, and winning all the time. She was winning because after living in Shanghai, and working in an international hospital, she knew a number of rich Chinese families. And they sometimes took her to their houses of gambling, so she understood the games very well. She was one of the few foreigners they allowed in. And they started gambling on the ship—there was nothing else to do—for entertainment. And Nina kept on winning because she had a great talent for these games. So we arrived in America with a little more money than we had expected to.

I didn't do any gambling. I never learned it. It was stormy, and I was miserable, seasick, but it wasn't tragic. It was like so many other times, I didn't eat. So I was very happy when we reached, after 11 days, the port of San Francisco. And when this enormous ship finally docked, it was a very nice day, everybody was anxious to get off, but they didn't let us get off right away.

So, I came out and stood on the deck, and I saw one thing that caused right away a little bit of confusion. I saw that the cook was opening up the doors to the big refrigerators of the kitchen. And they were schlepping out, as we say, half a beef. Half an animal, half! They were still wrapped in cellophane, very beautiful. One after another, one after another, they brought them out, and what did they do? They threw them into the water. Into the water!

I had just come from a country where a million people are dying of starvation every day. And here, they were taking food—not just beef, but other food too, bread and vegetables and whatever—they were just throwing it right into the water. Some they put on a cart to go into the city. The rest was thrown into the water.

I was astounded. And though my English wasn't good, I slowly approached the fellow, I smiled at him, he smiled back. And then I said, "Tell me, what is the great idea? To throw these things into the water! There are such hungry people all over the world. And especially from the place where we just came. I don't have to tell you, you were there.

So, he fell back and looked at me with great exasperation—"Who is this guy? He will never understand, no use telling him." But, he tosses off, and he said, "We just now crossed the Pacific. Many people didn't eat, because as you know there were storms, and many people were seasick. So we are left with a lot of these things. And we have orders, no matter what, we must clean out the refrigerators, because there on the dock are waiting already big trucks who have to fill them up again. That is the way of America. You have to do this so they can bring more stuff and the people will work and be paid and there will always be prosperity. You understand?" So, this was my first important lesson about America.

We finally left this liberty ship and came to our hotel in San Francisco. This was arranged for us, of course, by the Jewish Agency, because I was still a part of this group, which was trying to help refugees. And here in San Francisco I had a very pleasant impression. My wife, too.

Everybody who comes to America comes with great expectations. Many who come say that it is overwhelming, huge, and unusual. But Nina and I did not have this reaction to America, because we had come from a great metropolitan city. We had lived in Shanghai, which has eight, ten, twelve—nobody ever counted them—million people. And there was the *Bund*, the business center of Shanghai overlooking the water, and it is so tremendous, with all the high rise buildings of all the great companies of the world, and the masses of people running here and there, and the flickering lights. You really were in a very big place, you had to always raise your head, to look up and to see.

So, when I came to America, to San Francisco, I wasn't overwhelmed. It was a lovely town. We walked the fine streets of San Francisco, and what we see are street cars—ding, ding, ding goes by on this side, then ding, ding, ding goes by on the other side—it is like a children's storybook. It was so nice. People are not hanging on the outside of the cars like in Shanghai, they are sitting and enjoying the ride. The buildings were not huge, not overwhelming. You could stroll quietly in the streets. Children skipped. This was San Francisco, a little romantic town. Fine. Things to see, it was very beautiful, very beautiful.

In the evening, we went out. Once, perhaps the first or second evening, we went to eat at a cafeteria. This was a new thing, a cafeteria. But when we got our food and came back to our table, a man had also come and sat down. Our things were on the chairs but it was a big table. We didn't say anything. His coat collar was up. He was an older man, not shaved. He didn't say hello, didn't say anything, just sat down, and with some hesitation, he reached over and pulled our bowl of soup over. We were literally just off the boat, as they say, and perhaps he understood that we would not know what to do about this thing. And we didn't. We sat as he sipped and sipped the soup without saying a word. I said to Nina, you know, they told me there were poor people even in America, too. But I didn't understand that it was true. I never imagined to see such a sight here, in this charming and lovely San Francisco. This was my great naiveté. I thought that America would take care of these people, such fellows, give them a place to eat. Well.

We were in San Francisco five or six days, and we made a call. I had relatives in Glens Falls, New York, an aunt and uncle, my father's brother Laser Evry, who also had a son. They knew that I was coming to the United States, because at the beginning, it was they who sent to Japan, through Nahum Goldmann and the Jewish Agency in New York, papers for me to come to the United States.

Therefore I thought it important to call these relatives who had tried to help me by sending the documentation—too bad it didn't help—and of course they were very happy to hear that finally I came to America. My aunt was overwhelmed. And they said their son Lenny, a GI who just returned from the Air Force, was just beginning his schooling, at Clark University in Worcester, Massachusetts.

I told them that we were staying in San Francisco a day or two, and would come to see them. Whether she told me I should come to Chicago or to come there, I don't remember. Maybe she thought that we would not find our way. But somehow there was a mix-up. It went like this: Since I was a member of the Jewish Agency of the Far East, some members of the Jewish Agency in America told me that they would like to see me and they will send me a ticket to come to Los Angeles. There they have a kind of a center, and there are people who are interested in seeing me. We didn't think anything of it, we went to Los Angeles for a few days. And Nina wanted to see Hollywood, so we saw Hollywood.

We had a place to stay, we went around, we talked to people. Los Angeles was busy, busy. Jewish people were coming to Los Angeles—some were refugees like me, but most were from other place in the United States—where there were two well-established Jewish communities. The Congregation B'nai B'rith had been in Los Angeles since 1861, and there was also the Wilshire Temple, which was a reformed temple and very affluent. There were others as well. When I arrived, the Jewish Community Centers Association had formed and people were busy organizing a Jewish Theological Seminary and other institutions. The war had awakened something in these people.

Well. We enjoyed ourselves, and we didn't know that my aunt was waiting for us in Chicago. She called every day the hotel in San Francisco, and the hotel said they left, and they didn't leave an address. Why should I have left an address? But this was a great misunderstanding.

We liked Los Angeles, and we forgot about my aunt, who was sitting in Chicago, in a hotel, waiting for us. Well, the Los Angeles people told me they will send me to New York, to the Jewish Agency there. So, we left Los Angeles and went on to Chicago, and found my aunt, and told her the whole story.

Wherever I went, I heard the same story from the people of the Jewish community: they needed teachers for the Jewish school there. And always they explained to me, whether in San Francisco or Chicago, that this city is the nicest place to live in America. They wanted me to stay. The Los Angeles people didn't tell me this, because the Jewish Agency had already told me to go to New York. But in Chicago, right away I was called on to run one of their schools, they wanted me to stay and teach.

Well, Chicago made a very serious, concrete, no flip-flop impression on me. That is Chicago. A little bit cold, I knew it was cold. But the people there, everybody knows where he is going, what he is doing. There are no little charming things, like in San Francisco, with the ringing streetcars. Chicago was something different, completely. And I felt it. I really thought that Chicago could be a good city to be in. No nonsense.

But, there wasn't an immigrant who would come to America, whether from the East or from the West, who did not want to see New York. You have not really been in America if you have not seen New York. Period! I said, I will not make any decision yet. I will see New York, and I will then make my decision.

So we left this no nonsense place and my aunt brought us to their little town on which there was ten, twelve feet of snow and ice. San Francisco was very pleasant, but it was still winter in New York State, and there were canyons through the snow. She and my uncle and their son were very, very warm and kind to us. And I found at their home a table on which were exhibited all my family pictures. I had not known of these photographs— my photographs. My bar mitzvah. But my father kept on sending them to these relatives, whatever the occasion, and they put them on this table. I was very happy to see them. I thought, well, I will need them someday, especially since at that time I didn't yet know what had happened to my family.

This little town, Glens Falls, was very nice. It was, and maybe still is, a town of insurance companies, and it is near the great summer resort place, the Adirondacks. We stayed for a little while, and it was a happy thing to be among family again. My aunt, she dressed us up like Yankee doodle. My wife already, when we left, as soon as she was on the train, she took off her hat and said she is not going to wear this. She wrapped it up. But never mind. We saw their way of life, and the people who had lived there a very long time. My uncle's grandmother was still alive and in her 90s. She gave Nina a ring that she had received in 1898, when she came here as a bride. She wanted Nina to have it.

The whole family had settled there in 1895 or earlier, and it looked to us like a town where people lived a settled life, nothing compared to my home in Poland, nothing compared to the cities, where people are just dust, riffraff. These people just lived, this is their home, they were born there. Even in their daily talk, they are relaxed. They were so very engaged with little things, it was charming. They were not great millionaires of Wall Street, but they had what I never knew, the feeling of security. Nonetheless, this could not be my paradise. I wanted to go to New York City.

One great thing that I learned after I got to New York City is the nervousness of many people there, especially Jewish people. They don't have the security of the small town life, although they are all doing well. They didn't have roots there, they don't feel they have a place to go back to. They had come to this big city as immigrants and now if they are thrown out, where will they go?

When I arrived in New York, I had two fine offers, right away, with two great higher institutions of learning—one in Boston and one in Baltimore. One was Boston Hebrew Teachers College, the other one was Baltimore Hebrew College. Well, I was in New York, and beyond New York was the Atlantic. I had to finally make a decision.

Well, Boston Hebrew Teacher's College was a very fine and well-funded institution, and they wanted me to come and see them right away. So did the Baltimore school. It was now the middle of summer, the school year will start in September. Goldmann had invited me to stay in New York and look around a little bit. This was very nice. And once you sign with us, they both told me, we will come to New York and move you. So there were two possibilities for me.

I smiled toward Boston. Not so much because of all the fine institutions there, such as Harvard, but because of a name that had been like a charm for me for a long time, and was the reason that I came so willingly to America even though I thought my place, my true place, was in Palestine. And this was the name of the great archaeologist and biblical scholar William F. Albright. I had heard of Albright during my graduate studies in Warsaw, at the Higher Institute for Jewish Studies. My professor, Moses

Schorr, was a great admirer of Albright and introduced us to his work. So, I wanted to go to Boston, because I thought that there I will find this Albright, and I will continue my studies.

This was my dream, not to be a teacher—I would be a teacher because I had to earn a living—but to continue my studies and be a scholar. My education was interrupted in 1938 by the war, and I felt as though I had been wasting my time for nearly ten years. So even on the ship, as I was crossing the Pacific, when I would sit and think, I thought that, well, I am not going to Palestine, I am going to America so I will find Albright and I will continue my studies. This is what will give me the greatest satisfaction.

Someone from Boston came to New York, met me and also Nina, because he said, we are like a big family, and we want also to meet your wife. And I let them take me to Boston, and they let me see their institution, which was first-class.

As we were in the school buildings, and very unexpectedly, they asked, would you like to go into a class. Well, of course I said yes, but it was a little trap. We sat and listened to this professor for a while and then they asked me, "Are you familiar with what the teacher says?" Yes, of course. And then he says, "Would you like to take over?" Take over in the middle of someone else's lecture! I was completely unprepared! But I knew exactly what the professor was teaching, and I knew I could find my way very well because it was a class in Hebrew literature. This made a tremendous impression, a great impression, even on the professor himself. They knew I still had to prepare lessons and learn the American way of teaching, but they had me sign a contract, right away. So, my home will be here, Boston.

Then I went back to New York, and I told my acquaintances about Boston. And I was happy that I was about to continue my studies after ten years of wandering and that I was close to my dream of studying with Albright. And then I heard the bad news. They said, you have made a mistake. This Albright, that you are so taken with, he is not in Boston. He is in Baltimore, at Johns Hopkins University. In Baltimore! I had the wrong city beginning with "B!"

So I went running to Baltimore. It was a great shock. After I learned, and all of my friends told me, what a very nice city Boston was. But Albright is in Baltimore, not Boston. And here was the mess—I had signed a contract. I didn't know what to do. Goldmann, my friend, took me to Baltimore, to the Baltimore Hebrew College. And in Baltimore I didn't have to undergo this whole unholy ritual. He showed me the school. It wasn't so imposing. If I had been a layman, I wouldn't have been impressed. I didn't observe any students, any teachers. I only saw the office, and they wanted me to stay.

Now, in Baltimore, my wife had a friend, named Hanya, who was a pediatrician at Johns Hopkins and who is also the friend who had sent Nina the money from Switzerland that she needed to pay the Intourist, to go through Russia and escape to Japan. Hanya had studied medicine in Switzerland, and had then come to America. All of her family was in Baltimore. Hanya, really, had saved Nina's life. Nina and Hanya were very close, and Hanya wanted Nina to come to Baltimore.

Well, we went to Baltimore and it seemed sweet. Here is a good friend. And we stayed with her, with Hanya, no more hotels. And here is Albright, although I hadn't yet spoken to him. Here is Dr. Louis Kaplan, president of the Baltimore Hebrew College, who wants to give me a teaching position.[1] What else could I want? There was only one thing—I had signed a contract in Boston. But this Dr. Kaplan said to me, we have also lawyers in Baltimore, and you leave it to us.

In the meantime, we decided, at the advice of all the people we knew, to stay in New York for the rest of the summer. We had a very lovely place in New York that friends found for us, in a nice apartment house, on Second Avenue. We were completely organized, except we didn't have to organize because we didn't have anything. We still carried only a satchel.

So this was my coming to America. There is one other thing to tell from this first summer of our new life. This was the time when the United Nations was debating the questions of Palestine and the Jewish state, the sovereign State of Israel. The Jews had become a great question after Hitler's program, his attempt at extermination—the latest in a long history of attempts to kill all the Jews—had become known after the war in Europe ended. And the United Nations was talking about the idea of a Jewish homeland. The British were giving up trying to please the Arabs, and also with trying to deal with all of us uncooperative refugees who refused to return to Germany and Poland. They were giving up, and had turned the question of what to do with Palestine over to the United Nations.[2] It was very exciting. Since I was still a member of the Jewish Agency I was invited to go and be part of the delegation. I even had an automobile sent for me, and I was there, watching the proceedings. This was a new, unexpected thing.

It was the summer of 1947. And the world was watching as the British Navy rammed a ship loaded with Jewish refugees—the British called them displaced persons, or DPs—to keep them out of Palestine. The ship was in the Mediterranean, and it had been named the *Exodus*. After they sank the *Exodus*, the British put the DPs on a transport and took them back to Germany. But when they arrived, these refugees refused to get off the ship, no matter what. They would rather die of starvation or an epidemic than set foot in Germany.[3]

So it began to sink in that maybe these Jews, these few who had survived Hitler, will not just pick up their lives again in Europe and go back to the way things were. This is what Britain thought, that they will go home and help rebuild Europe. But it was not working out that way. These Jewish refugees insisted that they be allowed to go to Palestine and have a place to call their own. So Britain had turned over the question of Palestine to the United Nations in April. And now the United Nations was really debating the existence of a country of Israel in Palestine! This was unbelievable, to those of us who had dreamed of a homeland, all the Zionists of world Jewry, the idea that now it will really happen!

I came to know, first of all, the representatives of the Jewish Agency, which was functioning as a kind of shadow government of the Jewish settlement in Palestine. I discovered that Moshe Shertok, who was the director of the Jewish Agency Political Department at the time, knew my brother Benjamin in Israel. I also came to know David Horowitz, and the head of the Jewish Agency delegation to the UN, Abba Eban. They spent nearly all their time talking to delegates at the UN about a Jewish State in Palestine. They greeted me, and they told me where I could sit and listen. In August, the UN Subcommittee on Palestine made its official recommendation, to partition Palestine into separate Jewish and Arab areas.[4]

One day soon after this, I learned, by just talking with Shertok and Horowitz at lunch time, that the next day they had to go and speak to the Chinese delegation, to encourage them to vote in favor of the partition. Soviet Russia was in favor of a separate state of Israel, and the Americans too of course. So now the Jewish representatives had to convince all the delegations of the other member nations, including the Chinese. And it would not be so easy for them to talk to these Chinese. First, the Chinese have a different attitude, a different way of thinking.

I said to them, I know a young man named Yosef Tookachinsky. He was my student in Shanghai. He was the fellow who came with his sister to the ghetto in the white car. Well, his parents were wealthy importers and exporters, and as soon as the war ended, he was on a plane to America to study law at Harvard. He had become a learned and accomplished young man. And I could get him, I knew he was in New York because only a few days ago I met him coming out of the subway. Imagine this! I am coming out of a subway in New York and I meet a student I had tutored in Hebrew in a Shanghai prison camp. And we spoke, and he had asked me, "Moreh?"—he still called me teacher—"Can you take me for a day, to the United Nations?" I did it, I brought him with me. I got a ticket for him the next day, and I brought him, he was here with me yesterday. I said to them, "If I would have known it, I would have brought him here today."

I said to them, "He knows Hebrew—he was my student—and he also studied at the University of L'Aurore in Shanghai, and he knows French very well. He speaks Russian, first class, and English. But most importantly, he grew up in Shanghai, and he knows and speaks Chinese very well. You have a better person?"

"Call him up! Call him up!" they told me. So I called him up. All that I said about him, when they met him, he was ten times better. They said, we need you right away, now you cannot leave us. And he did as they wanted. He immediately went to speak to the Chinese delegates. In later years, he changed his name to Tekoah, which means "blow the *shofar* [ram's-horn trumpet]," and he became the Israeli ambassador to Brazil, and then, in 1966, he became director of Israel's Ministry of Foreign Affairs after Golda Meir left the position. Later he became Israel's ambassador to the United Naitons and then president and chancellor of Ben-Gurion University of the Negev.

And of course, I was very happy to be in New York. I offered what I could to people and went wherever I wanted to and it was a very nice time. And I one time went to a public Hebrew lecture by a great Jewish theologian named Abraham Heschel, he was speaking about prophecy in Maimonides.

So I went, and I found a group who had arranged this lecture, and they all knew each other. When I came in, the fellow who was presiding came over to me and said, you must be a new person. I said yes, I am new. He asked my name and so on. And at some point he said to the others, "I want all of you to greet this person, this fellow who is now in New York." And after the lecture ended, two people approached me and said, "You are Iwry? The name of your father is Jacob?" And then they told me, "We are your relatives."

I remembered that the night that I left home, my father, who thought that perhaps he would never see me again, said, remember in America you have this uncle, my brother, in Glens Falls. And also there are other Iwrys in America, in New York City, two brothers. And these were the two brothers. One has a son, Alfred Ivry, who is now a professor at New York University.

The only difference between them and my family is in the spelling of the name. They spelled it Ivry, as it should be. I have this "w" in my name because the Polish doesn't use a "v," the "w" is used instead. But Iwry is not a Polish name. It is a Hebrew name—Ivry is the transliteration of the word in the Hebrew language that means "Hebrew."[5]

Well, then came the time in September when I had to go back to Baltimore. There was already prepared an apartment for us, and things were starting the sixth or seventh of September, more or less. They had already settled things with Boston. Kaplan told me on the phone that he told them "I have a better battery of lawyers than you." So somehow the contract with Boston was ended and I was able to go to Baltimore.

Anyway, at the beginning of September, we packed our two satchels, and we went. We took the train to Baltimore. Nina had already found us an apartment, and school was about to begin. I had the address where Kaplan lived, and he had told me that when we arrived, we should call him. So I called, but there was no answer. So Nina calls up Hanya, but there is no answer.

Well, I said to Nina, I don't know what to do, we don't know who has the key to the apartment, I don't know where to find Kaplan. Hanya is not there. Where do we go? Well, she says, we have lived up to now in hotels and other temporary places, let's go to a hotel. We didn't have any big things to carry. It turned out that the day was Labor Day. I didn't know it was a holiday.

It was some days later that I met Albright. It was a tremendous thing, to meet Albright. He had a great informal way. And I am wondering how I might talk to him, how to get along and get on with my life that now depends on him. Well, I told him that I am from Poland, and I went through the times, how I left Poland, was stuck in Shanghai, but now I have come to America, and I had spent all my life studying the subjects of the Bible, and the languages of the ancient Near East, and I would like to see if I could continue with my graduate work. So he asked me, what is my academic background, he listened. And the minute I mentioned Moses Schorr he jumped! "You're a student of Schorr? Moses Schorr?" He asked, "What did you take with him?" I told him the subjects, Beginning Akkadian, Hebrew Grammar, History of the Near East. He kept answering, "I know, I know, I know."

But then came my terrible moment. I had to tell him that I had no papers, the ones that are needed to get into any institution of higher education. I had nothing. No documentation, no graduation certificates, no diplomas. What happened to my college documentation is this. The last year before the war, everyone wanted to get out as soon as possible. The only way I could escape to Palestine was as a student at a university. So I sent my papers, all my documents from Schorr, all my papers from the University of Warsaw, everything I had, and applied at the Hebrew University. And they accepted me. But the war broke out, so I couldn't go. Instead, I left Poland and went to Vilna, carrying only safe and minor identification. So now, I am sitting in front of this great scholar and I have nothing. I told Albright, in a blunt way, I didn't have any papers, no diploma, nothing. And I didn't even tell him where I sent them, because I thought they were probably lost.

He said to me, "No documentation? No diploma? So? Well, you don't need any documentation. If I say you're in, you're in. You will stay here and study. I will call and make arrangements. We start at the end of September." So I was in.

But first I began teaching at the Baltimore Hebrew College, and the story went like this. They hold classes in the morning, in the afternoon, and also in the evening, because people have to work or do other things. The teachers don't want the late classes, they want to be free in the evening. So they saw me, and the teachers, they think, "Here comes some kind of a greenhorn. What does he know?" They knew I was a scholar, that I could teach, but they think, let's see what we can do with him. And they thought they could take advantage of me because I was new.

They didn't give me one class in the morning. Not even one in the afternoon. All the classes I was assigned to teach were in the evening. I made a face, as if they had exploited me, discriminated against me! But I was laughing inside. This enabled me to be a free man during the day. I did not have to teach until around six o'clock. Without my asking, they set it out for me. I could have dinner and then teach from 6:00 or 7:00 until 10:00. They were happy that I didn't object much at the meeting.

So the Baltimore Hebrew College, where I was a full member of the faculty, was very cooperative with my other plans. I taught a limited number of classes, two evenings a week. The other three evenings allowed me to do other things, and I was happy with my schedule. I was fully free all day from seven in the morning until six in the evening—all five days—to spend my time at Johns Hopkins like any full-time graduate student, and I never missed a class. I had my place in the library and I didn't feel that it is too much for me, because I wanted to catch up, for all the years that I missed during and after the war. I wanted only the opportunity to grow and learn and progress in scholarship. I believed that I was in some way continuing a long process that started with the Bible, and finally I'm able to catch up with something that is warm and healing and carries some kind of higher aspect for me to hold on to. I was going back to the things I did as a young man in Poland, going back to an atmosphere that I found interesting. In this I felt that I am doing what I was supposed to do, what I was meant to do.

This, to my great satisfaction, worked very nicely at both institutions. Also, Hopkins was very happy that they got me after the war, when they didn't have any young scholars, they were in need of new European scholars, and here I came, and this was fine, they are very happy that I am going to get a PhD because it would mean for them a great thing, just as it did for me.

I told Nina, what a chance this is. I have met Albright, I am accepted at Hopkins. And we have a place to live, I have a place to teach, things are not bad. I am a good teacher and I can get along with a class very well, I didn't have any difficulties at the college.

I learned to communicate with these American students. They said of me that I have a ready smile, which is as it should be. And they know this is Sam, he is not aloof, not concentrated on himself. I started the conversations, I opened up little doors, I tried to get along. And I liked my students very much.

Years passed very fast. At the end of the 1950s, after the great hullabaloo over the New American of the Year, I became, as near as I can feel, more and more Americanized. It is very difficult to tell it, how a newcomer gets into the rhythm of life in this country, the kind of metamorphosis that happens to a person who comes to America already aged 36, with a well-developed view of life and an inner adaptation to a certain environment.

I knew that I came to this country not as a tourist, but as a man who will stay here, with a wife who is a foreigner like me and who had a child born here. Together, we tried to build a home here, especially for our son— an American boy born to foreigners.

When Mark was very young, and he would sit on the porch with his mother, playing with blocks, and here would come the neighbor boys and girls, who knew that my wife has a command of five or six languages. They had to do their homework, whether French, German or even Spanish. So they would come to Mrs. Iwry and ask her, and she would help them as a neighbor who knew their parents. And Mark would sit and listen. One day, one of the boys or girls told Mark, "Your mother really knows languages." Says Mark, speaking with his child's lisp, "Yes, she knows languages, but English she doesn't know."

But Nina, too, felt at home here. Soon after we came to America, Nina, though she was still in her first months in an English-speaking country, took the train to Washington, D.C. and went to Congress. She had the nerve to go to the office of Senator Millard Tydings, Sr., and plead her case. Well, she succeeded. The files of her dear sister Lilly, Lilly's husband Genek, and her brother Sevek were found and Nina was able to bring them to Baltimore. She brought them out from Auschwitz, with their numbers on their arm. So she felt at home in Baltimore, with family nearby.

I was more mixed into this life, just because I had to do with hundreds of students. I think, not with too much self-aggrandizement, that I was a very good teacher. Students not only tolerated me, took some notes, but they looked to me, smiled to me. They could agree with me or disagree with me, but they stayed with me, in class.

And also I must say, I never went into the class with the attitude here I am, let's start. I always had my little sacrificial lambs, I would tease a boy who a week ago forgot his satchel. I would make a remark to one student, even if this would concern only him. And I would always start with a thing, a little bit of today, a little bit of yesterday, but with something that would draw their attention.

I was very strict, however, with the question that bothers every professor—did they read what I assigned? In this too I would ask questions in such a way that they could not say no or yes, but they had to understand what they read. But I knew that some will and some will not. When I wasn't happy with a student, I would call on him or her to illustrate some example of what I had just said. However, I was never seen in class mad or unhappy. I was very much into teaching, and it was because of my own interest that I drew them to my subject.

Attendance in my classes was very good—almost 95 percent. I saw always that when I came out of class, some students would follow me. I had very good students, and I called on them for very specific questions. I saw that often a student who took one class with me, perhaps in Bible, would also take my class in modern Hebrew literature, although these are two different subjects and both might not fit well with their own curriculum.

I was happy that I was a teacher. When Albright would leave to travel, I would sit in his place, and fill in, teaching the seminar for all the graduate students. I never got up in the morning and said, I don't want to teach class today. I tried in the evenings to sit and prepare. This is, I think, my European background. My own teachers were like this. At night, I always asked myself, what more do I have to do?

However, I will tell about an incident in which I was not so great. The thing that I emphasize with this is that to make a little bit lighter remark here and there, it is okay. But when I tried to make a big joke, I discovered a joke can be a non-joke.

At the Baltimore Hebrew College, I had tremendous classes, big classes. And normally, you know the students, some of them, from a former class, a former year. And then you don't call them Mr. Sovolevsky or Mr. Greenberg—you call them Howard or John or whatever. The girls, normally, at the beginning, I would call by their last name. She would sometimes correct me, "Miss!" or "Anna!" or "Mary!" Then one time I made a declaration, my non-joke.

I told my students, classes are not getting smaller, they are getting bigger. I am not getting younger, I am getting older. Let me make it easy for us. As to the girls, what did they insist? They insist I call them also by their first names, like the boys. So I will make a deal with you. Since most of you are named Susan or Debbie, I will call all of you either Susan or Debbie. They didn't like it at all. And this statement I made was told around very quickly. Later in the week, when I went to Hopkins to teach, even the students at Hopkins knew. I found they talked about me, and I was an example of something exotic.

That day, before my Hopkins seminar began, some of the girls were sitting around the table, talking to one another. Before I opened my mouth to begin the seminar, one said to another at the end of the table, "Do you want to be Susan? Then I will be Debbie!" Well. I got the point.

Overall, I didn't have any problems in my long teaching career. I made very good friends, and they were my friends for a long time. I began spending my days doing what was required for me to do, and one action leads to another action, and then I find that I have a daily routine. I never thought I would have such a simple thing as a daily routine: Who thinks of a daily routine after such a catastrophe? But my daily routine became everything. Many, many times, in the many years that I have been here, I think, how was it?

This is how it was. When I came to America, I came with the mood, that first of all, I will continue my life and my studies. As time went on, it was clearer and clearer and clearer from the reports that followed the end of the war, that concerning my family, there was no room for hope or great illusions. I understood now from the newspapers and otherwise that they had all perished. I didn't know how or when, but I thought that I would always walk with ashes on my head, and it would take all my life to comprehend this great catastrophe that had happened to my people. I felt it, always, at that time. I taught, I studied, I smiled, I talked with people, yet always at that time I thought I would wear the dust of war forever.

EIGHT

The Master and the Scrolls

Baltimore was and is a wonderful place to be a Hebraist or Jewish educator. Besides the presence of Albright and the Department of Near Eastern Studies at Johns Hopkins (then known as the Oriental Seminary), there were also two prominent schools of higher Jewish learning: the Baltimore Hebrew College (now the Baltimore Hebrew University) and the Ner Israel Rabbinical School. Baltimore has a great tradition of Jewish education, as the first Hebrew school in Baltimore opened in 1842, and over 90 percent of Jewish children attend Jewish schools. Samson Benderly, considered the father of modern Jewish education in America, began his innovative work in Baltimore and his successor as director of the Board of Jewish Education was the man who hired Sam Iwry to teach, Louis L. Kaplan.

Albright's way of doing things was to have some 15 or 20 people sitting in seminars. These were his chosen, selected students. Some of them were Jesuits, including my friend Glantzman, and also there were my two friends who laughed at me, guided me and teased me, Frank Moore Cross and David Noel Freedman. They were nicknamed "Murder, Inc." They were later considered to be the best students of Albright, and are today still the most eloquent names in Near Eastern and Biblical scholarship. Freedman edited the encyclopedia, the *Anchor Bible Dictionary*. And of all the work on the Dead Sea Scrolls, the best was by Cross. And I had to follow the work of these two people, whom I could not imitate in any way.

I learned how they worked. I would find them in the library, Freedman standing up there on the ladder, at the top shelf and Cross, always the quieter, with the polite demeanor, would be standing down on the floor.

Freedman would open a book and tell him this and that was written there. Cross would write it down and ask, "what is in the bibliography?" And Freedman would call out the citations, the page numbers and dates, and Cross would write it down. They were already the advanced students when I was in my first year, the fall of 1947 and spring of 1948. They had both already been to seminary, they were American, they knew the short cuts, what to do. I was like a person who does not know how to use a computer today, and who cannot do anything.

Everything they wrote, they did together, even their dissertation. When they handed their dissertation to Albright, camera-ready for publishing, only two days before sending it to the registrar to complete their doctoral requirements, Albright took the dissertation and he broke it in half, and he wrote on one half "Cross" and on the other "Freedman." It is so until this day, in two halves.

I admired and enjoyed them. They worked together in such a lively and a resourceful way, and they made me wonder, what is it that is demanded of a person, to bring out things like this? And when I listened in the seminar, when they participated, they had all the knowledge, and never did they make a remark that was not relevant. They were more than a decade younger—I was an old man of 38—and they looked at me as an eccentric, a person who needs a little bit of help, at least in using the library, and they said to me, "You go around with us." So I did.

Also, I admired the Jesuits who were part of the class. They know how to take a lesson, listen to it, make notes, and they have it in full on a single page. They don't just copy the lecturer. They put it down in a strategic way. They apparently were taught this in their three years of training. Tremendous discipline, they had.

Well, you must understand a little bit about the atmosphere. Albright was physically stiff—he had broken a vertebra, and four fingers also, in a farm accident when he was young. He was also mentally exact, and demanding, but in his warm way. I remember one fellow, who was not going to say something wrong, he only wanted to recall something, and he began to speak, "I once read in a book . . ." Albright stopped him dead, and he said "We don't talk like this. We say, there is a source, the book, page, author, this is what you will say here."

Anyway, I didn't open my mouth too often. But, it was possible for me to do the work, and I never felt like I was behind the class or not prepared. I did what I could. I was always prepared for the next class. I read up on whatever I could, all of what was necessary, and somehow, I passed from one class to the other, and they let me go further. Of course, the second year I was already much better at the work. My third year, perhaps others looked up to me.

I was also taught in the first year by Louis Kaplan, who was head of the Baltimore Hebrew College, who I have already mentioned. Kaplan came to Hopkins to teach the History of Hebrew Language and Comparative Semitic Grammar, and everybody had to sit through these classes. He called Albright Billy, or Willy, because he knew Albright was sitting in on his class to learn. Albright was in his 50s, and a scholar already known around the world, but still he studied, always learning. Kaplan became a great friend to me, perhaps because we had a little in common. He had been born in Russia, and came to the Unites States when he was seven or so years old. We had similar interests as scholars, as well as our childhood memories of Russia.

Two days a week, Albright gave seminars, one in Biblical Archaeology, one in Ancient Near Eastern History, and one in Biblical Readings. (This seminar in Biblical Readings was the one that I was destined to take over from him, but at the beginning I didn't dream of it.) So the classes were very demanding. It was graduate work, and we had to read up enormously after that, to be ready for each class. I was lucky that in the morning I didn't have classes.

And after my first three or four months as a graduate student, participating in the seminars, and understanding it well, I was expected to write a paper. A paper! And here, also, happened something unusual.

The seminar in Biblical Readings that particular year[1] was on the topic "Forty years after Charles's Apocrypha and Pseudepigrapha." The Pseudepigrapha—the word means "falsely attributed"—are a number of documents that were written in Palestine about the Greek and Roman times more or less, and many of them are supposedly written by Moses and Abraham and other Old Testament people. But of course, their true authors were only inspired by these great historical figures. The Apocrypha, on the other hand, is a group of 13 books that were more or less removed from the Bible because they didn't really fit in.

Well, about the beginning of the 1900s, there was a fellow named R. H. Charles who collected all the writings in the Apocrypha and Pseudepigrapha together into one book, with the best commentators, and he edited it. It was called *The Apocrypha and Pseudepigrapha of the Old Testament*. It was published in 1913 and it was *the book*. So in this seminar, Albright took these writings and he said, each of you takes on one book. So, he divided them up—"Who wants to take Enoch? Who will take Baruch? . . . As to you," he says to me, "I will give you a special case."

There was one book in the collection called the Damascus Document, and Charles was very criticized, he got a lot of flak, for including it. Scholars said it was a hoax, that it was not known whether it was really from the ancient times, like other parts of the Apocrypha. But Charles put it in. Albright says, "This is really the only book in the whole collection which is in Hebrew. You take it." This set me up to scholarship. And this was my first attempt, and I am still dealing with the Damascus Document today.

And some months later, I came out with my paper. It wasn't a brilliant paper, it wasn't very fine in form or in language, but I presented very good evidence that the document really was authentic, written more or less in the second century B.C.E. The language reflected the Greco-Roman times in Israel and foretold something great. I presented my paper, and gave my argument that it was authentic, though there were few others like it to use as comparison.

But then, you will not believe it, but it is true—during my presentation, Albright's telephone was ringing. He was called to his office to answer a call. Somebody was calling him from Jerusalem. Albright was known all over the world, and he was called immediately with the news that the American School of Oriental Research in Jerusalem had some of the Dead Sea Scrolls!

They were of course Hebrew scrolls, and so Albright asked me to come to the telephone, and the student there in Jerusalem, named John Trevor, read to me some of what he was holding in his hand. I knew right away that this was from the book of Isaiah, the Hebrew prophet, and we grew increasingly excited by what we heard. I was convinced immediately from the spelling and other details of the language that these scrolls were authentic, that they were written in the second century before Jesus and were the most ancient version of these texts yet discovered.

Now, the first of the Dead Sea Scrolls had been found more than a year ago, in the spring of 1947. More scrolls kept on turning up as the looters and archaeologists searched more and more of the caves above the Dead Sea. And it was a great surprise, that a scroll with the whole book of Isaiah was found in the very first cave. And there is a great story about these scrolls and how they were sold. Eventually they were bought by E. L. Sukenik, a professor at the Hebrew University and the father of Yigael Yadin, the Israeli archaeologist and military commander. I will tell more of this later.

But the first seven scrolls were found in 1947. And there were four complete scrolls, one of which was the Isaiah Scroll. For a long time, nobody knew what they were. A dealer sold some of these scrolls to a person with the title of Syrian Metropolitan Athanasius Samuel of St. Mark's Syrian Orthodox Church in Jerusalem. He had bought them for almost nothing because their real value was not yet recognized. But this official suspected they were extremely valuable, and in February 1948, the very day I was reading my paper, he sent some of the scrolls over to the American School of Oriental Research—it was nicknamed ASOR—to see if someone could tell what they were. Well, John Trevor looked at them and thought they looked authentic, but he couldn't be sure. So he called around the world to the one person who would really know—Albright. Albright had been the director of this institution in the 1920s. (It is now named the W. F. Albright Institute of Archaeological Research.)

Not long after, some part of the scrolls themselves came to us at Hopkins, and I immediately began to examine it, studying the language, the style, the way the letters were formed. And I was soon convinced that this was the real thing. So even though it was two in the morning—I had worked late into the night—I called up Albright and told him the news. These Dead Sea Scrolls were authentic!

As I already mentioned, they were eventually sold to Professor E. L Sukenik. This official of St. Mark's Syrian Orthodox Church in Jerusalem was about to sell the scrolls to Professor Sukenik, but before the transaction was complete, Israel was granted statehood—it was May 14, 1948—and the War of Independence began. After the war ended, this official refused to sell the scrolls to an Israeli. So he refused to deal any more with Sukenik. But then in 1954, he came to New York to try to sell them. He put a little note in the Wall Street Journal: "Ancient scroll for sale." Two lines. Now, it happened that Yigael Yadin was in New York and someone pointed out the note to him.

Yadin called Albright, and they discussed this matter and eventually he got Harry Orlinsky, who was a professor at the Jewish Institute of Religion in New York and also a former student of Albright, to pose as a buyer named Mr. Green. The price for them was set on the phone. Orlinsky met the seller in a warehouse and decided the scrolls were authentic, and bought them for Yadin and Sukenik. So the scrolls went home, to Israel.

But this was years later, after the first discovery in the caves above the Dead Sea. At first, there was a great battle over the scrolls, and the battle was over whether or not the scrolls were really authentic.

Albright, and myself also, said right away that the scrolls were authentic. But Solomon Zeitlin, a professor at Dropsie College, which was a college devoted entirely to Jewish scholarship, said "No!" Now, Zeitlin was a great rabbinical scholar, and he said the scrolls are medieval, that someone had found some material from medieval times and threw them in the caves to make them appear to be older.

That is how he talked. I remember that he was so sure of it, that any paper that came in to be published in his journal—he edited the *Jewish Quarterly Review*—that was for the authenticity of the Dead Sea Scrolls, he printed a eulogy after it, set in a black frame. And he would write that this scholar doesn't know anything, and he would point out where the author was mistaken. Well, Zeitlin once asked me to write an article about the Isaiah Scroll. I told him, I will write, but you will print it without your eulogy. And so it was.

But it was 1964 or 1965—almost twenty years after these scrolls were found—before the debate finally ended, the great debate between those who said this is the greatest archaeological discovery of all time, and those who said the scrolls are not worth even the parchment they are written on. We now know that these scrolls were written—some were written and some were copied—around 125 B.C.E. This has been confirmed by carbon-14 dating.

And these scrolls are still considered the greatest archaeological discovery of all time, because they are our main source of information about Judaism after the time of Alexander the Great and about the Jewish background of Christianity. It was later found that these scrolls were written by the same people who wrote this mysterious Damascus Document.

In the meantime, I began doing more work on the Damascus Document. Albright immediately appointed some students to help with my paper, to get it into shape. And this document I used later in my dissertation. Since I wrote the first dissertation about the Dead Sea Scrolls, Albright advised me not to publish it, because every day new scrolls were being found in the caves above the Dead Sea. He thought it was important to wait, to see what more scrolls will say, after they are fully deciphered, or well deciphered. So I never published my dissertation. And I regret it even now.

Also, I wrote a number of articles, and my work as a scholar began in earnest, though it was my first year. The next three years were very busy and difficult. I had to participate in seminars, read papers, take classes, take exams, know what I am trying to do. And I was also teaching at the Baltimore Hebrew College at the time, where I gave classes in Biblical studies and Jewish history and also in another field that I happened to love, Jewish literature.

I had always believed that literature, in any language, is the art of the highest level. I know Russian literature well, I know of course Polish literature. But my favorite, which I taught at the Baltimore Hebrew College, was Modern Jewish Literature. And I will tell you only a very little about this subject.

Jewish men and women started writing, about everything, at the beginning of the nineteenth century. Before this time, in the mid-1700s, there was the great writer-philosopher, Moses Mendelssohn—the same family that distinguished itself in music and everywhere. He was a logical, rationalistic thinker. It was only a little bit later when Emmanuel Kant came, and said that there is a limit to the human mind, that there is more beyond the rational universe. And then another new trend started in literature, Romanticism. And here, when Romanticism was in full bloom, was where the Jewish writers picked up.

These writers were people who still went to yeshiva and excelled at Talmud, but they, illicitly even, read and enjoyed this literature. It was considered bad by the Talmudic leaders as it was not rational, it was enticing. But the yeshiva students would read these books in secret, hiding them under their Talmud!

The first great Jewish Romanticist was Abraham Mapu (1808-1867), and he was the creator of the modern Hebrew novel. He wrote *Ahavat Zion* (a love of Zion), which has been published in English with different titles, but it was first published in Vilna in 1853. This novel was a fictional account of the time of the First Temple, when we were a healthy people, like all the peoples, and there he created very natural heroes.

After Romanticism, came another trend that was called Naturalism, which explored the reality and ugliness of life. This lasted until about the 1890s and then there came a great writer, who was the founder of Jewish Realism, Mendele the Bookpeddler. Mendele the Bookpeddler is a nickname for Mendele Mocher Sforim, and this name was a pseudonym for Shalom Ya'akov Abramovitch (1835-1917). He is known as the grandfather of modern Jewish literature.

One of his stories I should mention because it is a favorite of mine. The title is *The Book of Beggars* and it is about a beggar who drove a big covered wagon from town to town, according to a plan. He had ten or twelve invalids with him, and he gave them only food to eat and nothing more. When he came to a little town, a *schtetl,* he parked the wagon and then he would take one after the other—they all were some kind of an invalid—and put them at different corners of the town. He would return in two hours to see how much they made begging, and then he would put in somebody new.

One of his beggars was a woman, a hunchback, but very lovely, and they had a romance. This was one of the best romances in this realistic style.

Mendele the Bookpeddler described his characters in a very realistic, sometimes ugly, sometimes naturalistic way. But above all he had a love for people, for ordinary people, which made his stories great.

Realism lasted through the 1800s. Just before the 1900s began came Neo-romanticism, and new Jewish writers came up. One of the greatest was I. L. Peretz (1852-1915), a lawyer and official of the Warsaw Jewish community. Peretz liked people. He saw the ordinary Jews as poor but virtuous, loving and wanting to help others. But he also criticized them, and wanted to free his people from their superstitions and meekness, and to encourage them to have self-respect. It was I. L. Peretz who wrote the famous story of *Bontshe the Silent*. Bontshe was a poor man who lived a terrible and hard life, and endured it all without complaining. When he died, he found himself in Paradise and was offered anything he wanted. But this poor man who never complained—when he is offered anything he wants, what does he ask for? He asks for a hot buttered roll every morning for breakfast!

His stories are all like this. In his way, he wanted to show that no matter what a person does or does not have, he is a human being. He has himself, he has a soul and his feelings and what circumstances he is given. There is a writer in America called O. Henry, who writes a little like this.

Another of my favorites is the best humorist of the Russian Jewry, Solomon Rabinowitz, and he used a pen name, Shalom Aleichem, which means greetings, peace to you. He was born in 1859 and he was the best humorist there could be. He used a pen name because he was also a rabbi and a scholar, and it was considered improper for an intellectual to be writing popular little stories in Yiddish.

He showed his fellow Jews in Russia their contradictions, their weaknesses, their striving so high, and yet they are so low, and poor, and small. The very first thing he wrote, as a teenager, was a list, a dictionary, of his stepmother's curses. His writing was so funny that the Soviet authorities, who hated Jews and Jewish culture, permitted his books to be read. It was Shalom Aleichem who wrote a number of stories about Tevye the Dairyman, and these tales are famous today because they were made into the story called *Fiddler on the Roof*.

When he came to New York, where he died in 1916, the American writer Mark Twain came to see him. And Mark Twain said to him, you don't know me, but I am the Shalom Aleichem of America.

Sam and Nina Iwry in the 1950s. Nina Rochman's promising journalistic career in Warsaw was cut short by the Nazi invasion. After escaping Poland as part of the Polish Government's news agency, she also was a refugee in Lithuania, crossed Russia by herself on the trans-Siberian railway, and reached Japan, where she and Sam Iwry met. He declined her request for an exit visa to Palestine, as she was single and each precious visa could cover an entire family. Just after Pearl Harbor, Nina left Japan, the only woman passenger on a Japanese cargo freighter sailing through heavily mine-infested waters to Shanghai, China. There Nina became the administrator of a hospital, which allowed her to escape confinement in the Shanghai ghetto and to save Sam Iwry's life after he was tortured. When the war ended, she accepted his proposal of marriage.

And after that came modern Hebrew literature, which was about the people who made an effort get out of all this exile culture, which they considered terrible and frantic, to build their own way of life, of a nation, Israel. And the spirit of the people in Israel—their initiative, their new way of looking at the world—this needed another great writer, Shmuel Yosef Agnon, which is the pen name of Samuel Josef Czaczkos. He was born in Poland, in 1888, and went to Palestine in 1908. He was the last of the Neo-romanticists, and he expressed the vision of the land, the great, magnificent effort to build a Jewish homeland. He was given the Nobel prize in 1966, and died in 1970.

To study all this literature is a revelation. And this is what I taught the students, both at the Hebrew College and later at Johns Hopkins. One of my students, a woman, did her thesis on Agnon and his feminine heroes. So my students were inspired to write papers and theses on Jewish literature. And when I saw my students doing these things, then I knew that even though I am still doing my graduate studies, I am right in my chosen field.

Besides teaching Jewish literature, I was also able, before I got my doctorate, to publish something in the *Journal of Biblical Literature* about the scholar Umberto Cassuto and his scholarly review of Exodus. And even though I wasn't Cross or Freedman, because of my European education I could make other contributions. I introduced, in the weekly seminar, the work of two scholars that U.S. students were not familiar with, this Cassuto whom I have just mentioned, and also another named Yehezkel Kaufmann. Of course, Albright knew of these scholars, but his students didn't. When I told them in a preliminary way who they were, they wanted to know more.

Cassuto was a great classical scholar and the director of a great Rabbinical seminary in Florence. His family had lived in Italy since the middle ages. But when Hitler and Mussolini made their pact, the family had to leave in a hurry, and so Cassuto went to Israel, and became a professor at the Hebrew University in 1939. Had I made it to Palestine after being accepted at this university, I myself could have studied with this great scholar.

Since the other students in the seminar wanted to know more, I gave a review of his book on Exodus, his approach, how he rejected the Documentary Theory[2] of textual analysis, how he said we have to look at the book as it came to us as an oral tradition.

The second scholar I introduced, Yehezkel Kaufmann, was born in 1889 in the Ukraine. He also became a professor at Hebrew University. Contrary to Cassuto, Kaufmann followed the documentary theory. And he produced an eight-volume book called *The History of the Israelite Religion*. Later, in 1960, this book was translated into English with the title *The Religion of Israel*.

Kaufmann thought that the idea of monotheism was a great intuitive discovery by the Hebrews. He illustrated the idea like this: If one stood in the middle of nowhere in Israel and faced the Mediterranean sea, you would watch the setting of the sun. To your right would be Syria and the routes to Mesopotamia, which the Israelites had rejected. It was their past. To the left is Egypt, which they had also rejected. At your back is the desert. Kaufmann said that when the Hebrews stood like this on the hills of Palestine, they could look in only one direction: up. And they saw that the whole world is one world, and God is also One.

Scholars of that time considered the notion of monotheism to be a result of the cross current of ideas, of the people, who traveled through the bridge that is called Israel, between Mesopotamia and Egypt. But Kaufmann said, no, it was an intuitive discovery.

Well, when I presented this, Albright's remark was that this notion of Hebrew intuition is a result of German romanticism. But in his later years, when Albright revised his book, *Archaeology and the Religion of Israel,* he stated that this idea of one God, of monotheism, is an idea of Hebrew intuition, and he put in some good words about Kaufmann.

But this change in Albright didn't have anything to do with me. I didn't pursue it. I didn't want to hear the words, "German romanticism" because I knew that the time of romanticism was the worst period in German culture. If you go back and trace the path, you will find that the image of Hitler as the redeemer of the German people comes from their romanticism.

During these student years, in 1950, was born my son, Mark. I remember coming to the Wednesday seminar and Albright announced that Sam Iwry became a father today. So I said, "Well it's great, but the world has seen already great things like this." Albright answered that yes, the world has already seen this, but, in your world, it is the first time. I felt very happy, I knew that my son was born at a good time, in 1950.

I remember that was when I wanted to buy my first car. I learned to drive, then I wanted to buy a car. When Mark was born, we had to take him to the doctor. I could come to the college by bus, which was how I came the first two years. But with Mark, we needed a car.

This was in my last year before preparing my dissertation, and I told this to the fellows sitting around me—Cross, Freedman, and others. One of them, my friend Mitchell Dahood,[3] said to me, "You will buy a car? They will have a customer! They will have a customer! I will go with you."

Well, he really was giving me something that I wouldn't have dared ask of him. This was on a Friday, and after classes, he went with me from one dealer to another. He was a sports car addict, fine. And he said, first thing, to the dealer, "Now listen, the car is not bad, but the price is bad. And you don't "Jew" him, you understand?" So, I heard it, and I ignored it. But then we went to another one, and he used another expression, "Don't Shanghai him!" I thought, "This is the way he talks?" And all the time he is with a Jew who comes from Shanghai! But he said these things.

Anyway, we bought from this "Shanghai" man, we bought a very nice gray Dodge, and we knew that it was good. Because the fellow says, "It is a used car, one year old, but this is the man who owned it, you can call him. He got married and they decided on the honeymoon to buy another and better car, new. So here you have the opportunity to get a good car." And Dahood helped me to buy the car.

When it was time for my oral exam, I was very nervous. I was worried about what they would want to hear from me. I was a student who came without any documentation. I was admitted only on Albright's faith. My Jesuit friend Glantzman said to me, don't worry. You go in, and I will be praying outside the door for you. I said, prayers are all right, it is nice of you, but also remember that you have to hold a cigarette ready for me, and already lit, when I come out the door.

I was a smoker then, like everybody else, and my idea, before I went in, was this. The professors will be sitting with their pipes, very comfortable, and they can smoke and play with their pipes to keep their hands busy if they want. And here I am, a smoker like the rest of them and I am also very nervous but I will not have a cigarette, and I will go completely out of my mind! So I told him, you stay behind the door and be ready with a cigarette—a lit cigarette—when I come out.

When the time came, they kept me longer than anybody else. It lasted one and a half hours, which is unusual. There were 12 faculty members from many different departments, including the elderly chairman of the English department. Everybody asked me a question in order. Some were interested in my background. Some asked me to explain the current European situation, and others dealt with history, European history, for instance, about the Congress of 1815. I also remember questions in other fields, in literature. I happen to know Russian literature, I know some Scandinavian literature, German literature, and English literature in translation. And Albright asked me a few questions to show off a little bit.

In general, they were smiling the whole time, they seemed satisfied. I knew how to answer most of the questions they asked me, I didn't have any difficulty. At the end, the old man who chaired the English department said, "Now, it is my turn. But I have heard enough of your English and I am not going to ask you anything."

When I came out, Glantzman was at the door, just as I asked, with a cigarette. I was told the next day—if they had told me then I wouldn't have heard them, I was so exhausted—that the committee decided to give me a Phi Beta Kappa, an award of high academic distinction, because I didn't have the opportunity to do my studies in my young years. I remember that they told me that there was a medical professor at Hopkins who had come from outside the country, and they awarded him a similar thing. So ended the most crucial time in my studies.

Later that year, on May 15, I was finally ready with my dissertation. The work of preparing at that time was enormous. There weren't any computers. I had to type and retype. I brought Albright chapter after chapter. And the writing wasn't so easy. I had to write a couple of pages, and always rewrite it, all by hand, and all in English, which was not one of my first five languages. I would give it to somebody to correct, then bring it to the Baltimore Hebrew College, where the secretaries typed it up.

The Baltimore Hebrew College was not like Johns Hopkins. Albright had hardly any secretarial help. I remember one of his students, her husband was an archaeologist who was killed in Cyprus, she was a student and she also ran the office. Before her there wasn't any secretary at all. Once a week, a man or a woman would go from department to department, and bring two blue carbon papers for making copies on the machine. Two carbon papers a week. No more. This was how things were at Hopkins. Albright never protested, who could protest? So here at Hopkins I could get no help. There weren't any secretaries. Who gave me such great help? The people at Baltimore Hebrew College.

First of all, they had two secretaries and many other helpers in their office. And Dr. Kaplan said, "His work comes first!" So when I needed help, to type my handwriting and retype all the remarks, they were helping me, doing anything I needed. And they didn't count the number of rewrites.

And also my friend Glantzman, who was a Jesuit, helped me with the bibliography. He told me, "The bibliography will be my job." And he really did it. But when the day came, and I had to bring in my dissertation (the rule was that it had to be turned in two weeks before the end of the year) after I passed my comprehensives, after I passed all the examinations, the two secretaries were helping me, and they were putting it all into a book, making two copies, and all of a sudden they found out that one page from the bibliography is missing. A page is missing! How can I deal with that? One of them said, "Don't do anything, just pack it. When they find out, you will already have your doctorate."

But I was nervous, because I was unwilling to do that. So I called up Glantzman, who lived in a dormitory at Loyola College. I said, "Remember the bibliography? One of the pages is missing!" He said, "If it is missing, it is my fault. No one else touched it, let me go in and see." And he comes back, "Is it page seven?" "Yes!" I told him. "Well, take a taxi, please, and bring it to 2497 Eutaw Place, Baltimore Hebrew College, and quick!"

He came. He called a taxi and he got in. So here he is, a priest, a very nice-looking young man with impressive looks, and he tells the Jewish taxi driver, "Make it fast! Take me to Baltimore Hebrew College at Eutaw Place! Hurry!" The Jewish taxi driver turns around and says to him, "So at Baltimore Hebrew College somebody is dying and they need a priest?"

While I was still a student, Albright gave me classes to teach, like other advanced students. After I finished my doctorate, Albright told me that although he didn't have any funds in his budget, he would make an effort to get some money for me, from the outside, and he would make a proposal to appoint me as a member of the faculty. Well, Albright had very little. He himself earned at that time, as the chairman, only $6,000 a year, which was already out of date. So he got for me, $3,000.

I couldn't ask more of him. He wasn't a man who knew the world, especially business matters. He was all scholarship. So, I started with $3,000 a year, and one day the president of the university called me in for about five minutes, and he said I am happy to tell you that you are appointed a member of the faculty. It was a very short visit, apparently it was more ceremonial than anything else. Since then, well, I stayed, teaching both at Hopkins and at the Baltimore Hebrew College.

I began teaching a course that Albright used to teach, Textual Studies of the Hebrew Bible. All of the students attended this course, and it was a very good opportunity for me to teach. Albright was happy that I was taking over for him. And all the rest of my career at Hopkins, I taught this course and other courses. My greatest years were when Albright would leave to travel and I would sit in his place, and fill in, teaching the seminar for all the graduate students. And I also introduced new courses, Modern Hebrew Language and Modern Hebrew Literature.

Albright's personality defined the department, even though he wasn't always there. When he was gone, I had to report to him how the seminars were going. He wanted to know about every one of them. He often went to Saudi Arabia, and when he returned, it was always a great day. He would tell us about the excavations, what he did, what he found, what he was looking for. And he told us that the Arabs considered him a great man The people who worked with him, who dug, who helped and brought up the dust thought he was a great man. Why? Because they knew he had four sons. To them, there could be nothing greater than this.

So scholars and his Arab helpers thought he was a great man, but not everyone regarded him with awe. Not Mrs. Albright. She was a kind, but formidable woman. Her name was Ruth, and she was an expert in Sanskrit, a scholar in her own right.

One day, during the seminar while a student was reading his paper, there was a knock at the door. And who was standing in the doorway? Professor Albright. He had just returned from Turkey—he was invited to go to Turkey by the government because he was interested in the Hittites, an ancient people of Asia Minor who are mentioned in the Bible. It was winter, the collar of his coat was raised, and he was wearing his hat. It was such a great surprise that the student who was reading his paper felt that all his teeth were falling out! We didn't expect him.

So I got up, and said, Dr. Albright! You are here. We are so happy, come sit down. He says, no, no, you sit and continue, and he took a seat somewhere in the back where the students sit. And the student who was presenting his paper, the poor fellow had dropped all his papers, he was shaking and having the hardest time collecting his papers and himself to continue. All the other students were trying not to laugh. But it was a comical situation.

And while we were wondering when this poor student could finally make himself continue, the door opened again, and we heard a little scream. And who is standing there? Mrs. Albright! And she says in front of everyone, "Look at him. He is here. He didn't come home. He came straight from the plane. Here! Because he knew that this is seminar time!" And she didn't say to him, "Bill, what are you doing here?" She knew what he was doing here. Instead, she said to me, "Sam, I never expected you to be a fool like this. Don't you know it! The man comes straight from the plane, he doesn't come home even to wash up and take a glass of water. He may be a great intellectual, but he is not very intelligent."

From time to time, I would have lunch with him, and he would order always what I ordered, because I didn't eat meat. He ate his meals at the

Hopkins Faculty Club often, but when I joined him, he would always order what I would order, telling the waitress only "The same for me." One time, the waitress, who was very clever, told him one day, "Dr. Albright, Mrs. Albright wouldn't like this, what you ordered." They would never say anything like this to anybody else, but they would say it to Albright. And they really did know Mrs. Albright, as they both would come there to eat.

Many times, she would say to me, for some reason or another, "That's your fault, Sam." Sometimes I would go to his home. This was not often, but on occasion I would want to discuss something, and he would say to me, all right, we will discuss it, come over. And Mrs. Albright would tolerate me. One time, we were traveling on a train to a conference in Philadelphia and she was with him. I got on the train, and she says to me, "You want to sit with William? You can squeeze his brain here, too." Nevertheless, after he died, Nina and I would go to see her often. She was progressively going blind. And many times when we came to visit, she could tell by the sound of our knocking at the door, that this was Sam and Nina.

But Albright was not attentive to many things. Just before Mark was born, Mrs. Albright was saying to Nina that she had not yet finished the sweater for the baby. And Albright turned to Nina and asked, "Are you pregnant?"

But he was a very friendly man, an eloquent man, and one who showed great humility. Many years after he had retired, and was becoming older, Mrs. Albright would take him to church if he was feeling well enough. I told him one time, that if she cannot take you, I will drive. I was still somewhat young at that time, the father of a boy who was growing up. He says, I don't go every Sunday, but I told him, whenever you want to go, you call me.

Well, from time to time, I would take him. And I would sit with him in the back, and then I would take him home. One time I said to him, that I of course cherish the privilege of taking you to church, but I was wondering about this fellow who delivers the sermon, I am sure that he wouldn't qualify to be your graduate student. He got a look on his face, and he became very serious. He said, "When a man advances in years and he becomes somewhat distinguished or famous or known, there is one thing that he may lose. And this is humility. Humility is an important Christian thing. When I come to church and I sit with all the housewives, all the other people—never mind what the preacher says, I know these things—it adds to my self satisfaction, that I learn to be a good Christian. I remember to be as everybody else, going to church with everybody else." This is a great thing to remember. People who rise in a profession, who become known, are in danger of losing their humility.

Albright also had a sense of humor. Once I was sitting with him in his office, and somebody knocked at the door. And in came a young man, dressed like a clergyman, a very nice-looking fellow with a satchel. He tells Albright his name, says I am Mr. So-and-so and I am applying to the graduate program, and I have an appointment with you. I got up and left, but Albright asked me to come back in five or ten minutes. Albright questioned the fellow—what is your background, why do you want to study here, all kinds of questions. And he also asked him is he advanced in Greek? does he know Latin? and more importantly, how much Hebrew does he know? Well, the man said, among other things that he knew Hebrew.

So when I returned, Albright said to me, "Sam, would you please see how his Hebrew is." I got a Hebrew Bible and the fellow read it. I asked him a couple of questions, and he answered. And I told Albright, "O.K." Albright told the young man, "I am very satisfied and I will let you know."

So, Albright and I sat down again to continue our discussion, and there was a knock at the door. The fellow had returned, and he said, "I am sorry but I have left my hat." So he takes his hat and he leaves. A few moments later there is another knock, and it is the young man again. He said, "I have left my pen." Albright found the pen and gave it to him. And we sit down again, but he knocks a third time. And he had left the satchel. Yes, the satchel is there. Albright gets up, stretches himself to his full height—he is a tall man, thin—and he says, "Young man! I want to tell you something. Absent-mindedness is a privilege of professors, and only FULL professors!" I never saw the fellow again.

NINE

Teacher, Scholar, Grandfather

Sam Iwry was a teacher throughout his career, and through his many students, he has had great influence on the full range of Hebraic and Judaic studies, from ancient to modern. He also played an important role in scholarship on the Dead Sea Scrolls from the beginning. His great teacher and mentor, W. F. Albright, was immediately thrust into the center of the discussion, and Albright, who had great respect and admiration for the depth of his student's learning, turned regularly to Iwry for consultation and discussion. This was partly because Iwry had already begun an in-depth study of the Damascus Document (discovered in an old Cairo synagogue near the end of the nineteenth century), which could be appreciated and understood only by someone of Iwry's extraordinary mastery of the Hebrew language.

Research conducted by Iwry and others showed that the Damascus Document derived ultimately from the same community that left the scrolls at Qumran. So Iwry and those who consulted with him had an important head start in understanding the larger historical issues posed by the Dead Sea Scrolls. Perhaps the most important single result of this research was Iwry's landmark 1969 paper, published in a volume honoring Albright and entitled "Was There a Migration to Damascus?" In this paper, Iwry proposed his original and sophisticated theory concerning the origin of the community at Qumran. Iwry took great pride in his scholarship, perhaps only second to his pride in family. His sojourn through life encompassed both and enhanced all he touched.

In the year 1953, it finally happened. I made my first trip to Israel. It was just after the time of Joseph McCarthy and his witch hunt. And even at

Johns Hopkins, McCarthy made a stir. There was a fellow, a professor here, of Far Eastern Studies, and McCarthy accused him of betraying America, and even being almost a spy, in good relationship to Soviet Russia. And he made him out to be a symbol of all liberals and Jews and immigrants and professors from different universities. The whole campus was shivering.[1]

I remember at that time, that Professor Boaz of the Philosophy department had been called to counteract this, and support the defense of this professor. And he started to collect money from the faculty. And I was approached and he asked me, can I get from you something? Well, I was still a poor fellow, but not so poor I couldn't give him five dollars. So I gave him five dollars.

When Albright found out—Albright was a very strict man—he says, "You gave him five dollars? Did you ask me?" I said, "No, I just gave him five dollars, what is the big deal?" Albright said to me, "You shouldn't have given it, and I will go to him and tell him to return your five dollars, and take you off the list. You shouldn't be on a list like this. He may publish the list, or the list will go around."

"It is like this. If any of the other graduate students or young professors get involved, well, it is their business, what can he do to them but call them Communists. But you are an outsider. From Poland! And Poland belonged to Russia! And not only from Poland but also a Jew! And you don't yet have your citizenship. So you will be thrown out right away." He said, "Are you going to mix in it? No. Go and take away from him the five dollars, and I will tell him he should take your name off the list, and I will explain to him."

This is registered in my mind. The whole McCarthy era brought bad memories. I remembered Poland under the Bolsheviks and I know what this means. But McCarthy's threats did not last too long, because later in 1954, the government scolded McCarthy—censured him—for abusing his authority. I read this in the newspapers, and everyone relaxed a little.

But even before this, in 1953, after I fulfilled my five years in America, I got my citizenship and then I applied for a passport to go to Israel. This is when Albright told me, if you will want to go out, to visit Israel, you will not want to come back. Even so, I got my citizenship and my passport and I made my first trip to Israel.

I went there to see my younger brother, Benjamin. During the war, I had lost contact with him. Then after the war, he wrote me. He found me in America, somehow. And he wrote me—and this is very characteristic of him—that when the war first broke out, he was the number three Israeli to

Sam's brother Benjamin settled in Israel as a halutz or pioneer, in 1936. When World War II began, he enlisted in the British army and served in North Africa as a tank specialist fighting against Rommel. Pictured here with his French-born wife, Ora, an artist, and their first son, Tsour, Benjamin founded a kibbutz, Yagour, and was a key member of Israel's intelligence community. He later became chief operating officer of Zim—Israel's dominant cargo and passenger shipping company. Zim carried hundreds of thousands of refugees to Israel and played a critical role during Israel's War of Independence.

volunteer into the British army. The second was Moshe Shertok, my acquaintance from the Jewish Agency in New York.

Benjamin became a sergeant-major in the British army's Jewish Legion. He spent the war in Egypt and Libya, fighting against Rommel. He commanded tanks. And then the war ended, and the first thing he did was, he went home to Bialystok, as a soldier. He wrote me and told me that he had found nobody. It was all gone. He wanted me to know. Also at the end of the war, he was with the army on Rhodes, the island in the Mediterranean, near Israel. While he was there, he dismantled a whole military radio station, and brought it in parts, on ships, to Israel, and put it back together. He was much stronger than I, always, and he had a fine mind, an engineer's mind.

Benjamin also was a key counterintelligence officer in Israel's War of Independence, and he was sometimes at odds with Israel's military genius

General Moshe Dayan. Benjamin thought that Dayan needed to pay more attention to routine security matters, and decided to give him a reminder. Benjamin sent some of his men to sneak into Dayan's headquarters in the middle of the night and "borrow" the maps and battle plans that had been left about on a table. They brought these papers to Benjamin and he waited quietly with his pipe in his mouth. After about 24 hours, Dayan realized that Benjamin might have done this to him, and of course the great general did not appreciate this "lesson."

Benjamin was always in action, always doing. He graduated from gymnasium in 1926, I think, and my parents made it possible for him to go study in France. The idea was to get training, to bring skill to Palestine, to help build the land. His plan was to go to Palestine as a *halutz*, a pioneer. And he did this. Later, in the 1950s, because of these connections, Benjamin played a key role in Israel's relations with France. But he also was for a while a journalist, and he covered the civil war in Spain. When my parents heard it, they said, "Of course. It is dangerous. So he must be there. Everywhere he must be, he must be in a dangerous place!" But he covered the war, and he made a reputation for himself. And as he was returning to France, Benjamin heard that the famous Soviet, Maksim Litvinov, was in Paris.

Litvinov was the senior Soviet official who was sent to promote the idea of collective security—Russia's attempt to get cooperation from France and Britain against Nazi Germany. And this Litvinov was the man that everyone wanted to interview. And my brother sent this man a little note, in Yiddish, that read "How would you like to talk to a man that, like you, went always around the city watchtower?"

He sent this note because Litvinov was not really Russian—he was a Jew from Bialystok. He had been born Meier Wallach in the 1870s, and had gone to yeshiva just as I and my brother had. But then he went to Russia and became a Bolshevik, changed his name to Maksim Litvinov, and became great under Lenin. But he was from Bialystok, and the watchtower was a symbol of the city. Bialystok is a medieval city, and wherever you go, you are always walking around the watchtower. So Litvinov knew. And he agreed—he gave my brother this prized interview. They laughed together, and my brother had the nerve to say, after they had remembered their boyhood days, "Let's talk about bigger matters, what is your purpose at the League of Nations, and what do you hope to achieve?" And Litvinov gave him a perfect interview. And this was printed in the newspapers in London, and also in the papers in Bialystok, and my father and I read it in our local paper.

He could do these things. After that, he returned to his training, and he earned degrees in law and agronomy at the University of Toulouse in France. He married a French girl there, named Ora, and they went to Palestine together, where they were part of a group of pioneers who founded Kibbutz Yagour near Haifa, and had two boys. The last I heard from him before the war was that they were in Haifa.

As the country began to grow, Benjamin learned about shipping. He helped to build Zim, the Israeli shipping company, and became chief of Operations. But I did not know this at the time, I had not heard from him since after the war, when he had written to say that there was nothing left.

In 1953, I thought I would go and see him. When I came to buy my ticket, from the Zim office in New York, somebody said, "Iwry? Are you a relative of this Benjamin Iwry?" I told them I had a brother Benjamin, but I didn't know he was with Zim. They told me, he is at the top! And they said, we will arrange for you, that when you come to Israel we will make it a surprise for your brother. So they arranged passage to Marseilles—in 1953, their ship only went from Europe—and from Marseilles I got on the Zim ship to Israel, to Haifa. And he didn't know I was coming.

When the ship reached Haifa, only one of my brother's coworkers knew I was there, it was kept a secret. So they arranged for me to be with the first party landing, seven o'clock in the morning, and he was there to meet me. They brought him down, telling him only at the last moment, your brother is on the ship. "Nobody told me! It's the truth!" he said to me. His people answered him, "Why do we have to tell you who is on the ship, there are many passengers." This is how I met him.

And my first visit there was very impressive. Israel was already a state, though it was a poor country fighting every day for survival. When I came there, an army colonel named Gamal Abdel Nasser had just overthrown the government of Egypt. This Nasser had collaborated with Hitler, and now he was in control of Egypt and already beginning to threaten the new state of Israel.

My brother and some acquaintances gave me a very nice reception, took me all over, showed me everything important to see. I was really impressed with the beauty of the land, especially the Golan Heights and the northern part of the country, the Galil. But most of all, I was impressed with Jerusalem. I thought Jerusalem would be the place for me. I could touch the spirituality of Jerusalem. And when I say it, I am not exaggerating. I knew all these places, both the new and the old. And you can walk in the street and hear the echo of your own footsteps. There is something—even in the middle of the day, when everyone is busy and cars are running—there is a certain stillness of Jerusalem that cannot be disturbed. One who has an ear for it, has listened, knows about the stillness. Especially of course, on the Shabbat.

First of all, you will not believe it, I went to the Hebrew University and got my diploma. Yes! My documents from the University of Warsaw Institute of Higher Jewish Studies. They had them in their archives. Well, I got them, and I later showed my diploma to Dr. Albright. He had accepted me only on my word, that I said I was Professor Schorr's student, but now I had my diploma again. I still have it.

I made great friends at the Hebrew University. Some already knew me there, from before, from my involvement with the Dead Sea Scrolls. All the people who were dealing with the Scrolls and in Biblical studies were familiar to me, and of course I was a student of Albright, which was a great thing.

But there was one episode from that trip that I can never forget. After I had escaped Poland, I never knew what had become of my parents, my three sisters, their husbands, and their children. I knew that they probably died in Treblinka. I found out that much, that the people of my acquaintance were taken out in this and that period, from Bialystok, to Treblinka. But in Israel, I learned the whole story from a doctor, Tobias Citroen, in Tel Aviv.

We had known each other from childhood, we lived on the same street. He went to Prague, to the Poland medical school, for his education. He had survived the war and made it to Israel. He was the same age as my oldest sister, Fanya. So he told me the following. We were sitting in a little hotel, the Jordan Hotel in Tel Aviv, on Ben Gurion Street. We sat all night until three o'clock, and he told me what happened in Bialystok.

The Germans who were holding the Bialystok ghetto[2] and taking everyone out in parties to send them to the Treblinka concentration camp, they had one thing in mind, that epidemics should not happen, because they can spread, turn into a catastrophe that would destroy the Germans also. So the Jews who were doctors were treated a little bit differently. They were asked to supervise anybody who was sick and notify the Germans. The sick were taken out of the ghetto immediately.

Tobias was the head doctor of this group who watched the sickness in the ghetto. He took in my sister Fanya, to work with him, to give her a little protection. Her husband had been burned alive at the beginning of the Nazi takeover of Bialystok, when they collected 3,000 Jewish men in the high synagogue and set it on fire. So my sister went to work with this doctor.

He told me how she had tried to save my parents. She didn't get them registered and let them be taken to the ghetto like everybody else. Because she was one of these five or seven people who were assigned to work with the Germans, she knew that the people in the ghetto were eventually sent to Treblinka or other places and were burned or gassed there. They were not supposed to tell anybody, because the Germans would have executed them immediately.

The people still thought at the beginning, they go [from the ghetto] out to places where they will work in agriculture. But finally they learned the truth, and my sister thought, no, she will not let her parents be taken. And in Bialystok, near a bridge, there were a lot of little caves. She placed them there as in a shelter, and covered the opening.

She was alone, her husband, our sisters, their husbands, were all gone. And our parents were getting older. She put them there and kept them alive for many months, bringing food to them. Until one day, one of the neighbors told the police, who told the Germans. The soldiers came, and they opened the cave, and they brought a machine gun, and tut tut tut tut tut tut. That's how they died. Tobias told me.

When the day came that my sister was ordered to go to the concentration camp, she said no, she would die here. So Tobias gave her a poison. She drank it in full consciousness, full willingness, and she died. And this he told me, how she died.

My stay in Israel, which I made three weeks, was like three days. I wanted to see everything, and meet everyone. At the end, when it came time to leave, my brother told me, even though he was chief of operations of Zim, that the ship will go here and there. I will change your ticket to a flight, so we will have more days to spend together.

So I did it. And after the time had ended, I came, happy, back to my wife and child, who said, "you didn't call too often and you didn't write." Mark was asking "Where is daddy, where is daddy?" And it was true, true. It was not like today, there are phones everywhere and you can pick up a phone and make such a call very easily.

I was very happy to have finally seen Israel. I was also lucky to have continued my education at the time of the discovery of the Dead Sea Scrolls.

Because of my interests, I studied the scroll containing the book of Isaiah, looking for the uniqueness of that text. We know now that the scrolls were written—some were written and others were copied—sometime around 130, 125 B.C.E. So this is the earliest copy known of the book of Isaiah. But there was not only a modern battle of the scrolls, about when they were written, and about whether they were authentic. There was also a battle inside the scrolls. The scrolls that were written, and not simply copied, at that time, tell of a battle between the writers of the scrolls, who were a group of Sadducees, and the established religious leaders of the time, the Pharisees.

In one of the scrolls, the authors write, ". . . the teaching of their lies," meaning the Pharisees. The writers of the scrolls were extreme conservatives. The Pharisees were trying to bring the Levitical law into tune with their own times, which were Greek times. The Pharisees said, well, we live in Hellenistic times. And this culture has filled up our lives, in science, in philosophy, in art, everywhere. And we cannot escape it. We will have to accept that we live in this time, despite the Hasmonean war, which we won, somehow, as independents. But we will take these Hellenistic teachings only on our own conditions.

This is why the Pharisees, in my view, started to explain and expound Jewish law, in a way the people of their time would be able to follow. However, the people who wrote and copied these scrolls disagreed, and they attacked the Pharisees and accused them of teaching lies.

All my theories and my identification of them was based on a phrase that repeats itself five times. And this phrase says, "The Zadokites, children of Malachites, these are the returnees to Israel, who spent a lot of their time outside, but descend themselves from Judah, the old Judah." And here they are.

The key to this idea was the translation of a certain word. The two great scholars who interpreted the Damascus Document before the Dead Sea Scrolls were found, translated this word, plus the name Israel, as either the "eldest of Israel" or the "repentees of Israel." But I kept on saying, even until now, that this phrase means the "returnees of Israel." When these returnees came to Jerusalem, they found there was no place for them there. This was not the promised land that they wanted. So they left Jerusalem, however, and they went to Qumran.

I published this in an article that appeared in 1969.[3] This was the time when I got a lot of flak, clatter, when I was reading my papers and having people agree with me, or disagree with me. Finally, I felt that I am "in it." And I was enjoying myself very much.

So in the 1960s, I had already made my entrance into scholarship with the Dead Sea Scrolls. But even before then, I published an article in the *Journal of the American Oriental Society*. Well, after this I became more widely known.[4] And the great Israeli scholars then looked upon me as a fellow whom they would like to have among them. And I was recommended for a Fulbright scholarship.

At first, the Fulbright officials said, "An exchange professor to Israel in Biblical studies? This is an export business for Israel. What do they need you for? Well, it is a waste of money. We can give it to another fellow." But a letter from Albright, apparently, was convincing. And the Israelis also said that we want to hear what he has to say and to see how he teaches, because Albright's school was very great. So it went through. I went to Israel. Mark was now 14, my wife Nina was fluent in Hebrew, and in 1964 we went to Israel, and we went very well equipped.

At that time the ship, *Shalom,* the luxury ship of Israel, was cruising from New York directly to Haifa. Before we left, we exchanged our automobile for another one, a fire-engine red Plymouth Valiant. It was very nice. We took the car to New York and it went with us to Israel. And then as to books—the people in Israel told me, "Remember that if you need a certain book, then twenty of your students will also need this book. So you do as we do, we have here our private sources." So, since we were going by ship I took 200 books with me. Baltimore Hebrew College let me take out any book I wanted. Some books I had already, and some I bought. And we packed it all very neatly, and where did we put them, do you think, 200 books? In the car! In the trunk and in the back seat. This was a very good thing. The car held whatever we needed.

So in August 1965, with our car and the books, we started out for New York, for the ship *Shalom.* And on the ship, we had a second honeymoon. It was very nice. There was music every night, dancing every night, we went first class. Not because of my brother, but because the Fulbright people paid for it.

In the cabin next to us was Abba Eban. We knew each other slightly, Eban and I, from before, when I had attended the UN sessions over the fate of Israel. Eban was Israel's deputy prime minister and at other times foreign minister. He was an elegant spokesman for Israel, and one of Israel's greatest intellectuals. He was educated at Cambridge University and never became a true Israeli. When he appeared before the United Nations, they called him the little Churchill.

The trip was more than ten days but it went quickly. There were two orchestras, you could hear classical music. As for movies, the newest and best was there. And the best food. Mark was always going down, with Eban's son Eli, they became great friends, to see the car, and to pat it. It was like a little dog, his pet.

When we got to Jerusalem, we were lucky and got the apartment of some people who left for America for a year. So we had a fine American apartment with a piano. We had many emotional reunions with some of Nina's classmates and teachers from Poland who had survived the Nazis and come to Israel, so she had friends there. She found her favorite teacher, Dr. Hayim Ormian, who taught psychology. She found him in Israel, teaching there and he was very happy to see her. Dr. Ormian, who was a fine and formal European gentleman told Mark "Your mother, Nina, she always had a bold opinion and expected her opinion to be heard. But she was an outstanding student, the cream of the crop." And our very American 14-year-old son answered "yes—the sour cream!" So Dr. Ormian knew that Nina's strong opinions were an inherited trait.

Besides these friends, my brother Benjamin and his family were there. Benjamin's elder son, Tsour, became an agricultural engineer as well as a commando in Israel's armed forces. He was also a successful artist. That was the way things were in Israel, everyone's talents were put to use. The younger brother, Erez, became chief engineer of Israel's merchant marine, following in his father's footsteps, on Zim cargo ships and tankers. Erez also became secretary general of his coworkers union.

Besides my brother Benjamin, Nina's aunt, Rita Bande Rutenberg and her son and daughter-in-law, Kazik and Ada Rutenberg, and their children, were in Tel Aviv, after miraculously surviving the war. So we had friends, we had family, and we spoke Hebrew, and we felt at home. The difficult thing was to get Mark into school.

The best school in Jerusalem—there are many good schools in Jerusalem—I knew about it, because it had been there since the beginning of the century, in the center of Jerusalem. Many of the leaders of Israel went through this Hebrew Gymnasia of Rechavia, as it was called, so why shouldn't Mark go to there also? But the principal told me, it is full. They have 40 students in the class where he would go. Well, I was told that if he added Mark to a class to make 41, it would cause a general strike of the teachers, because it is in their contract that there will be no more than 40 students. And it is true. No more! And it is not only this one school, but all over the country. They are a tremendous union. So I wrote a letter in Hebrew to the chairman of the union, and I said, "If you have the guts to refuse my son when I am a teacher, and I came here to teach, and so on." And I waited to see what they would reply.

And now you won't believe. A few days later, there came a letter from the teachers' union. They had a meeting of their board, the Israeli All-

Country board. They decided to make an exception in this thing, and the principal agreed to it. They had already cleared it, you can come Sunday morning—this was the beginning of the week, in Israel, students have only Saturday free—and he will be accepted.

When we went on Sunday with Mark to the school, the principal met us with a smile, and he was admitted to the school. In the meantime I was told that the committee was led by Yigael Yadin. He was a friend of mine, and he told the committee to make the school accept Mark Iwry.

Of course, for Mark, being there was not so easy. He wasn't fluent in Hebrew, so he did not understand what the teachers were saying. And the school had high academic standards. Their expectations were much higher than even a private school here in America. Mark said that most of the time, he could not even tell what subject was being taught. When the teacher of mathematics put algebra on the board, then he knew it was math, but that was all. The rest was all blah blah blah. It was very hard for him. The first month, he used to come home green-faced from school, throw away his books and lie down.

I knew this would only last the first few weeks. But the second week, one of Mark's teachers came to see us at our apartment. His name was Mr. Kamenetzky, and he was unhappy to have this American boy in his class. He told us, "Mark really should not be in my class, I have very good students and I teach at an advanced level. Mark should be where he can catch up. He doesn't even understand Hebrew." So I said well, "I could have helped him with Hebrew, and I will certainly help Mark with Bible." And he said, "No, it is not the Bible you know, we study Bible as with Kaufmann, with other scholars." I said, "Is that so? I want to tell you, that I happen to know this too." He was surprised. "You know Hebrew? You have studied Kaufmann?" I said, "I am coming to be a professor of Bible at Hebrew University." He said, "You are the new man? I am your student! I am working for my PhD there." I said, "You better take care of Mark." And he did.

And I told the principal that Nina and I know Hebrew and we will help. We also asked him to send us a student tutor, and I said, he will get paid in dollars. When I said "paid in dollars," that was something. Back then Israel was poor. Today it is a rich country, but not then. So the director sent their star student to be a tutor.

He was a very nice fellow, from the twelfth grade, and his name was Dan Meridor, and he is now a leading member of the Israeli parliament and former finance minister. Several times a week, Dan would come and help Mark with the schoolwork, and explain it to him. But finally, after four or so months, Don came to me and said, he doesn't need me any more. He is very good, he gets A's even in Hebrew.

We were very comfortable this whole year because we brought our automobile. And when we went out in this automobile and drove the streets of Jerusalem and the road to Tel Aviv, everyone looked at us, at the fire-red car. And we drove to and from the American Embassy in Tel Aviv. All our material needs, because we were there on a Fulbright, were arranged through the American Embassy. We would go there once a week, or once every two weeks, to the American "PX" [post exchange] and fill up the trunk of the red car with anything we needed, except meat, which we didn't buy from them. Israel had a supply of its own.

Whatever you could need—socks, anything—they had it, you didn't have to pay. Of course, you couldn't sell it. But when we arrived, my name was on their list, given to them by the secretary at the embassy who deals with all the Fulbrights. We didn't have to go and ask, "Where is this, how can I buy it?" or deal with the black market. The embassy provided everything we needed. At that time, because of Israel's policy of importing only necessities, and exporting everything possible, anything that was considered a luxury was not available. But we had available to us everything that they considered luxury!

In Israel, American cigarettes like Chesterfield and others were only bought on the black market. And our friends knew that Sam Iwry got them—two cartons!—from the Americans, those crude people. I told them, I can get cigarettes, but I am not allowed to sell them, but just to go around. So whenever I smoked a cigarette, and the way of a gentleman at that time was if you take out a cigarette, you offer first to your friend. But these men, who knew all of your secrets, didn't just take the cigarette. They took the pack. So I had to get another. This was their way of doing business.

Well, we gave more than cigarettes. We didn't sell, but we gave to our friends. And because of my long-time connections with the Jewish Agency and my many colleagues at the universities, we had a very rich circle of friends. The social circling, the going around, started on Friday, in the late afternoon. Our friends would come Friday or Saturday afternoon, after doing their errands to prepare for the Shabbat.

Everyone goes home at midday on Friday. In my time there, this was the way. Normally, you stop and buy flowers and bring them home to your wife. The flowers are put in a container of water, this declares that it is the Shabbat. Also, there were many stalls in the streets, selling the newest books and journals. Many people would buy a book instead of flowers, and they would put it on the table and declare Shabbat.

But even then, in 1964, when Israel was still a young and poor country, there was a great debate between the religious and the nonreligious people. The secular Israelis also savor the flavor of Shabbat. (Although a few of them, I am sorry to say, disregard the religious rules—such as the ban on dribving on Shabbat—in order to make the religious Jews, the "fanatics" as they call them, angry. When one time I asked a young Israeli friend how long it takes to drive to the beach from his home in Tel Aviv, he answered, smiling, "Usually 20 minutes, but on Shabbat only ten, and five on Yom Kippur!") It was not just about theological arguments, because at that time, the Orthodox religionists were fighting with the government over who was and wasn't a Jew and who would be given citizenship.[5]

The year we lived there, the country was still very vulnerable. Egypt under Nasser was very threatening. Since 1955, about the time of my first visit when I came to see my brother, the Soviets had been sending weapons to the Egyptians, and only nine years earlier, in 1956, Egypt had grabbed control of the Suez Canal. They shut off the canal and would not allow Israel's ships through, and this provoked the Israelis to launch their Operation Backlash. And in the north, there was much fighting and a lot of terrorist activities along the border with Syria and with Lebanon. It was in 1964 that the PLO, the Palestinian Liberation Organization, was formed, and it was only a few years later, in 1967, that Israel had to fight again, in the Six-Day War, to protect itself.

And yet, this was the time when the Israelis felt that they were finally at home, though they knew that their claims would be put to the test. It was a romantic time of Zionism. You could feel it. Even the people who had just come, who walked in the streets with their little satchel that held all their possessions, they would say, "See this? This is our bank. See this? This is our . . ." It was an intimate, very nice society. Many of them were, of course, survivors of the Holocaust. But most of the people who lived there were the old *halutzim*—the pioneers. They came because living in Israel was the dream of their life, and this showed in the way they lived.

When the time came to leave, it was very difficult. But our year ended, and we made our plans, reluctantly, to go home. At this time, Shai Kamenetzky, the teacher who was one of my students, and who was upset that Mark was leaving his class, came and told us, "Listen. Mark is a real Israeli. I am a decent person, my wife is great. Leave Mark with me. He will really be at home with us. Leave him here." And Mark didn't say no. But Nina, she couldn't leave Mark there. However, Mark after that returned several times for the summer, to work in a kibbutz and other things, and made friends that he still knows.

I can say that when we came back to Baltimore, we found everything easy. Our home was as we left it. But the main thing was, again, a school for Mark. We had here a little scholar. Mrs. Albright recommended the Gilman School, and Mark was admitted even though he had not signed up with them in September when we returned.

I returned to my routine. It was at this time that I decided that I had oversmoked, especially while I was in Israel. Of course, not just because it cost 13 cents a pack, but because being such a smoker was not good for me. I was now suddenly in my 50s, and I had to think about these habits I had that I knew were not good. So I started looking for ways to stop. It was very difficult.

But then there came an occasion when I was operated on, a hernia. Afterward, the surgeon came in and offered me a cigarette. He was smoking too. But my internist said to him that this is a mistake. He said, you shouldn't do this, and he told the surgeon some things. And I listened to him. When I came out, I didn't smoke. I made it almost imperative, to get away from it. And I did. It was a great feeling, when I stopped. I didn't feel the ringing in the back of my head, I didn't feel the dryness in my mouth.

Things went on in the most regular way. I was teaching in the evenings at the Baltimore Hebrew College, where I later was given the title of Distinguished Professor. Because the Dead Sea Scrolls were of such great interest, a lot of students were interested in these texts, and they took my classes. I taught modern Hebrew literature and Hebrew language for undergraduates, and for the graduate students I taught Biblical texts, and Aramaic and Hebrew language classes.

And I published a couple of articles on which I began the work in Israel. And I went to the meetings of the Society of Biblical Literature, and meetings of the American School of Oriental Research, and I presented some papers. And things flowed very quietly until Mark graduated from Gilman.

I remember one day, we found out that on the SATs Mark had made an 800 in mathematics and 777 in verbal. So when I got home, I said, shame on you Mark, a fellow who made an 800 in mathematics, why did you make only a 777 on the other part? Mark knew it was a joke. But here he was raised in a home of foreigners, yet it goes like this, that even so he was accepted to Harvard, and with a four year National Merit scholarship and Harvard National Scholarship, and he got a sophomore standing.

About this same time, I was called by the chairman of the department of Near Eastern Studies at Harvard. And he wanted me to consider if I would join the faculty. It was very difficult to decide. Nina and I were close to accepting. But around that time came the letter that Mark is accepted, and he would be going to Harvard. And right away we thought that we will not go to Harvard. Mark lived all his life with foreigners. He needed so much to get away.

We knew it! For the first time he can live it up. And if we went to Harvard too, it would start again, like he was a child. To call him up in the morning, did you have a glass of milk? When did you come home last night? So we answered no. Just to give him his chance. But besides this, we had family here. Nina's beloved sister Lilly and her husband Gene lived nearby, and their daughters Gitelle and Annette also. We did not want to leave them.

Well, there was one other thing, his mother. Nina didn't want him to start as a sophomore, because of the war in Vietnam. Well, she says to Mark, maybe you should start as a freshman, and we will see how things go. And it was not a terrible thing. So Mark left for college.

My life went on here very nicely. During this time in the early 1970s and 1980s, I was in many cities of America, lecturing. Some very pleasant things happened. For one thing, the group B'nai B'rith sent me on a lecture tour, with Nina. For three years in a row, we visited several Jewish communities in the Caribbean, on St. Thomas, Puerto Rico and then we would finish up in Curacao. This is a great irony, because Curacao was the place where I was afraid to go while I was a refugee in Vilna, and looking to escape both the Nazis and the Russians. While we were in Curacao, we found the grave of the sister of Spinoza. She had fled the Spanish inquisition and was buried there.

I also participated in the World Congress of Jewish Studies. This started in Israel right after Israel was established as a nation, and it drew thousands of scholars from all over the world—Christians, Moslems, but mostly Jews. This is a great congress, because besides the meeting every four years, they also publish a series of scholarly books called *Eretz Israel* (*The Land of Israel*). It is for archaeology, literature, other related things. Each book is dedicated to a prominent scholar. My article about the Dead Sea Scrolls was published in *Eretz Israel* no. 8, devoted to Albright. I started participating beginning with the fourth. This congress is the highlight for Jewish scholars. Many people from here, from Hopkins, go to this congress. And one time, they asked me to open the congress. Open the congress! This

With Israeli Prime Minister Menachem Begin, a political antagonist from university days in Poland. Iwry traveled to Israel almost annually, including a year in Jerusalem as a Fulbright Scholar, teaching at the Hebrew University in Jerusalem. He was periodically invited to lead the monthly seminars of biblical scholars and archaeologists hosted by Israel's Prime Minister at his residence. Iwry took one such occasion to use his authority as a Biblical scholar in an attempt to change Begin's policies by persuading Begin that his firm position laying claim to the territories of Judea and Samaria on religious grounds was in fact not well grounded in scripture.

was a great thing. With me on the platform was the prime minister of the state of Israel. So I gave a short address, and opened the congress.

When I came back to my seat after speaking, the first person who was on the platform to greet me was Moshe Shamir, the great Israeli novelist and intellectual, who was sitting between me and the prime minister. Apparently, Shamir had gotten some details about me, that I was really from Poland, from Bialystok. When he heard it, he jumped off his seat. You are from Bialystok? I was in the gymnasium, the Hebrew gymnasium, the same school! How come you never came to see me? I said, "The same thing was asked of me by your friend Menachem Begin, who is also from Poland, and I will tell you what I told him."

It was in Menachem Begin's house. There was a tradition of the president of Israel, that scholars, biblical scholars and archaeologists, would meet in his house once a month. This was especially true when Zalman Shazar was president. He was very interested in these matters. After Shazar was no longer president, Menachem Begin took the gathering to his house, because the new president was a different sort, a scientist who had no time for such interests. And I was invited there, to Begin's house, by Yigael Yadin. When the discussion ended, Begin asked me to stay behind for a "glass of tea." And I remained even though it was already very late. His wife said goodnight. And he said, why didn't you come to visit me here? He was from a place called Brist, which is near Bialystok. And I answered him, and I answered the same to Shazar: I didn't come to see you, although it would be a great honor to be received by you, because I am not fully at peace with myself.

This haunted me all the years. I explained it to him like this, and I will say it here also. "You, as well as the others, came to Israel and were the great heroes of our time. And I landed in America. And I couldn't stand not being in Israel. Even though I truly loved America and wanted to study with Albright, it grieved me—would grieve me forever—that I was not in Israel. And to look you straight in your eyes, as though you didn't know as well as I that after the Holocaust my place should have been in Israel—I couldn't do it. How could I come to you, any of you, whom I consider heroes, in these later years after the work you have done and the struggles you have endured and say, look at me, I am here. It was too hard. So I didn't."

Well, in later years, I used to go to Israel almost every summer, to visit and study. Of course, the year that I taught there gave me a little bit of relief, to think that I had made some contribution after all. And I knew that not all my plans depended on me, that there were many circumstances outside my own limits that made my decisions necessary. How could I have turned my back on a chance to work with the great Albright, or a visa from a GI, given as a wedding present, when the Communists were at my back door?

I have gained also a great liking for this country, even though I thought that I should not have been here, but in Israel. I liked many of the circumstances that I found here, the directness of the people, the simple relations that people establish with each other, not like the pompous European ways.

One day in 1985—I was suddenly in my 70s—I was told by my colleagues at Johns Hopkins that there would be a kind of a celebration, and the chairman asked everyone to come. And they told me, bring your wife. The wives were often invited to these things, and so I came with Nina, very innocent. I didn't know what it was.

But when the door opened, everyone applauded and started laughing. I found out this was an event to present me with a *festschrift*—a collection of 29 articles by scholars from around the world. They collect the articles and put them in a book and it is then presented as a tribute to another scholar. This *festschrift* was collected and edited by two of my fine younger students, Ann Kort and Scott Morschauser. This was a very beautiful gift to me. It was my 75th birthday. It was published the next year, and there were articles not only from local scholars, like from the Baltimore Hebrew College and Hopkins, but also from around this country and from Israel. It was presented to me not yet finished, not printed, was because they waited for one last article to come. And this was from Yigael Yadin, the great Israeli archaeologist and general, and my great friend.

Yadin had been in the Israeli government at that time, he had a very important position, and he wasn't writing articles in archaeology. Finally, he retired and he said, now that I am out of the government, the first thing is to write this article for Sam Iwry. He sent it, and shortly after that, he suddenly died. And the book became a more important one because of Yadin's contribution. Many people wanted to have a copy. So this was a milestone in my life. I felt that I didn't deserve a thing like this, but at the presentation they all laughed at me and said yes I did and made a big hullabaloo.[6]

Another thing that came unexpectedly to me in my later years, in 1986, was this. Two of our great friends in Baltimore are Alvin Blum and his wife Millie. Their children Marc, Jim, and Claire are also great friends and supporters. Well, Alvin is a very successful businessman, and he came to see me one day, unexpectedly, and invited me to lunch. While we were sitting, he and I, he says, "I have something to ask you." He says, "I have decided to make a contribution to Johns Hopkins, where I was an undergraduate, and I want it to be called the Samuel Iwry Lectureship."

I was stunned. I said, "What has it to do with me? You want to make a contribution, that's very nice. But how do I come in here?" He says, "You come in here because I think that if they agree it will be very nice for me and for you." Well, I told him I was completely unprepared for it, but grateful, and if it will be, I want it to be called a Hebraic lectureship. In other words this will be for Hebrew language development, for stipends to students who will study Hebrew, and for scholars who will come here to give lectures in Hebrew, about Hebrew, and so on.

Well, he told me he talked to the president of the University, the president is very happy with the name. Since then, the Samuel Iwry Hebraic Lectureship has brought scholars from Israel, has sponsored lectures and seminars, and has given financial aid to students who needed it to really

Iwry, in his 70s, always had a natural way with children. He had a soft spot for them, and they responded to him. During this period of his life, he received a *festschrift* volume in his honor, which contained articles by fellow scholars from around the world and an honorary degree, Doctor of Hebrew Letters, from the Baltimore Hebrew University. He was further honored by the establishment of the Samuel Iwry Faculty Fellowship Fund at the University of Maryland.

make some progress in Hebrew. And later, in 1999, this tremendous friend with his wife and son Marc did even more. He gave a commitment to Johns Hopkins to establish the Blum-Iwry Professorship in Near Eastern Studies.

In 1991, the time came to retire. I felt that I had already overstayed my time. Nobody pushed me to it. But I said to myself that the reason why I stayed longer was to erase my memory of the eight years that I spent everywhere but in my chosen profession, from 1939 when I said good-bye to my family and escaped the Soviets and Nazis both, until 1947, when I really began my studies here with Albright. I wanted to regain those years that were taken from me.

Yes, I knew retirement would bring a change in my routine. But I continued to take some students, when Hopkins had a student here or a little group there that I taught, even at age 83.

My retirement came with some big news, in April 1991, which was reported in the university newspaper, the *Gazette*. The headline said "Iwry's Dead Sea Scrolls Theory Confirmed." Under this headline, it read, "Carbon-14 Test Proves Professor Accurately Dated Dead Sea Scrolls Forty Years

Ago." It was at this time, when I got a call from a journalist, who told me that a special new test was made in Switzerland on a fragment of a Dead Sea Scroll. And this very scientific way of dating things had shown that the Scrolls, including the Damascus Document, were written in the beginning of the second century B.C.E. And this journalist read somewhere that I had said they were from the first to second century B.C.E, somewhere around 125 B.C.E. This was a great gift as I was retiring.

So the time came to begin my new phase of life. A phase in which I am taking my time. And taking it easy. I used to say that in that cherished time, when I am retired, I will do a lot of things. Perhaps everybody thinks such a thing. My wife has always said that I have never learned to have a hobby. But I think that when I can sit and read and do whatever I want, it is like a hobby. I take a walk in the mornings, and do my calisthenics. And I enjoy life, as my health is good to me.

As I speak, I am now in my eighties. It's quite a nice age. Somebody said one time that—I think Montesquieu said it—"I hope I would die young only I hope that it would be very late." I'm happy that I reached this age and I feel quite comfortable in these years.

I do not exclude myself from anything that the everyday life demands or brings. And this is because of a certain philosophy. I really feel—and it is all the time that I have this feeling of being ten years younger. When I was 70 and I should have really thought at that time about retirement, I thought I was only 60. And this is because of the years I lost before, during and after World War II.

But to my own great surprise, on March 18, 1992, I became a grandfather. To become a grandfather is perhaps not a very great thing to many people, but I am astonished to have lived to see a grandson. I never believed that I would be in a kind of a position in which I will go around with photographs and showing my grandson.

My son Mark and my lovely daughter-in-law Daryl told me some time ago that I'm going to be a grandfather. The day this happened, not to miss anything, I left with my wife Nina and took the train and a taxi to the hospital, and we found a baby born at midnight, or so, late at night, and his name is Jonathan. And when we came into the room around noon the next day, we found a little "blondie" being wrapped up. His face was very clear and he even opened for a minute his eyes, and you can see his nose and his eyes. Nina thinks he looks like Mark, but you can't always believe a mother. So we will have to wait and see.

Iwry, age 83, enjoying his grandson, Jonathan, age 1. At this stage of his life, Iwry was honored by the establishment by the Blum family of the Samuel Iwry Hebraic Lectureship at Johns Hopkins and, later, of a chaired professorship, the Blum-Iwry Professor of Near Eastern Studies. (The first person to hold this chair is Professor Theodore J. Lewis.)

He cried a little bit and then he stopped and I had this unusual experience of seeing a new creature less than a day old. And it's a phenomenal thing, to see a baby in the first hours of its life.

And here is this that I think about: In 1996, there was a great celebration in New York. It was a celebration of all the Jewish refugees who had been granted transit visas by the Japanese official in Lithuania, Chiune Sugihara. They honored this Japanese man. His wife and son came, and the Japanese community of New York took part too. He had come to Lithuania as a consul, and the Jewish refugees were there, trying to get exit visas to Japan. This man worked and worked, writing out thousands of visas by hand. Even though his government did not approve, he wrote the visas anyway, for purely humanitarian reasons. He, like many others, helped to save so many people, and I was one of them.

Dr. Samuel Iwry died in Baltimore, Maryland, surrounded by his family, on May 8, 2004 (17 Iyyar, 5764), as his story was being prepared for publication.

May his memory be for a Blessing.

Nina Rochman Iwry

by J. Mark Iwry

The unsung hero of my father's story is my mother. Although both grew up in Poland, they did not meet until the 1940s in Japan. Nina ("Ninotchka" to family and friends) was born in the city of Lodz, Poland, to Mordecai Rochman and Gulia Bande Rochman. The family was well educated and well to do: her father owned a textile factory, and Nina, her sisters, and brother received a fine secular and Jewish education. Nina was the top student in her school, beloved by teachers and students—sweet, with a slight streak of mischief.

After completing a master's degree in journalism at Warsaw University, she began her journalistic career with the Polish government-sponsored daily newspaper in Warsaw. By the time Hitler invaded Poland, Nina was, in my father's words, "a young practicing journalist . . . already published . . . in the daily press." With a group of colleagues, Nina escaped Warsaw by train, having had 20 minutes to pack a few things and dash for the station. (To her surprise at the time, the first item she grabbed during those frantic minutes was her Bible.)

They disembarked in Kovno (Kaunas), the capital of Russian-occupied Lithuania. Nina found work writing for a local newspaper (where, mysteriously, she never met the colleague who was translating all of her articles; she later learned he was working as a spy in the underground). Nina's and Sam's separate lives in Lithuania—she in Kovno, he in Vilna—must have resembled in some ways the shadowy, multi-lingual world of cafes, underground activity, counterfeit passports, espionage, and treachery that was dramatized and romanticized in the classic Bogart film *Casablanca* (he as the resistance leader Victor Laszlow, she as the beautiful Ilsa, played by Ingrid Bergman).

Like the other refugees in Lithuania, Nina had her passport confiscated by the Russian occupying authorities. Most could never retrieve their passports, were therefore prevented from exiting the country, and were eventually murdered. When Nina tried to retrieve hers, two circumstances saved her life.

First, while in Poland, Nina and her brother-in-law, who also later escaped to Lithuania, had been advised by a mutual friend to have their passports bound in red rather than the traditional dark binding. The friend, a lawyer, had a hunch this could be useful some day. He would prove to be right.

The second lucky circumstance occurred at the Russian embassy in Kaunas, where Nina, ever the optimist, queued up with hundreds of other foreigners seeking their passports. Nearly everyone felt hopeless, as the stone-faced clerk in the passport office had turned a deaf ear to countless previous requests. But when Nina finally reached the front of the line, she was able to tell the clerk they had something in common—both were named Nina. This earned my mother the bureaucrat's cynical permission to take five minutes to try to find her passport in a room where thousands of ostensibly indistinguishable passports were piled randomly on tables. To the clerk's surprise, my mother located her passport—the red binder saved her.

She then pressed her luck by hazarding a further request: for time to search for the passports of two others trapped in Lithuania—her brother-in-law and the lawyer friend. Permission was granted, she found their red passports, and the two men were able to exit the country and save themselves.

Meanwhile in Poland, Nina later learned, the Poles and Germans were expropriating, rounding up, and terrorizing the Jewish population. The trusted, long-time senior manager of the textile factory that her father owned appeared at the family's apartment and peremptorily demanded the keys to the factory. There was nothing to stop him. In the Winter, when Nina's family and the other Jewish families in the building were evicted from their apartments with only their blankets and hats to protect them from the bitter cold, the friendly, trusted watchman and security guard of their apartment complex—who had worked for them for years and had looked after the children—forced every adult and child to turn over their blankets and hats to him as they left their home for the last time on the way to the camps. Nina concluded that the Jewish people needed a land of their own, where they would be welcome and no longer defenseless.

Nina left Lithuania alone, escaping the Nazis by taking the "insane risk" (as my father put it) of crossing Russia. After 14 days on the trans-Siberian railway, she reached Japan, where she did not know a soul. Fascinated by the country and culture, she found a job in the city of Kobe. In my father's words, Japan was "like a fairy tale" for Nina—and the Japanese took to her as well. Her long-term plan, however, was to settle and start a new life in Australia.

Nina arranged passage there on a British vessel. On December 6, 1941, the day before her departure, she paid a final visit to her dentist, Dr. Shiga. Surprisingly, he was dressed in full military uniform. He regretfully told her that her ship actually would not be sailing because war in the Pacific was imminent. And he had a special request: please remember Japan as you have known it until now; do not judge us by the way we behave during war.

When Nina went to the dock the next day, 16 colleagues and friends, European and Japanese, came to see her off. But Dr. Shiga was right: it was the day of Pearl Harbor, and her ship would never sail.

Moreover, Japan was now incarcerating foreigners in internment camps. The Japanese authorities, based on their discreet but unremitting surveillance of Europeans, told Nina that she had been "very, very honorable" while in Japan. By way of reward, they offered her an alternative to internment camp: leaving Japan as the only passenger in the hold of a Japanese cargo vessel bound for Shanghai, China, through heavily mined waters. Without hesitation she chose the passage to Shanghai.

Before Nina left Japan, an acquaintance requested a favor: to smuggle American dollars into Shanghai and deliver them to his relatives there (with some additional cash for herself). Although this compounded the danger to her—the only female on a cargo vessel—Nina agreed. The bills were sewn into the large custom-made buttons of her dress.

Nina survived the voyage—mines, sailors, and all. In Shanghai she delivered the cash, and used her portion to rent a room advertised in the classifieds. The room was in an apartment owned by a well-to-do Russian Jewish family, the Citrins, who were deeply impressed by Nina's qualities and educational background. After Nina had found a job and begun work, a key management position in a hospital in Shanghai's French Concession unexpectedly opened up. The Citrins, who sat on the hospital's board, asked Nina, as a favor, if she would fill the position temporarily. Despite a longstanding fear of hospitals, Nina consented. The way she conducted herself and carried out her considerable responsibilities soon earned the respect and affection of those around her, European and Chinese.

This administrative post probably saved Nina's life by exempting her from Shanghai's Hongkew prison camp (described in my father's narrative), where nearly all Europeans, including my father, were interned. Nina is sure she would not have survived the camp. At the hospital, her duties included managing the payroll and other administrative functions, as well as maintaining data on European refugees in China, in order that the international Jewish community might give them financial and other assistance.

At this time, inflation in China was rampant: wages that bought a cup of rice at the start of the pay period would buy only a fraction of a cup by the time they were actually paid. The hospital's Chinese employees asked Nina for informal advances on their pay. Yet if any one of them caused any loss to the hospital, this irregular practice would almost certainly cost Nina her job and her exemption from the internment camp. A faithful senior employee, known as Number One, told her that the other workers were fundamentally untrustworthy, and would readily cheat and lie to foreigners. But with her, he claimed, they would be honest, because she was so well liked and respected. She trusted Number One, gave the advances, and Number One proved to be right.

At one point, the hospital's Chief of Medicine, Dr. Steinman, told Nina that a patient, a religious young man hospitalized with a life-threatening illness, had just learned that the Nazis had murdered his parents and entire family. Despondent, he had no further desire to live, and the doctor told Nina he now doubted the boy would survive. Nina went to visit him in his hospital room every day to encourage him and show that someone cared. He gradually began to fight for survival, and eventually recovered.

Nina and Sam each became well known in the Jewish community in the Far East and had heard of one another before they met in Japan through mutual friends. In view of Sam's key position in the "underground," Nina asked him whether he could help her obtain transit papers to a safer place. He declined. Visas and passports were scarce, and each covered an entire family; he could not justify using one for a single person when many escapees from Europe had families. His answer earned him her respect.

As recounted in Sam's narrative, several years later, when he was beaten unconscious by the prison camp guards, Nina found out, and sent her Chinese employees to find him and bring him to the hospital. This probably saved his life.

After the war ended, Sam was among many who courted her. Eventually, Nina agreed to marry him. In an unexpected twist, their friendship toward a young GI helped them escape Shanghai just before it was taken over by Mao and the Communists. A "slow boat from China" brought them to San Francisco and freedom. Sam then describes how Nina, newly arrived in the States and still learning English, took the train to Washington and went to the office of United States Senator Millard Tydings (D-Md), where she successfully arranged for her sister, Lilly, her sister's husband, Genek, and her brother, Sevek, to be brought out of the displaced persons camps in Europe and admitted to America.

Nina's promising career, launched in the 1930s, was another casualty of war. Following her early accomplishments in journalism and, later, as a hospital administrator in China, she never attempted to resume her professional career in this country, although she performed translations—both professionally, on contract with the United States State Department, and as a favor to friends in the literary and scientific communities. Nina felt that her skill as a journalist rested largely on her ability to use the written and spoken language (for which she has a rare and remarkable gift). But that language was mainly Polish (her first language), not English (her seventh).

After all Nina and Sam had been through, bringing another child into this world involved a terribly difficult choice and, ultimately, a deliberate act of faith. On Nina's part, especially, it was an expression of hope and optimism. Once they had a child, Nina's desire and, she felt, her proper role, was to focus on being a mother. In this, she was enormously successful—an extraordinary, loving mother and wife, devotedly caring for her family. In fact, Nina saved Sam's life again four decades later in Baltimore: when he became critically ill, and the doctors had lost hope and given up, she insisted on and arranged the kind of care that ultimately enabled him to recover. And for the four years of Sam's final illness, Nina cared for him at great cost to her own health.

Giving and selfless to a fault, Nina has helped others in countless ways, especially at times of great need. When a seemingly fatal disease struck our dear friend Kathy Mendeloff in her early twenties, Nina's love, intelligence, and fighting spirit were instrumental in enabling Kathy and her parents to survive the ordeal. When our lifelong friend Dr. Andrew Becker was afflicted by grave illness, Nina's creative intervention proved critical to the ultimate success of his treatment (and Andy's constant devotion and loyalty have been invaluable to us, especially during my father's final illness). We have been blessed with many friends in America, Israel, and around the world, and Nina's dedication to family and friends—her kindness, compassion, optimism, and *gemilut chasadim* (acts of loving kindness)—are legendary among all who know her.

Modest and private, my mother objected strongly to the preparation of this epilogue or any other presentation about her. But her dear and wonderful friends, Toby Mendeloff, Millie Blum, and Jeannette Fineman, encouraged me to go forward with this, and seek forgiveness in lieu of permission.

May 25, 2004 (5 Sivan, 5764)

Suggestions for Additional Reading

The selections that follow are intended to be only a supplement to this oral history, for those interested in a more complete picture of Iwry's particular experiences. A number of the topics referred to here are the subject of a considerable literature. These suggestions offer only a few selections, most of which intersect in some way with Dr. Iwry's story.

Those looking for additional material on the Eastern European Jewish culture prior to World War I will enjoy Martin Buber, *The Legend of the Baal-Shem* (Princeton University Press, Princeton, NJ, 1955), Elie Wiesel, *Souls on Fire: Portraits and Legends of Hasidic Masters* (Random House, New York, NY 1972), and also Miriam Weinstein, *Yiddish: A Nation of Words,* (Ballantine Books, New York, NY, 2001).

For an excellent general history of Poland, see Adam Zamoyski, *The Polish Way: A Thousand-Year History of the Poles and Their Culture* (Hippocrene Books, New York, NY, 1987).

A vibrant picture of Jewish life and educational institutions in Vilna before World War II can be found in Lucy S. Dawidowicz, *From That Place and Time: A Memoir* (W. W. Norton, New York, NY, 1989). Vilna's refugee days are related by Hillel Levine, *In Search of Sugihara: The Elusive Diplomat Who Risked His Life to Save 10,000 Jews from the Holocaust* (Free Press, New York, NY, 1996). The fate of Vilna and Vilna's Jews under the Nazis is related by Yitzhak Arad, *Ghetto in Flames: The Struggle and Destruction of the Jews in Vilna in the Holocaust* (KTAV Publishing House, Hoboken, NJ, 1981).

A wider perspective on attitudes held by the United States toward Hitler and the Jews, as well as U.S. immigration policy, can be found in David S. Wyman, *The Abandonment of the Jews: America and the Holocaust, 1941-1945* (Pantheon Books, NY, 1984).

The complex attitudes of the Japanese toward the Jews are explored in David Kranzler, *Japanese, Nazis and Jews. The Jewish Refugee Community of Shanghai, 1938-1945* (KTAV Publishing House, Hoboken, NJ, 1988), in Herman Dicker, *Wanderers and Settlers in the Far East: A Century of Jewish Life in China and Japan* (Twayne Publishers, Inc., New York, NY 1962), and also in Marvin Tokayer and Mary Swartz, *The Fugu Plan: The Untold Story of the Japanese and the Jews during World War II* (Paddington Press, New York, NY, 1979). For another account of the Shanghai ghetto, see James R. Ross, *Escape to Shanghai: A Jewish Community in China* (Free Press, New York, NY, 1994).

For additional material about Shanghai and its famous Jewish *taipans*, see Stella Dong, *Shanghai: The Rise and Fall of a Decadent City* (HarperCollins, New York, NY, 2000).

The turmoils and international conflicts over the creation of the state of Israel are explored in detail in various works, including Tom Segev, *One Palestine, Complete: Jews and Arabs under the British Mandate* (Henry Holt and Company, New York, NY, 1999).

Those interested in the Dead Sea Scrolls and their many controversies will enjoy Lawrence Schiffman, *Reclaiming the Dead Sea Scrolls: The True Meaning for Judaism and Christianity* (Doubleday, New York, NY, 1994). There are many other treatments of this subject, both scholarly and popular.

Notes

Forword

1. E. Solender, "Time Traveler," Baltimore Jewish Times (June 20, 1986), pp. 56-58.

Chapter I

1. Dr. Iwry here refers to his mentor and teacher, William F. Albright (1891-1971), professor of Semitic Languages at Johns Hopkins University.
2. The Russian revolution broke out in 1917; the tsar abdicated March 16, and soon after, Aleksandr Kerensky was named premier of Communist Russia. The Ukraine declared its independence, but the Communist Red army invaded immediately and the new Ukrainian government collapsed. The battles between the Red army and the White (anti-Communist) army continued for five years. The Communists won, and in 1922, Communist-run Ukraine joined Soviet Russia, Byelorussia, and the Transcaucasian Republic to become a founding member of the Union of Soviet Socialist Republics.
3. Between 1648 and 1658, followers of the Cossack leader Bohdan Khmelny-tsky persecuted and destroyed countless Jewish communities. Jews were banned from the professions, craft guilds, farming, and large commercial enterprises and forced to survive by small, petty commerce.
4. As Dr. Iwry and his family were not Ukrainians, and could somehow prove their Polish citizenship, they were allowed to leave the newly formed Ukrainian SSR and go back to Poland, which had been independent for only three years.
5. Following World War I, representatives of the United States, Great Britain, France, Italy, and other nations met in Paris in January 1919. This meeting is known as the Paris Peace Conference. At this time, the Treaty of Versailles was negotiated, which specified the disarmament of Germany, required Germany to make extensive financial reparations, and established the boundaries and sovereignty of Belgium, Poland, Czechoslovakia (now the Czech Republic and Slovakia), and Austria. The Versailles Treaty was signed June 1919.
6. Yiddish is actually a Germanic language (about 85 percent of the vocabulary is German, 10 percent Hebrew, and 5 percent Slavic, plus words from other languages), though it is usually written with Hebrew characters. It is spoken mainly by Eastern European Jews. Hebrew is the language of ancient Israel.

Chapter 2

1. At the end of World War I, the territory now belonging to Lithuania was disputed between Russia, Poland, and the Lithuanians, who wanted their independence. Various regions were occupied in turn by the Polish and Soviet armies as well as the Lithuanian nationals. The League of Nations tried to mediate, but ended its involvement in January 1922. The following February, Pilsudski and his followers again called for "restoration" of the Vilna region to Poland, which was confirmed by Allied powers. Vilna remained a part of Poland until the beginning of World War II.

2. In the mid-1700s, Poland was weakened by civil strife, while imperial Russia was expanding by military means. Alarmed at Russian ambitions, and seeking to shift Russian expansion into Poland, Prussia and Austria signed a series of treaties with Russia that divided more and more Polish territory among the three other powers. Poland was powerless to resist and by the end of the 1700s, the country had been fully divided among Russia, Prussia, and Austria and had ceased to exist.

3. Born to missionary parents in Chile in 1891, William Foxwell Albright was the foremost Biblical archaeologist and Near Eastern scholar of his day. He was a professor of Semitic languages at Johns Hopkins University from 1929 to 1958, and also served as the director of the American School of Oriental Research in Jerusalem. He died in 1971.

4. Palestine had been placed under British authority in 1920. Alarmed over violence between Arabs and Jewish settlers, Britain in 1922 issued a White Paper limiting the number of Jewish immigrants to Palestine's estimated economic capacity. In 1929, disputes provoked further violence, and Britain in October 1930 issued the Passfield White Paper that completely halted Jewish immigration. However, protests by Zionists convinced Prime Minister Ramsey MacDonald, in February 1931, to revoke the Passfield Paper and return to the 1922 White paper.

5. In the event of a deadlock among Poland's many political parties, the prime minister can dissolve the *Seym* (parliament) and call for new elections. During many of the years between 1919 and 1939, the *Seym* often had a majority party, which was won through the illegal (and often violent) means of Josef Pilsudski, who despite his questionable methods did not hate the Jews. However, when elections were held in 1938, the parties gaining the most seats were those with a strong anti-Semitic agenda.

6. Hitler had hoped to employ Poland as an ally against the Soviets, but Poland would not cooperate. Hitler then went to Stalin, and signed a nonaggression pact on August 24, 1939. This pact secretly divided Poland between Russia and Germany. With the Soviet confrontation thus delayed, Hitler invaded Poland on September 1.

Chapter 3

1. When the Soviets returned Vilna to the Lithuanians, on October 29, 1939, the Lithuanians began several days of riots against the Jews, who were often

perceived to be pro-Soviet. One man was killed and over 200 wounded, and Jewish shops and synagogues were broken into and looted.

2. By June 1940, the Nazis were approaching Paris and the French government left for Tours, declaring Paris an open city. The Polish government-in-exile then fled to London.

3. Fridtjof Nansen, the inventor of the *sauf conduit,* was the ambassador from Norway, and the League of Nations was headquartered in Geneva. The Dutch officials were likely, the refugees thought, to recognize forgeries.

4. The Lithuanian NKVD showed an unusual level of cooperation, largely because of the intervention of the Kaunas physician Elkanan Elkes, who had many contacts in the diplomatic community. Dr. Elkes worked tirelessly on behalf of the local Jews and the refugees to smooth over difficulties with the Soviets.

5. The refugees' treatment of this wineseller and their demand for his signature show their utter desperation. As Polish citizens, they could not ask Jan Zwartendijk for a Dutch visa, yet they needed a destination in order to get a transit visa. Because Curacao was their only hope, they went to this wine seller for an "official" statement of Curacao's welcome.

Chapter 4

1. The attitudes of the Japanese toward the Jews during this time have been well documented and analyzed by David Kranzler in his book *Japanese, Nazis and Jews: The Jewish Refugee Community of Shanghai, 1938-1945* (KTAV Publishing House, Inc. Hoboken, New Jersey, 1988).

2. This ship was a barely seaworthy tramp steamer, crowded to overflowing with as many as 550 people and running at an enormous profit. The trip normally took 36 hours, but would stretch to 60 hours in severe weather.

3. Gerechter headed the volunteer Jewish Committee from Kobe, which was funded mostly by the Joint Distribution Committee and Vaad Hatzalah. This committee arranged for the train trip to Kobe, as well as for food, housing, medical care and occasional employment for the refugees. Gerechter was also kept busy as a cultural ambassador, such as when he had to explain to the Japanese authorities why the yeshiva students refused to sign their landing papers on the Sabbath.

4. Although Curacao did not require a visa, a landing permit had to be obtained from the governor of Curacao. Even a desperate refugee could not hope that this governor would grant thousands of landing permits to shiploads of penniless refugees who arrived at his shore.

5. Starting in the late 1930s, U.S. immigration policy was very restrictive. Provisions that were strictly enforced included exclusion because of an illness (aliens were considered a risk to public health) or any factor that could make a person "likely to become a public charge." There was also widespread anti-Communist hysteria and fear of espionage.

6. The British were still issuing very limited certificates for emigration to Palestine, but without direct contact with a British embassy, there was no hope of getting a certificate. The nearest British embassy was in China. The

British had maintained a strong presence in Shanghai since 1843, when England had defeated China in the first Opium War.

Chapter 5

1. As a result of a treaty and additional agreements signed in 1843 at the end of the first Opium War, China was forced to open Shanghai to British trade, and a section of the city was set aside for British residents. France and the United States soon demanded and received similar privileges. The Japanese presence in Shanghai began to grow dramatically in 1895, after Japan defeated China in the first Sino-Japanese war.

2. There may have been other opportunities in Asia, but Shanghai required no visa, had extensive transportation contacts with the West and had the cheapest and most room, given the relief organizations involved, for such large numbers of people. And the International Settlement at least provided an element of familiarity to the European refugees.

3. *Poppy* could be derived from the Polish term *popis* that means "showoff," or could simply refer to a British expression to describe the often flamboyant, arrogant behavior of wealthy Europeans in China.

4. From before Pearl Harbor and through the postwar times, there were between five and seven of these facilities operating. The first, the Ward Road *heime,* had a kitchen that served up to 7,000 meals a day. Until Laura Margolies arrived, there was not a single professional relief worker involved—all were staffed by volunteers. Funding came mostly from the JDC, which was cut off when the war in the Pacific began, although the Shanghai residents contributed a great deal. Unfortunately, the refugees themselves had no say in how the *heimes* were run.

5. During World War II, the Japanese used prisoner of war labor to build a railroad between Burma (Myanmar) and Siam (Thailand). It was said that one man died for every rail laid. The Japanese also forced about 70,000 American and Philippine prisoners to march through the jungles of the Bataan peninsula. As many as 10,000 died from starvation and brutality, and it became known as the Bataan Death March.

Chapter 6

1. The Japanese formed the Vigilance Corps, called the *pao chia* in Chinese, to assist in Ghetto police duties. The *pao chia* consisted of 3,500 male refugees aged 20 to 45, and their performance was closely monitored by the Japanese. Rule breakers were required to be handed over to Okura, and punishment for neglecting duties was severe. When the war ended, the *pao chia* prevented looting during the celebrations that followed.

2. Rabbi A. Kalmanowitz, through relentless efforts with the U.S. Department of State, the British authorities and private supporters, managed to get transit visas for all 300 members of the group to Japan, to care for and feed them while they were in Shanghai, and after the end of the war, to bring them all to New York City.

3. Between 1939 and 1945, there were approximately 1,580 deaths among the 17,000 refugees, including 36 suicides. Such a low fatality rate (less than ten percent) given the Shanghai living conditions is a testimony to the care received by the refugees.

4. Whether *popoloved* is an idiom in Russian, Yiddish, Polish, Shanghai slang, or simply a result of Dr. Iwry's colorful gift for self-expression is unknown. However, the term certainly describes the mood of the times as bottles were opened in celebration of war's end.

5. When the war ended, the British officials were released from their prison camp and stranded in Shanghai for a time with all the other refugees. Contacts with the West were restored, but the status of the former British embassy (during the summer of 1943, the British, the Americans and the French all signed treaties with the Chinese renouncing their rights and settlements in Shanghai) and how the certificates for immigration were handled during this chaotic time is not known.

Chapter 7

1. Louis L. Kaplan was born in Russia in 1902 and was brought to the United States at age seven. Besides serving as president of the Baltimore Hebrew College, he was also on the board of governors of Dropsie College in Philadelphia, the Board of Regents at the University of Maryland, and ably headed the University of Maryland, Baltimore Campus.

2. In 1945, Britain was still committed to the friendship of the Arab world and considered the partition of Palestine and large-scale Jewish immigration to be unacceptable. In response, Zionist forces in Palestine attacked British installations and conducted a guerilla campaign against British policy. As sympathy for the refugee population rose in the United States, a joint Anglo-American committee was formed, but London rejected its recommendations. This was followed by the Morrison-Grady Plan, which suggested a partition between Arab and Jewish provinces and better represented Britain's interests. However, a deadlock ensued between Britain, the Uited States, the Arabs and the World Jewish Organization. Prime Minister Bevin announced on February 14, 1947, that he would refer the issue to the United Nations. This occurred the following April 2.

3. The *Exodus* was a small ferry ship, which set out from France for Palestine, loaded with refugees, in early August 1947. It was met by British destroyers in the Mediterranean, and just outside Palestinian waters, the British attempted to board. A shipboard battle ensued and ended only when the British began to ram the ship, threatening to sink it. Eventually the refugees were put on a British transport ship and taken back to France, where they refused to disembark and to receive medical care. They were then taken to Germany where they again refused to disembark. The British finally forcibly removed them and took them to a refugee camp in Germany. When British officials asked them questions, the refugees would answer only with the words *Eretz Israel* ("land of Israel"). The incident lasted several months and was extensively reported in newspapers around the world.

4. The idea of dividing Palestine between the Arabs and Jews was decades old, but had gone nowhere until after World War II, when Britain turned the question over to the United Nations. The UN Palestine Committee debated the question from April 2 until November 25, 1947, when it passed by a vote of 25 to 13. It was then submitted to the General Assembly on November 29, where it passed by 33 to 13.

5. In the fourteenth chapter of Genesis, verse 13, the bible refers to Abraham as *Avram Ha'Ivri* or "Abram the Hebrew." The word *ivri* (spelled ayin-vet-reish-yod in the original Hebrew), or *'ebiru* originally meant "he who crosses over," or "easterner," that is, east of the river Euphrates.

Chapter 8

1. Albright's classes met once a week for several hours, and were entitled seminars rather than classes for several reasons. Albright did not lecture. His students were very advanced and instead were given research assignments. During the seminar time, the students would present and discuss their results under Albright's direction. The theme of these seminars varied from semester to semester, depending on the latest archaeological and other discoveries.

2. The Documentary theory is the idea that the Pentateuch was not written by Moses as tradition states, but is instead a compilation of four separate sources that were written at different times, mostly after Moses. The four hypothesized sources are labeled J (or Yahwist, based on the name this author used to refer to G_d), E (for Eliohist, based on the name this author used to refer to G_d), D (the book of Deuteronomy), and P (the priestly source, considered to have been added after the Babylonian exile).

3. The colorful and popular Mitchell Dahood was a Jesuit priest and in 1956 became a professor of Ugaritic language and literature at the Pontifical Biblical Institute in Rome. He died in 1982.

Chapter 9

1. Dr. Iwry is referring to Owen Lattimore, a Harvard-educated scholar of the Far East. Lattimore served as a U.S. government advisor on Chiang Kai-shek as well as in other capacities. In 1950, while director of the Walter Hines Page School at Johns Hopkins, Lattimore was accused by Senator Joseph McCarthy of being "the top Soviet espionage agent in the U.S." The charges were eventually dismissed as a hoax.

2. The Nazis established a ghetto in Bialystok on August 1, 1941, and confined about 50,000 Polish Jews there. It first served as a labor and industry camp for the Germans. Within a year, an underground resistance had formed. By August 1943, the population of the ghetto had been reduced to 30,000 and the Germans issued orders that the remaining inhabitants be moved to Lublin. On August 16, when the evacuation began, the Jewish resistance began a battle to escape to the forest. The fighting lasted five days, ending only when the Nazis brought in tanks and armored cars. A few of the ghetto residents escaped and survived. The remainder were sent to Treblinka,

Auschwitz, and other destinations. Iwry's former neighbor, Tobias Ciitroen, wrote a book documenting the Bialystok uprising.

3. Dr. Iwry's revolutionary article was entitled "Was There a Migration to Damascus? The Problem of *ʾby yr'l,*" *Eretz Israel* 9:80-88, 1969.

4. This paper, "New Evidence for Belomancy in Ancient Palestine and Phoenicia," was published in the prestigious *Journal of the American Oriental Society* (volume 81, pp. 27-34, 1961). It concerned an early Phoenician artifact from the ancient city of Byblos, an arrow on which was written a series of names. By analyzing this arrow, together with a similar artifact, and then drawing broadly on pertinent information from the Bible and elsewhere, Iwry was able to construct a theory concerning the use of belomancy in the ancient Near East. The word belomancy comes from the Roman goddess of war, Bellona, and refers to a form of divination using arrows. In this instance, the objects were used to settle conflicts: They were thrown in a specific manner and the names that appeared right side up were the winners.

5. Israel's Law of Return granted citizenship and nationality to any ethnic Jew. However, the law did not adequately define who a Jew was. As a result, the rabbinate at times would impose limitations on burial, marriage, and other privileges based on Jewish Orthodox Law, which stated that intermarriage in an ancestor rendered an individual a non-Jew. Ultimately, the Orthodox acquiesced to Civil law, which decided who was a Jew, for civil purposes, based on nationality, thus separating Jewish nationality from Jewish religion.

6. Besides the contributions of many noted scholars, Iwry's *festschrift* was also generously supported by the Meyerhoff Philanthropic Fund, Alvin H. Blum, Daniel Gordon, Jerold C. Hoffberger (three of his dear friends), the Macht Philanthropic Fund, Mr. and Mrs. Gerald Eisenberg, Harvey M. Meyerhoff, the Joseph Meyerhoff Fund, Dr. Liebe S. Diamond, Abraham M Lilienfeld, Morton J. Macks, George Hugo Dalsheimer, Mr. and Mrs. Leonard Forman, Willard Hackerman, Bernard Manekin, Mr. and Mrs. Marvin Shapiro, and Susan M. Mower. It is available from Eisenbrauns, Winona Lake, IN (www.eisenbrauns.com).

Index

CPSIA information can be obtained
at www.ICGtesting.com
Printed in the USA
BVHW040220131222
654108BV00004B/241

9 781403 965769